Faith and Experience in Education

'This book is a must-read for anyone who is concerned about the current direction of schooling. It rightly challenges us to ask how education can authentically nurture care, love, trust, equality, justice and spirituality.
I have learned much in the past from Quaker thinkers such as Parker Palmer, and the contributors to this scholarly book have now challenged me further to think how we can make the educational system more humane and develop the spiritual qualities that will bring peace to our world.'

Dr Neil Hawkes, Founder, Values-based Education

'Education is a profoundly moral business. Every classroom is saturated with value judgements. For many people in education these days, this is an inconvenient truth. They like to present it as a merely technical matter of getting better grades and promoting national economies. Not, thankfully, for the authors of this timely collection. If we are truly to create a 21st-century education, it will have a heart as well as a mind. And these brave, unfashionable souls will be in the vanguard of that creation.'

Guy Claxton, Visiting Professor of Education, King's College London, and author of *The Learning Power Approach: Teaching learners to teach themselves*

'At a time when the school system is creaking under the weight of targets, audits, and performance indicators, this book provides a different and refreshing vision of education, inspired by the distinctive beliefs of the Quakers and by their long-established but seldom-acknowledged tradition of schooling.'

Richard Pring, Professor Emeritus, Department of Education, University of Oxford

Faith and Experience in Education

Essays from Quaker perspectives

Edited by
Don Rowe and Anne Watson

 is an imprint of

First published in 2018 by the UCL Institute of Education Press, 20 Bedford Way, London WC1H 0AL

www.ucl-ioe-press.com

©2018 Don Rowe and Anne Watson

British Library Cataloguing in Publication Data:
A catalogue record for this publication is available from the British Library

ISBNs
978-1-85856-838-6 (paperback)
978-1-85856-873-7 (PDF eBook)
978-1-85856-874-4 (ePub eBook)
978-1-85856-875-1 (Kindle eBook)

All rights reserved. No part of this publication may be reproduced, stored in a retrieval system, or transmitted in any form or by any means, electronic, mechanical, photocopying, recording or otherwise, without the prior permission of the copyright owner.

Every effort has been made to trace copyright holders and to obtain their permission for the use of copyright material. The publisher apologizes for any errors or omissions and would be grateful if notified of any corrections that should be incorporated in future reprints or editions of this book.

The opinions expressed in this publication are those of the authors and do not necessarily reflect the views of the UCL Institute of Education.

Typeset by Quadrant Infotech (India) Pvt Ltd
Printed by CPI Group (UK) Ltd, Croydon, CR0 4YY
Cover image ©Sally Sigmund

Contents

About the contributors   vii

List of figures   xi

List of abbreviations   xii

Acknowledgements   xiii

1   Introduction to Quakers, Quaker involvement in education, and this book   1
Don Rowe and Anne Watson

2   Whose values? Which values?   11
Don Rowe

3   Relational and restorative practice in educational settings: A values-based, needs-led approach   36
Belinda Hopkins

4   Building, maintaining and repairing a peaceful culture in school   57
Anna Gregory

5   Learning for emancipation   78
Tim Small

6   Equality, truth and love in subject teaching: Cognitive care in the case of mathematics   100
Anne Watson

7   The role and value of the arts in education   119
Janet Sturge

8   Early years education and Quaker concerns   139
Wendy Scott

9   Equality and the scramble for school places   163
Janet Nicholls

10	Reflecting on values emerging from practice and the value of reflecting on practice *John Mason*	182
11	When school won't do *Keir Mitchell*	202
12	Natality and Quaker education *Giles Barrow*	216
13	Friends' education: A reflective commentary *Kathy Bickmore*	231

Index 240

About the contributors

Giles Barrow
Giles is a teacher who has worked in both mainstream and specialist contexts. He currently works, on a consultancy basis, with teachers, informal educators and educational leaders in developing holistic approaches to education. Giles has a particular interest in social pedagogy, educational transactional analysis and the relational aspects of teaching, learning and school leadership.

Kathy Bickmore
Kathy is a professor in Curriculum Studies and Comparative International Development Education at the Ontario Institute for Studies in Education, University of Toronto. Her current research examines gaps (and bridges) between young people's lived citizenship experiences in violent neighbourhoods and their education in Canadian, Mexican, Bangladeshi and Colombian state-funded schools. She works and writes extensively on peacebuilding, restorative justice and democracy in schools and co-edited the book *Comparative and International Education: Issues for teachers* (revised edition 2017, Canadian Scholars Press).

Anna Gregory
Anna works for Peacemakers, a branch of Central England Quakers, providing peace education via practical workshops and experiences that develop social and emotional learning and understanding of how to resolve conflict creatively. Anna provides strategic support and challenge, training and development to schools to enhance teachers' work with children, young people, families and each other. Please see www.peacemakers.org.uk for more information.

Belinda Hopkins
Having been a secondary school teacher for 12 years, in the early 1990s Belinda founded Transforming Conflict, which is now one of the foremost

About the contributors

providers of training and consultancy in the field of restorative approaches to conflict resolution, nationally and internationally. She gained a doctorate in 2006 researching the implementation of a whole-school restorative approach. She shares passionately the ethos, principles and practices of restorative approaches that transform communities and institutions – especially in education. She runs training courses, writes books and articles, develops training materials and resources and speaks at conferences around the world. *Just Schools* broke new ground by showing how restorative justice principles could change school culture; *Just Care* remains the only book to show how important a restorative approach can be for looked-after children and how it can transform residential settings.

John Mason

John became a Quaker by convincement. He has BSc, MSc and PhD in Mathematics, and spent 40 years at the Open University, mainly in the Centre for Mathematics Education, developing open access courses. Throughout this work he has supported those who wish to develop their own mathematical thinking, or who wish to foster and sustain mathematical thinking in others. One of his many books, *Researching Your Own Practice Using the Discipline of Noticing*, is the result of twenty years' work articulating a phenomenological way of working. More information can be found at www.pmtheta.com.

Keir Mitchell

Keir chose to work in the education sector after a conventional childhood of academic achievement. He was a project manager for an education charity and worked with local education authorities (LEAs) and government departments in the UK and overseas, helping schools get built and become staffed. He then became a primary teacher and also trained as a Forest School leader. His chapter in this book describes his subsequent doubts and a journey of finding ways to nurture children that accord with Quaker testimonies.

Janet Nicholls

Janet attended a secondary modern school. After gaining five GCE O-Levels, she went on to gain three degrees, including a PhD on 'Education as a Political Issue', and later an Advanced Diploma in Therapeutic Counselling. As a university lecturer, she taught and researched the sociology and politics of education. Under the name McKenzie, she was sole author of *Changing Education: A sociology of education since 1944*. Janet has done voluntary work for Cruse Bereavement Care and for Support After Murder and Manslaughter. She now works as a psychotherapist.

Don Rowe

Don has been a Quaker for about forty years. After ten years of teaching in secondary comprehensive and middle schools, he set up a local authority publications unit working with teachers and local agencies on resources production. In 1984 he became director of the Law in Schools Project, and then co-founded the Citizenship Foundation. He has created and published training and teaching materials on a range of citizenship-related topics for teachers and students of all ages and has published research papers about citizenship, focusing particularly on moral education as a significant strand of citizenship education. For several years, he was part of the Council of Europe's international team for Education for Democratic Citizenship, working in a number of countries but particularly in Turkey and post-conflict Bosnia-Herzegovina. He has also written educational materials for young Quakers.

Wendy Scott

Wendy is a Froebelian early years teacher with extensive experience in practice, including headship of a demonstration nursery school and senior lectureship at the University of Roehampton. She has been an early years and primary inspector in London, and has worked as an Ofsted inspector. She led The British Association for Early Childhood Education and chaired the national Early Childhood Forum before becoming a specialist adviser to the Department for Education and Skills. She has worked with the British Council and UNICEF, and holds leadership roles in professional associations. She was awarded an OBE for services to education in 2015.

About the contributors

Tim Small

Tim taught English in seven comprehensive schools for almost thirty years, culminating in a headship in Wiltshire. He has practised for fifteen years as an education consultant, working across the UK and in Australia, Malaysia and the Middle East, and is now in his fourth year of advanced training in Transactional Analysis Counselling and Psychotherapy at the Berne Institute, near Nottingham. His father was a Quaker who journeyed ultimately to priesthood in the Church of England, while Tim has travelled in the opposite direction, towards Quakerism. He has been a member of the Governing Body of his South Gloucestershire village primary school for over ten years.

Janet Sturge

Janet was born into a Quaker family and taught art in comprehensive, grammar and Quaker schools. On retirement, she returned to art college, writing a dissertation *Art and the National Curriculum: Has art a raison d'être in the curriculum?* She is always interested in equality of esteem, whatever a student's ability, and is still learning about the connections between children's expression and their art. Alongside her work in the arts, Janet has undertaken voluntary work with Neighbour Mediation and, in schools, Peer Mediation and voluntary reading help. She has led two community art projects, at a youth club and in a child and adolescent mental health centre.

Anne Watson

Anne has been a Quaker for about thirty years. She has two Mathematics degrees and taught mathematics in comprehensive schools serving some fractured communities before moving into academic work, training secondary mathematics teachers and researching mathematics education. With a social justice agenda, she has focused on how young adolescents can become empowered through inclusion in mathematics. While a professor at the University of Oxford, she worked internationally and nationally with teachers and teacher educators and, more recently, has developed a critical and informed position towards policy and curriculum matters in England. See www.pmtheta.com for more information.

List of figures

Figure 4.1 The Relationship Triangle
Figure 4.2 The 'blame game' card
Figure 5.1 A CLARA profile
Figure 5.2 Jo's before-and-after CLARA profiles
Figure 5.3 Ollie's before-and-after CLARA profiles
Figure 6.1 Different understandings of 'doubling' a rectangle
Figure 9.1 A polarity of perspectives on equal educational opportunities

List of abbreviations

AVP	Alternatives to Violence Project
CLARA	Crick Learning for Resilient Agency
DCSF	Department for Children, Schools and Families
DfE	Department for Education
ELLI	Effective Lifelong Learning Inventory
GCSE	General Certificate of Secondary Education
GFE	Guild of Friends in Education
IIRP	International Institute of Restorative Practice
ILEA	Inner London Education Authority
K-6	Kindergarten to grade 6
KS1, 2, ...	Key Stage, 1, 2, ... (age-related phases of school education)
LEA	local education authority
NEET	Not in Education, Employment or Training
Ofsted	Office for Standards in Education, Children's Services and Skills
PET	planned environmental therapy
PVI	private, voluntary and independent
QF&P	*Quaker Faith and Practice*
RJ (or rj)	Restorative justice
RSA	Royal Society of Arts
UNESCO	United Nations Educational, Scientific and Cultural Organization
VbE	Values-based Education
VORP	Victim Offender Reconciliation Program
WMQPEP	West Midlands Quaker Peace Education Project

Acknowledgements

In producing this book, we have been helped significantly by Gillian Klein, our publisher, who has been wise and encouraging and helpful throughout; Elizabeth O'Donnell, whose chapter about 'Quakers and education' in the *Oxford Handbook of Quaker Studies* was immensely useful; and Heather Woolley, who undertook internal editing. We would like to thank Isabel Cartwright for insights from her work in Peace Education (see www.quaker.org.uk/our-work/peace/peace-education); the librarians of Friends House, London, for unearthing some hard-to-find sources; the Steering Committee of the Quaker Values in Education Group (www.qvine.org.uk); and many others, not least our spouses, Denise Rowe and John Mason, for tolerating our habit of filling our retirement with new tasks.

Chapter 1
Introduction to Quakers, Quaker involvement in education, and this book
Don Rowe and Anne Watson

In recent years there has been a rising concern among Quakers, along with many other people, about how the current state education system in Britain treats many children. Rather than focus on the whole, rounded and healthy development of children, the state-funded system is currently driven by data about test results and progress measures. Teacher morale is consequently low, resulting in poor teacher retention while they struggle to do more with fewer resources to meet the test targets on which the prospects of their schools and their personal careers can disproportionately rely. The well-meaning policy aim is to give more children the life chances and choices that are available to those who traditionally succeed in the system, but the methods designed to do so, as some of our authors argue, often pay little heed to the wider contexts of learning or, indeed, to the working capacities of those who come into the teaching profession, often with the highest sense of vocation. These difficulties are not, of course, universally experienced – there are plenty of success stories to be told about the enhancement of children's lives through education – but they are experienced in enough places to make us concerned for children, teachers and others whose lives are, to a greater or lesser extent, negatively affected by the current system.

In 2012, a group of Quakers in Cumbria came together to formulate their particular concerns locally and present them to the national Society of Friends. Subsequent discussions among Quakers at a national level in Britain led to the foundation of the Quaker Values in Education Group (QVinE). This book is one result of that group's formation.

Introduction to the Quakers
Quakers, also known as Friends, have a historical interest in education, which we outline here. The Religious Society of Friends, to give it its full title, was founded by George Fox as a denomination of Christianity in the seventeenth century, in the belief that each person is individually able to

directly experience or access the divine and that each person is equally a child of God. This means that everyone can have a personal relationship with God or the divine (however they wish to interpret that). Quaker meetings for worship are a form of corporate seeking of the inner light, or divine leadings, based mostly on deep listening and waiting. Children are born in grace as fully valuable people; there is no concept of original sin in Quaker belief. This leads to a yearning for equality, peace and justice among all people – ideas that lie at the heart of well-known Quaker concerns for prison reform, philanthropy and a wide variety of social action and peace campaigning. Quakers set great store by direct experience, their own and that of others, rather than the expression of such beliefs in the form of creedal statements, and the written testimony of Friends past and present forms the basis of books of discipline and guides for living the Quaker life. The British version of this collection of writings is called *Quaker Faith and Practice* and is referred to throughout this book as *QF&P*[1] along with the relevant paragraph numbers. *QF&P* is the primary written source for learning about our historic concerns or testimonies: peace, truth, equality, justice, simplicity and sustainability. These are not written prescriptive rules, but are descriptions of, and guidance on, how we live our lives as spiritual and social beings. Thus, Friends have a high degree of spiritual autonomy, but, to support our joint spiritual practice as Quakers, *QF&P* starts with a list of Advices and Queries to which some of the authors in this book make reference (viewable online at www.quaker.org.uk).

Friends' involvement in education in the UK

From the very early days of Quakerism, Friends were concerned about their children's education, girls as well as boys. Though Friends have never developed a distinctive philosophy of education, unlike, for example, Montessori or Steiner, their approach was grounded from the outset in the spiritual values they espoused. That said, it is not difficult to find many early examples of practices that fell short of their ideals, such as paying women teachers less than men and using solitary confinement as a punishment.

The early years of Quaker schooling were dominated by a concern to provide what was described as a 'guarded education'. For a long time, Friends were a people apart, with supposed peculiarities of dress, speech and worship. During the eighteenth century, the Society went through a period of inward-looking, self-regarding practice in which schools became a primary vehicle by which the Society of Friends reproduced itself. Schools were strictly for the children of Quaker families, although, as time went by, children of parents who had been disowned for practices like marrying non-Quakers or joining the militia were allowed to attend Quaker schools.

The testimony to plainness and a suspicion of the kind of classical learning common in the grammar schools of the time produced a curriculum that focused on the unadorned basics – literacy and numeracy plus some practical subjects (O'Donnell, 2013: 407). Perhaps surprisingly, Friends' belief in the leading of the inner light led them to reject religious instruction for fear it would interfere with divine inspiration. This practice continued throughout the eighteenth and into the nineteenth century until it was realized that new generations had an impoverished knowledge of the Bible, quite unlike the first Friends.

In the mid-1700s, Quakerism came under the influence of the evangelical revival. The peculiar practices that had kept earlier Friends as a separate collective now became an encumbrance and a barrier to new converts, as Friends sought to recover their dwindling numbers. One result of this new openness to the wider world was the undermining of the need for separate educational provision, and, after 1870 (when education became universal in the UK), the number of schools run exclusively by Friends gradually diminished, to the point that there is now only one remaining primary school that can claim Quaker origins (namely William Penn School, Coolham, West Sussex). As part of their mission to reach out, many Friends at this time became involved in the pioneering Adult Education movement, promoting literacy among the working classes while regarding this as a way of bringing social, moral and spiritual enlightenment to many. They also founded some teacher training colleges, recognizing that systematic training could lead to better, more knowledgeable, teaching, and many Quakers became involved with prison schools and the so-called ragged schools for destitute children.

With no need of an educated clergy, the early Quaker schools did not originally prepare their students for university. Quakers, in any case, along with other non-conformists, were barred from universities until 1871. After this, some Quaker schools began to compete with other secondary schools, preparing students for university with curricula that had little to distinguish them from those of the latter (ibid.: 411). The ethos and values of Quaker schools began to prove attractive to many non-Quaker parents, and Elizabeth O'Donnell notes that, by 1901, only 55 per cent of pupils in British Quaker schools were from Quaker families.

Thus, Friends in the late nineteenth and early twentieth century underwent a wholesale shift in the understanding of their relationship with schools and schooling. As the shift towards engaging with state-run schools gathered momentum and Quaker elementary schools either closed or were voluntarily incorporated into the state system and into state control, those schools that remained in the private sector came to be viewed with increasing ambivalence, even hostility, by the majority of Quakers, particularly in the light of the historic testimony to equality (see Janet Nicholls's chapter in this volume). Today, only 3 per cent of pupils and 8 per cent of staff in Quaker schools are practising Quakers, according to a recent study by Nigel Newton (Broadfoot *et al.*, 2016; Newton, 2016). Despite changes regarding the perceived role and purpose of Quaker education that have taken place over the years, many of the underlying values and concerns have remained the same, and these can be seen to be re-emerging in the writings of the authors of this book.

Above all, following Frank Pollard (1932), Quakers have believed that education should serve the spiritual purpose of enlarging young people's awareness of, and capacity to promote, the good. Pollard invokes the Quaker principle, possibly most commonly quoted by Quaker educationists over the centuries, including in this volume:

> It is justifiable then to take the doctrine if you can so call it – the hypothesis if you like – that there is something of God in every man [sic], not merely as referring to some restraining or guiding voice which we should revere and obey, but as implying the divine value of each human life not for what it is so much as for what it has in it to be.
>
> (ibid.: 15)

John Reader (1979: 44) supports Pollard in the suggestion that Friends developed no distinctive philosophy of education, but does contend that they played a pioneering role in the development of schools as sites of therapeutic practice in the twentieth century. One might hazard the supposition that this came naturally to Quakers, who were more concerned with nurturing the whole child than with academic development alone. John Lampen agrees, suggesting that:

> To see Quaker values in action in British education, we must look not to the recognised Quaker schools but to the 'planned environmental therapy' movement which Friends and others developed to meet the needs of difficult evacuated children in the 1939–45 War.
>
> (Lampen, 2015: 295)

Lampen discusses the Quaker contribution to this pioneering work with emotionally damaged children in a number of schools, some of which are still operating. He points out that the developers of planned environmental therapy (PET) saw it as having four main elements:

1. A regime based on love
2. Shared responsibility between children and staff
3. An understanding of children's needs drawn from psychoanalytical thought, especially regarding the basic need to be loved in order to learn to love
4. Avoidance of punishment.

This latter notion was based on the belief that a system of restitution for wrongdoing is better than punishment, which fails to achieve moral growth and undermines the quality of the relationship between staff and students. Lampen argues that these practices can be seen as a forerunner of restorative justice (RJ) practices in the UK. However, much of the modern literature on RJ in schools credits these developments to work undertaken in the late twentieth century in Canada, New Zealand and Australia (see Belinda Hopkins's chapter in this volume). Since Quakers have also been prominent in this more recent RJ work, as they were in the earlier PET movement, it might be seen as the re-emergence, by another route, of a fundamental Quaker concern for the well-being of the whole child, first and foremost.

This Quaker involvement in restorative approaches in schools, including conflict resolution and peer mediation, is today widely regarded as the Society of Friends' most visible corporate contribution to modern educational practice. Quakers have a history of, and unending commitment to, trying to change the world for the better through faithful action, and the education system is a values-rich environment with the capacity to inspire and transform the lives of young people of whatever ability. Harold Loukes was a respected Quaker educationist with a strong interest in the education of children who had failed selection tests at 11 years old (note that one of our authors, Janet Nicholls, was such a child). He writes:

> Childhood ... is not to be thought of as the waiting-room for manhood [sic], a mere time of preparation for what is to come ... Children live a life of their own, with its own values and its own rewards; and those grow most successfully into ripe men and women who savour their childish life to the full while they have it. They grow by being themselves ...
>
> (Loukes, 1958: 8)

The Quaker understanding is that all people, including children, can, do and should seek truth through experience and discernment and, having found some truth, should commit to it. This points towards educational approaches that value questioning, doubt, uncertainty and exploration. As the American educator Parker Palmer says: 'To teach is to create a space in which obedience to truth is practiced [sic]' (Palmer, 1983: 69).

Themes emerging in this volume

Within the present volume, the authors' different approaches chime strongly with the concerns of preceding generations of Quaker educators. Among their primary concerns are authenticity; care and love; trust; equality and justice; and spirituality.

Authenticity

The authors see education and teachers' relationships with children as nurturing the latter's true selves rather than coercing them into jumping through externally imposed hoops. Therefore, interactions with children involve listening with respect and valuing young people's personal searches for truth. At the same time, the act of teaching is also an expression of the teacher's true relational self, not as a transmitter of agreed knowledge, but as a whole, complex, person trying to act with integrity and love. These teachers describe how they have been driven by their personally held beliefs to teach in particular ways, to be critical rather than acquiescent of the status quo where necessary, and to act in the worlds of policy and governance where appropriate.

Care and love

Many chapters in this book display care for learners as whole people with, *inter alia*, spiritual and creative dimensions, and concern for their development as autonomous, self-confident people who know who they are and are comfortable with themselves. Alongside this, they describe how the teacher should also display cognitive care for the nature of the knowledge they are exploring with students and the positive but also negative ways in which students respond and try to make sense of such knowledge.

Trust

Because Quakers see children as being worthy of as much respect as adults, the authors also see them as capable, from the earliest years, of thinking in critical and exploratory ways, of developing valid opinions and of moral reasoning – and hence of being trustworthy in the search for authentic truth and understanding. This approach to teaching requires one to take the long view, both in terms of pedagogy and organizational control, so as not to fall back on short-term disciplinary strategies that deliver immediate conformity but do not nurture autonomy in the longer term. As teachers, they trust the processes of teaching when practised as a caring profession, in the same way that they trust that the processes of their meetings for worship will lead to insight and transformation.

Equality and justice

Most chapters in this book convey a strong implicit or explicit belief that education should both uphold and embody the values of equality and justice in curriculum content, in pedagogical practices and in school behaviour systems. Teaching and learning are seen by all the authors to be deeply ethical matters, and schools as ethical communities in which institutions and individuals are capable of undergoing transformation, the latter to become better aligned with their inner moral compass. In a telling phrase, the work of Hannah Arendt is referenced in Chapter 12 as arguing that the structures developed by mortals will naturally decay and atrophy. Thus, to 'preserve the world against the mortality of its creators and inhabitants it must be constantly set right anew' (Arendt, 1961: 192). Each new generation must therefore be more than merely inducted into existing structures; it must develop a sense of critical solidarity with the world. In addition, equality and justice should be reflected in the overarching mechanisms designed to deliver educational opportunities equally and fairly to all students. In this respect, the authors regard the whole national education system in Britain to be deficient and hypocritical, and they also examine critically the contemporary roles of Quaker schools.

Spirituality

Throughout this book, there is a strong sense that the authors are engaging with educational practices as spiritual people and that, therefore, the values embodied in Quaker spirituality *must* be worked out in the daily routines of teaching, learning and managing education. They also regard students as spiritual beings whose spiritual lives are contingent, to a degree, on their abilities to think well and reflectively, to reason ethically, to be in healthy relationships with others and so on. The links between spiritual, moral, social and cultural development are regarded as seamless and holistic. If one dimension is impoverished, then all are impoverished. As Pollard put it, there should be:

> ... no unhealthy division of religious and secular, no Sunday faith and weekday atheism, no weak bowing to expediency at the expense of right, no handing over of the conscience to the care of the Government, no talk of brotherhood on the lips while denying it in act.
>
> (Pollard, 1932: 70)

The content of this book by chapter

We open the book with an essay by Don Rowe (Chapter 2) on the many current approaches to values education and their orientations and methods. It is argued that, in these and also in some kinds of peace education, the nurturing of moral reasoning and awareness, of which even young children are capable, has been seriously overlooked. This is followed by chapters by Belinda Hopkins (Chapter 3) and Anna Gregory (Chapter 4) on the development and practice of restorative justice in schools; their personal perspectives illuminate the chapters, Belinda's being her personal journey towards her current thinking and work, and Anna's being detailed descriptions of how she puts ideas into practice. Tim Small (Chapter 5) finds fulfilment and purpose in developing the ideas of Guy Claxton and Ruth Deakin Crick in transforming learning power in schools and classrooms across the world. Anne Watson (Chapter 6) introduces the notion of cognitive care, using mathematics as an example to show how the relation between the knower and the known can be nurtured.

This is followed by Janet Sturge (Chapter 7) writing about how an understanding of the importance of creative arts has grown within Quaker thought, and why it is still important for all children to experience the arts within a school curriculum. In Chapter 8, Wendy Scott describes the educational and ethical imperatives of early years' experience for young children. She narrates her ethical commitment in policy roles, and describes how her integrity has led her to pursue critical and oppositional avenues. Opposition to current systems and structures is also a feature of Janet Nicholls's work (Chapter 9), in which she analyses current educational practice, policy and systems and finds it hard to locate pathways that might satisfy the desire of equality, including among Quaker schools. The next two chapters are by John Mason (Chapter 10) and Keir Mitchell (Chapter 11), who both describe strong personal links between Quaker belief and personal practice. In John's case, this is a *post facto* recognition of alignment, while, in Keir's case, being a Quaker has played a central part in his realizations about what it means to be an educator. Chapter 12, by Giles Barrow, presents a fresh perspective that could transform thinking about education – Hannah Arendt's notion of natality as the foundational commonality of human existence. Having our birth in common, seen from the Quaker perspective of all being children of God, puts education and educators in the role of facilitating the unfolding of life, while they themselves are being similarly unfolded, to become the fullest spiritual beings possible.

Finally, in a reflective commentary (Chapter 13), Canadian Friend Kathy Bickmore identifies some powerful overarching ideas that were less obvious to us as editors during our work on this book. Her ideas are strongly aligned with Quaker thought and practice, namely the importance of uncertainty and trusting unprogrammed aspects of the educational environment to do the work of nurturing insight. Kathy also returns us to the Quaker commitment to peace, noting the interplay of personal peacefulness with the transformation of educational systems towards peace.

Voices in this book

This book contains reflections on personal and professional experiences within the state primary and secondary education system from Quaker perspectives. Some of the chapters argue for the restoration and maintenance of education as rooted in the whole of childhood experience. Some chapters focus on policies and their enactment and effects; some on personal philosophies and practices aligned with Quaker testimonies; and some on putting beliefs into practice when working in, or interacting with, the state-funded system in England.

In editing these different contributions, we have tried to preserve the varied ways in which people of different experiential background express the links between their Quaker beliefs and how they have lived these out in educational contexts and practices. Thus, for example, Janet Nicholls writes from the viewpoint of academic sociology, but with a personal background visible in her biographical notes; John Mason reflects, as a Quaker and a maths educator, on lifelong practices that were not influenced by Quakerism when they were developed; and Wendy Scott narrates a history of personal engagement with early years policy. There is a broad spectrum of ways in which authors connect their own beliefs to their educational viewpoints and practice. Keir Mitchell, in his chapter, writes in a traditional Quakerly style of his own spiritual journey and how he has been led to change his life and practice in response to an increasingly felt impulse to live as consistently as possible with Quaker testimonies. The short biographies will help the reader make sense of these differences in perspective and style.

Textual decisions

In line with our beliefs about equality and respect for all, Quakers do not use titles, and the first time we use a name we give the full first name and family name. For further reference to individuals, we follow academic norms for ease of reading.

Note

[1] *Quaker Faith and Practice* (5th ed.) is available to download at: qfp.quaker.org.uk (Religious Society of Friends, 2013).

References

Arendt, H. (1961) *Between Past and Future*. London: Faber and Faber.

Broadfoot, P.M., Yu, G. and Newton, N. (2016) 'How students learn within a Quaker School environment'. Online. https://research-information.bristol.ac.uk/en/projects/how-students-learn-within-a-quaker-school-environment(58a06ee3-9e6a-4559-89c5-de2380907179).html (accessed 5 February 2018).

Lampen, J. (2015) 'The Quaker peace testimony in twentieth-century education'. *Quaker Studies*, 19 (2), 295–304.

Loukes, H. (1958) *Friends and Their Children: A study in Quaker education*. London: Harrap.

Newton, N. (2016) 'Schools for Well-being: The educational significance of Quaker school culture – based on a mixed methods study in secondary level Quaker schools in England'. PhD thesis. Online. http://ethos.bl.uk/OrderDetails.do?uin=uk.bl.ethos.730837 (accessed 1 March 2018).

O'Donnell, E.A. (2013) 'Quakers and education'. In Angell, S.W. and Dandelion, P. (eds) *The Oxford Handbook of Quaker Studies*. Oxford: Oxford University Press, 405–19.

Palmer, P.J. (1983) *To Know as We Are Known: A spirituality of education*. San Francisco: Harper and Row.

Pollard, F.E. (1932) *Education and the Spirit of Man* (Swarthmore Lecture). London: Allen and Unwin.

Reader, J. (1979) *Of Schools and Schoolmasters: Some thoughts on the Quaker contribution to education* (Swarthmore Lecture). London: Quaker Home Service.

Religious Society of Friends (2013) *Quaker Faith and Practice: The book of Christian discipline of the Yearly Meeting of the Religious Society of Friends (Quakers) in Britain*. 5th ed. London: Religious Society of Friends. Online. qfp.quaker.org.uk (accessed 13 December 2017).

Chapter 2
Whose values? Which values?
Don Rowe

A personal perspective

In this chapter, I will give a brief account of my own attempts to operationalize Quaker values in education by supporting endeavours to establish good quality citizenship education in the English curriculum. More particularly, these efforts have focused on raising the profile of moral reasoning, not merely to enhance students' social and political thinking, but also to help them to become more morally aware and developed as individuals and citizens. I then want to argue that my own work is one of many contemporary attempts to promote values-based learning, both within the curriculum and across the whole school – including different forms of peace education. I will argue that Friends have corporately tended to focus on one form of peace education and that their educational vision would benefit from being recast to reflect a broader spectrum of Quaker values.

I spent the first five years of my career (1970–5) teaching religious and moral education, humanities, English and drama in secondary comprehensive schools. I then spent a further five years teaching almost everything in a 9–13 middle school, during which time I learnt a huge amount about the teacher's job as an explainer. Influenced by a Schools Council Integrated Humanities project, I became wedded to the notion of teaching for concepts, that is, emphasizing understanding rather than factual knowledge, an approach that stayed with me for the rest of my working life. I was interested in curriculum development from the start, and I took every opportunity to gain experience in the writing of teaching materials for my colleagues, others in the county and, to a minor degree, nationally. As a result of this, I was invited to carry out a feasibility study for a county publishing unit and was subsequently offered the chance to set it up. As part of that post, I worked with the local police force to redesign their schools liaison programme in collaboration with a seconded officer. Having retained a keen interest in moral education, I was keen to move the police away from their default classroom stance of instilling fear of capture into their young audiences, towards helping them explain *why* certain actions were wrong and harmful and, hence, illegal. A further dimension of this initiative was to help the children understand that the police were public servants, accountable to the law and not themselves makers of it – a common misconception among young people.

I then took on a new role that was national in scope, developing teaching materials about the law aimed at 14–16-year-olds, on their rights and responsibilities, the law and democracy. The project was funded by the Law Society but run under the auspices of the government's then curriculum body, the School Curriculum Development Committee. A five-year curriculum development and dissemination project led, in 1989, to the establishment of an independent charity called the Citizenship Foundation, and, after a brief spell as chief executive, I settled into the post of head of curriculum resources for the rest of my working life.

Our work and positioning were fortuitous, and when the National Curriculum was introduced by the Conservative administration in 1988, citizenship education was identified as an important cross-curricular theme and I became closely involved in the development of the new (non-compulsory) framework intended for all four Key Stages. When David Blunkett became the new Labour Secretary of State for Education post-1997 he introduced citizenship education as a new National Curriculum subject, compulsory for all secondary students and a recommended strand of personal and social education (PSE) at primary level. Thus, I found myself writing curriculum guidance, developing teaching materials and running in-service training up and down the country. In essence, this subject is about inducting young people into public discourse, which is, of course, political but also profoundly moral, focusing on issues such as fairness, the nature of rights and responsibilities, what kind of society we want, what happens when individual rights conflict with the rights of society, what is the role of the law and what values underpin democracy. A primary task of the curriculum, if conceived as continuous and progressive throughout the Key Stages, is to encourage young people to think more deeply and sensitively about the moral issues underlying human relationships and interactions, as it progressively becomes more political and generalized in the upper years.

Prior to 1988, civic education (as it had been called) had been conceived as something reserved for secondary students because the focus was institutional and on their future status as citizens, rather than concerned with the rights and responsibilities of young people here and now. It had, in any case, largely disappeared with the demise of the secondary modern school. The conception of citizenship education that was developed for the National Curriculum post-2000 was of active, engaged citizenship in which social, moral and political understanding is combined with the skills and motivation to make the world a better place. At primary level, a strand of personal and social education encouraged primary-age students to get involved with their school community, help create and sustain the school rules, sit on school councils, support charities, understand their rights, learn to take responsibility, develop their own ideas and learn how to argue for them while respecting the views of others. At secondary level, engagement in the school and the community can deepen while students progressively learn to apply their thinking to the wider world. The concept of society, as an entity in its own right, begins to have salience around the age of 14 (for example Kohlberg, 1984; Rest *et al.*, 2000) and moral and political thinking becomes much more abstract and complex.

I became inspired by the research that Jean Piaget (1932) initiated into the moral development of children and young people. Piaget's work was taken forward by Lawrence Kohlberg (ibid.), John Gibbs *et al.* (1992), James Rest (ibid.) and many others all pointing to one underlying conclusion: that children's development as morally conscious beings is continuous and progressive, and shifts from concrete egocentrism towards various forms of more adequate (or inclusive) and more abstract reasoning. Further, in *The Beginnings of Social Understanding,* Judy Dunn (1988) demonstrates how young children begin to grapple with moral concepts such as fairness, responsibility, rights and so on, way before they go to school. On this premise, then, schools should consciously nurture and support the transition from heteronomous morality (as laid down by parents, teachers and others) to internalized morality (in which young people become self-controlled and increasingly mature and responsible in making their own socio-moral judgements). Kohlberg contributed much to our understanding of the cognitive stages through which young people pass on their way to maturity, and his work inspired some direct teaching of moral education using dilemma discussions, but, by the time I began teaching, his work had become largely discredited, not least because he claimed that morality was mostly about justice. This had been argued against by Carol Gilligan (1982) and Nel Noddings (2008), among others, who pointed out – rightly – that care is also an important moral motivator. Kohlberg's six levels of increasingly abstract moral reasoning leant support to the misunderstanding that moral maturity was not reached until level six, at which point thinking prioritized universal human rights; this level was attained almost exclusively by educated Western graduates. John Gibbs (ibid.), one of Kohlberg's students, later argued (much more plausibly, in my view) that moral maturity begins with the development of empathic ways of thinking in early adolescence and occurs as the young person develops self-control and autonomous moral decision-making.

For young people to become responsible, caring and wise in their judgements (schools focus too much on knowledge and not enough on wisdom, in my opinion), they need to be helped to master the language and procedures of moral thinking and this must begin from an early age to avoid developmental delay. I was concerned that there was very little attention given directly to this form of reasoning and so I developed with colleagues a range of morally rich stories for KS1 and 2 (Rowe and Newton, 1994; Rowe, 2014) revisiting the same concepts (justice, care, rights, responsibilities, friendship, community and so on) in progressively complex ways, specifically to give the children practice in analysing and *talking together* about the moral issues underlying a range of familiar everyday situations. The lessons typically use circle time techniques (for example Bickmore, 2013; Mosley, 1996; Mosley and Tew, 2014; see also Anna Gregory's chapter in this volume) and strongly promote what Neil Mercer (1995: 104) has helpfully called 'exploratory talk'.[1] This approach closely aligns itself with the Philosophy for Children[2] movement – it is, after all, a form of moral philosophy.

For this work, I developed a three-step methodology for analysing situations of moral conflict or ambiguity (Rowe, 2014). This approach encourages teachers to reject the instructional or 'assembly' mode (as in 'The moral of this story is: don't steal') in favour of systematically deconstructing situations with the involvement of the whole class, encouraging the most complex analysis that the children can achieve together. The first of the three steps looks at the moral issues raised by the surface events as presented in the story, encouraging the group to offer a range of different perspectives, which will, inevitably, be at differing levels of moral maturity. Second, we use the incidents to develop more generalized thinking, such as 'What would happen if everyone behaved like that?' or 'Do you think that the saying "cheats never prosper" is true?' The third step is what I call 'community building', in which students are encouraged to talk about their own feelings or incidents in their own lives relevant to the story. This stage is highly effective in nurturing empathy and trust in the group and these are key components in the development of moral maturity.[3] Crucially, the stories, even in KS1, should be non-didactic, morally rich, ambiguous, arousing of sympathy and curiosity, and age-appropriately complex. In one story, for example, a Year 1 boy experiences a moral dilemma in the form of a conflict of loyalties, about whom to play with at school (namely, a choice between his best friend and a girl who is a neighbour and who, out of school, he

Whose values? Which values?

often plays with) (Rowe, 2001). In the course of my work, I met many teachers who took the view that children are not able to think critically until upper KS2 and that they should not be exposed to multiple moral viewpoints too early, on the grounds that this confuses them. However, it is clear that they are already able to wrestle with moral complexity as demonstrated by the fact that, when asked to vote on whether Johnny had done the right thing in not wanting to play with his neighbour, even after being asked to by his teacher, one class was split equally. Their teacher was then able to encourage the children on both sides to develop the arguments for and against Johnny's decision[4] and respond to each other's thinking.

At secondary level, we published material about the law and how it affects young people (for example Rowe and Thorpe, 2002), but, critically, we regularly required students to act as citizens and ask: 'Do I think this law is fair?' or 'What changes would I like to see made and why?' Around this time, I was afraid that the introduction of compulsory citizenship education might lead to the return of dull, fact-based courses in civics taught, for example, by untrained and reluctant form teachers in schools where citizenship education and PSE were held in low regard. For this reason, I and my colleague Ted Huddleston developed a series of secondary lessons focusing on the principal concepts underpinning citizenship discourse (Huddleston and Rowe, 2001, 2015). This material was specifically designed to help students progressively understand and use socio-moral concepts such as fairness, rights, duties, welfare, tolerance, diversity and so on in increasingly complex settings, from KS3 through to KS5. One example that worked particularly well was a story called *The School on the Edge of the Forest*, in which two neighbouring communities living in suspicion of each other – one on the plains and the other in the forest – were persuaded by a young, progressive teacher to allow him to set up a school on the edge of the forest where the children of both communities could learn together and overcome the hostilities that existed between their peoples. For a while it seemed to be succeeding but then, one day, the people woke up to see that the school had been burnt down – end of story. Students are then asked to think about 'Who might want to do that?', 'What could the school have achieved had it lasted?', 'Should it be rebuilt?', 'What can be done to overcome such barriers between peoples?'[5] and so on. Other projects I led under the broad banner of citizenship education focused on issues such as anti-racism (see Rowe, 2010), which I also approached from an exploratory, non-moralizing point of view, a project about handling radical and extreme views in class (Crombie and Rowe, 2009) and a project for use with young offenders that majored on self-awareness and empathy development (Rowe and Dickson, 2006). I also became a member of the Council of Europe's human rights education team for some years, working in post-communist Central Europe, Turkey and particularly in post-conflict Bosnia-Herzegovina, where we majored on the teaching of human rights (Gollob and Krapf, 2008).

I believe that citizenship education is about helping young people understand and exercise their own legal and moral rights and thus become more respectful and tolerant of the rights and opinions of others (a central question of citizenship education being: 'What do *you* think about this issue/law/problem?'). Through moral education within this framework, young people become more sensitive and self-aware, more empathic, more able to make complex justice judgements and hence become more responsible and engaged in public issues (Rowe, 2000). They will also, I think, be more likely to flourish in their personal development and relationships and more willing to work for a world that is humane, caring, tolerant and non-violent. I believe this makes a significant contribution to the quality of our democracy and to what many Quakers call peace education. However, this raises, for me, the question of whether the term 'peace education' is adequate – would 'education for peace and justice' not be a more adequate and inclusive label? I will return to this issue later in the chapter. As a Quaker, I have felt this work, which helps young people to follow the 'promptings of love and truth' (*QF&P*, 1.02, 1), to be entirely in line with my own values. Quakers are also encouraged to remember their responsibilities as citizens 'for the conduct of local, national and international affairs' (*QF&P*, 1.02, 34), and citizenship education is an important way of helping others to do the same.

When working with teachers, I also tried to stress the importance of bringing whole-school practices, including behaviour policies (Rowe, 2006), into line with the concepts of justice, care, rights and responsibilities being taught in the classroom, such that teachers were not saying one thing while doing another. Thus, among other things, we advocated restorative practices, drawing on a range of 'just school' literature (for example Hopkins, 2004; Power and Higgins-D'Alessandro, 2008; see also the chapters by Belinda Hopkins and Anna Gregory in this volume) and the democratic involvement of students in school life as encouraged, for example, by Michael Fielding (Fielding and Bragg, 2003), all of which are morally nurturing. Some will argue that the main vehicle to develop children's pro-social values is through the lived experience of a caring school where teachers model values authentically. I believe this to be necessary but not sufficient. Others (such as Neil Hawkes, as we will see) have argued the case for teaching primary children to be able to name values so that teachers, for example, can commend positive behaviour. But I believe schools should go further and actually teach moral *reasoning*, so that students can see a situation, recognize what kind of issues are involved under the surface and know how to resolve them fairly. To do this, they need to know how to use the 'forms of thought' (Hirst, 1974) specific to moral discourse. Since the 1950s, there have been a number of attempts to introduce moral education *per se* into the curriculum[6] which, sadly in my view, were short-lived (as so often with curriculum innovations), and I have regarded much of my own work as another such attempt, this time taking advantage of the opportunities offered by the new subject of citizenship education. In support of my position, I have found very helpful the research undertaken some years ago by Robert Peck *et al.* (1960), who studied a group of adolescents between the ages of 10 and 17, conducting a wide variety of individualized tests which they triangulated with the views of peers, teachers and parents. They concluded that the most morally mature individuals displayed virtues combined with high levels of rationality and reflexivity in their moral behaviour and they called this the 'rational-altruistic' type:

> The Rational-Altruistic type ... are the most morally effective in the study. They have the best ego development of all. They are well-integrated, emotionally mature, and ... they have firm internalized moral principles which they frequently subject to critical inquiry and test to see if they work in practice. These principles are integrated into most of their thoughts and acts (compared to the rest of the population at any rate).
>
> (Peck *et al.*, 1960: 97)

Why has moral education failed to find a home in the curriculum when, after all, teachers have a duty to promote the spiritual, moral, social and cultural development of their pupils? One obstacle to undertaking moral education in common (non-faith) schools is the question of teacher confidence that what they engage in is defendable against objections by parents. The question of who decides which values should be privileged is one that, though rarely highlighted in official curriculum guidance, never goes away (Haydon, 2006; Stengel and Tom, 2006). And in the event of disagreement, whose values should be privileged – those of parents? Teachers? Governments? Having said that, it is encouraging to note the many current initiatives specifically designed to nurture pro-social values, though they adopt a number of different approaches and rationales in so doing. I want to review some of these but, first, I would like to make a few observations about the controversial nature of moral values in school. In fact, at one level, it is not unfair to suggest that schools are battlegrounds of conflicting values and that what is at stake are the hearts and minds of future generations.

Education and the good: Schools as sites of value conflict

Education has always been controversial and there is a long history of tension between those, on the one hand, who have seen it as instrumental to the economic needs of society and those, on the other, who view it as essential for personal development and fulfilment. In addition, there is a very long and honourable tradition of believing that education should be a means of social transformation. An early UK example is that of the nineteenth-century pioneers of mass public education. For example, in the 1850s, when most of the population was still very poorly schooled, activists such as the Quaker Joseph Lancaster and the Anglican Hannah More began to encourage mass literacy, but used the Bible as a basic reader to, as they saw it, lift people out of lives of moral degradation. Hannah More is a wonderful example of how interwoven educational ambitions and social values are. She is described as aspiring, through her writings, to transmit the virtues of 'content[ment], sobriety, humility, industry, reverence for the British Constitution, hatred of the French, trust in God and in the kindness of the gentry' (Wikipedia, 2017). And if we smile wryly at such dated views, we need to be aware that we are all, equally, children of our own age.

Quakers, of course, have their own history of educating their young (girls as well as boys) in their own schools before mass public education, as much to convey their own spiritual values as to provide a decent educational grounding. When the state, in the 1870s, finally began to provide universal education for children up to the age of 12, many of the established religious schools came to be supported by state funding, with the continuing freedom to promote their particular religious creeds alongside the conventional curriculum. Principally, in the UK, we have seen Anglican and Roman Catholic schools, but more recently there has been a proliferation of different faith schools. These, while preserving the family's right to 'provide their children with an education in conformity with their own religious and philosophical convictions' (European Convention on Human Rights, Article 2 of Protocol No.1), are giving rise to anxieties about children being brought up in cultural silos, less comfortable and familiar with people of different faiths. Various attempts have been made to counter this trend including school linking and, in Northern Ireland, an official cross-curricular theme called *Education for Mutual Understanding*, which Quakers, among others, have actively supported for years (Tyrrell, 1995).

I use such examples to demonstrate just how very powerfully and inextricably entangled education and social, moral and religious values are – and they are often in conflict with each other. These conflicts are less about good versus evil and more about competing conceptions of the good. Where schools openly commit to one set of values over another, it can prove hugely problematic for parents wishing to bring up their children uncontaminated by supposedly wrong beliefs or free from so-called forbidden knowledge, whether gained through the curriculum or in the playground. I think the objections of some Quaker parents to the military ethos being promoted in many schools at the present time (for example, the promotion of combined cadet forces, or the running of behavioural units by ex-military personnel in preference to teachers) are of a similar nature. Some parents go to great lengths to protect their children from what they perceive to be contaminating ideas by home-educating them, in preference to exposing them to negative spiritual or moral influences (see, for example, Keir Mitchell's chapter in this volume).

Teachers are often extremely wary of appearing to criticize the values of particular parents – school heads are generally very sensitive to parental opinion. But what is the moral duty of the liberal citizenship teacher in respect of children from families that espouse, for example, far-right politics, where this is not against the law? Is there a moral duty to 'enlighten' such pupils? If so, how? My answer, in brief, is to teach them the basics of philosophical reasoning and trust the leadings of truth.[7] Such problems of value conflict have led many teachers to accept the proposition that schools should not promote specific moral values at all. In my view, this is one reason that moral education is still not established as a subject discipline in English schools. Quakers and others who attempt to influence the school curriculum with, for example, peace and justice education need to have robust defences to the charges of indoctrination or subversion.

Values in the curriculum

During the period since the introduction of citizenship education into the National Curriculum, one very significant development has been the rising security threat from radical Islamic terrorism. While government enthusiasm for citizenship education has manifestly waned in recent years (Davies and Chong, 2016), there has been an equal and opposite emphasis on what the Department for Education (DfE) calls British Values (DfE, 2014), defined as respect for democracy, the rule of law, individual liberty, and mutual respect and tolerance of those with different faiths and beliefs. The importance currently attached to this duty is shown by the fact that schools that cannot show that they are taking adequate steps to transmit these values and safeguard students from extremist indoctrination can be described as 'failing', however good their academic record.

Other subjects, including religious education, English, history and science, are infused with certain values associated with respect for truth, evidence and integrity, and the content provides regular opportunities for students to discuss moral problems of both a personal and a social nature. Even subjects such as mathematics, which many would see as values-neutral, can be vehicles for the transmission of pro-social values (see Anne Watson's chapter in this volume).

Under the umbrella of citizenship education, there are other subsidiary areas of content that are extremely values-rich and often operate as what I will call 'quasi-subjects'. These are not formally recognized by any national curriculum frameworks but, in practice, they have become regarded as distinctive entities and they have each attracted a committed body of teacher enthusiasts, seeking to promote their particular 'education' within the broader curriculum. They are often promoted and supported by organizations outside formal education such as religious bodies, aid agencies and other charities such as Amnesty International and UNESCO. They typically privilege the values of justice, care, human rights, equality and environmental responsibility. A key characteristic of most of them is the aspiration for long-term attitudinal and behavioural change in students. Among these 'quasi-subjects' I would include: anti-racist education, multicultural education, anti-homophobia education, disability rights education, development education, global education, human rights education, holocaust education, environmental education and, not least, peace education.[8] In this respect, at least since the 1980s, Quakers have corporately attempted to influence what goes on in schools (leaving aside what Friends as individuals have achieved). Most notably this has taken the form of two curriculum packages focusing on peace education[9] and the work of a nationally appointed peace education officer.

Peace education has a huge literature of its own and is associated with a number of religious faiths. It is supported by, among others, Confucianism, Islamic Sufism, Judaism and Hinduism (Brantmeier et al., 2010), not to mention Christianity. Because peace is so central to Quaker values, we need to note some of its main characteristics here. Peace studies as an *academic* pursuit began in earnest following the world wars, with the emergence of supra-national peace-brokering bodies such as the United Nations, which, in turn, gave rise to a new body of expertise in conflict resolution. In 1975, American Quakers began to develop a conflict resolution programme, Alternatives to Violence (Wikipedia, 2018), for the inmates of a New York prison, and this appears to have subsequently influenced the production of school-level materials. It seems to have penetrated UK schools in the 1980s when Kingston Quakers, drawing on American and other sources, published *Ways and Means* (Kingston Friends, 1985) and the West Midlands Quaker Peace Education Project was established in 1987 (see Anna Gregory's chapter). Centrally, Quakers in Britain established a peace education post and related programmes around the same time. The dominant model adopted by these education programmes is largely based on conflict resolution, anger management, positive listening skills, empathy work, anti-discrimination and discussion skills. Closely allied to this approach are school peer mediation projects in which Quakers have also been prominently involved over the last thirty years or more. Generally speaking, peace education programmes have since broadened out into whole-school approaches, across all age groups from KS1 upwards, although the principal focus remains conflict reduction and peacebuilding through mediation and relational and restorative approaches (for example Cohen, 1995; Cremin, 2007; Dill, 1998; Drew, 1999; Schrumpf *et al.*, 1997; Sellman *et al.*, 2013).

Charles Harlock (2013) has studied the evolution of various forms of peace education in the English curriculum and points to a range of initiatives promoted externally by non-governmental organizations, peace activists and some educationists from within the system, including many I have already listed. Additionally, it is worth noting the World Studies (8–13) Project supported by the (Quaker) Joseph Rowntree Charitable Trust. Harlock argues that, following the introduction of the National Curriculum in 1988, many peace- and justice-oriented initiatives were squeezed out. This was not accidental, and at a time when the Cold War was still very influential on public sentiment, the official view of peace education was that it was an instrument of the political left and closely associated with the Campaign for Nuclear Disarmament – which, among other things, was funding an organization called 'Teachers for Peace' (Harlock, 2014). Around this time, I was reliably informed that human rights education was also regarded with suspicion by officials in the DfE. Harlock argues, however, that citizenship education has since then provided a curriculum location where much peace-oriented teaching can legitimately take place. Hilary Cremin and Terence Bevington (2017), on the other hand, point to the somewhat conservative, non-critical, state-centric view of the citizen set out in official National Curriculum documents. These authors support the Citizenship Foundation's assertion that schools should 'demonstrate citizenship through the way they operate' (ibid.: 107) and that 'education *through* citizenship and not just *about* citizenship lies at the heart of good peace-building practice'. This, they explain, is based on 'the authentic and truthful connection between the inner and the outer, between what is believed and what is practised' (ibid.: 108). What all this does show, of course, is that peace education is not a single entity but more of an umbrella term covering a very wide range of content areas, concepts, skills and pedagogies. It can also be controversial.

The very concept of peace is ambiguous, and this has regularly prompted peace educators to qualify it with the concept of justice, following Johan Galtung's (1969) distinction between negative peace (absence of war or conflict) and positive peace (absence of structural and cultural violence and the presence of justice). While negative peace emphasizes the importance of the reduction or removal of violence and conflict, striving for 'positive peace' stresses the importance of the *quality* of peace, which must be just and sustainable. Thus equality, justice and human rights all need to be promoted in the creation of lasting and just peaceful communities. A more recent extension of this approach seems to be an emerging emphasis on the creation of inner peace as a prerequisite for any kind of authentically peaceful outward behaviour.

The link between spirituality and peace education also manifests itself in the work of an organization called Spiritual England, which is currently promoting a Peaceful Schools project, in close association with British Quakers. Recently, and remarkably, one large Academy chain (run by Oasis, which describes itself as a 'ground-breaking global Christian movement'), has declared a commitment to introduce peace education across all of its schools as a strategic way of building resilience against Islamic radicalization, on the premise that young people need to have inspirational goals in life and that failure to provide such goals can leave young people vulnerable to less wholesome and violent alternatives (Chalke, 2016). Quakers have recently become involved with the Oasis Trust and Coventry Cathedral in organizing a national project known as Inspire. Inspire seeks to use the centenary of the end of World War I to help schools and youth groups to 'remember for peace' and encourage a questioning of what it means to be a peacemaker today.

Values across the whole school
a) Virtues-based approaches
There has recently been a surge in interest in what has become known as character education, or virtues-based education. Since 2012, the Jubilee Centre for Character and Virtues at the University of Birmingham has

become an important centre for the development of a range of curriculum projects focusing on virtues and the development of character, a term that hitherto has been more familiar in the USA than in the UK. In its own words, the centre's aim is to:

> ... promote, build and strengthen character virtues in the contexts of the family, school, community, university, profession, voluntary organisations and the wider workplace. We believe that character is constituted by the virtues, such as courage, justice, honesty, compassion, self-discipline, gratitude, generosity and humility. These virtues: 1) are critical to individual excellence; 2) contribute to societal flourishing; 3) can be exercised within all human contexts; 4) are educable.
> (Jubilee Centre for Character and Virtues, n.d.)

A strong pedagogical element of the Jubilee Centre's approach is that of students' reflection on their own moral characteristics. Students are presented with thought-provoking stimuli (such as stories of moral heroes) and are encouraged to reflect on aspects of their own character, in oral and written form, including journaling, becoming more self-aware in the process. Such processes are claimed to be effective in building moral self-identity (Carr and Harrison, 2015; Lapsley, 2008). By comparison with some of the approaches to moral education described here, there is relatively little focus on analysing moral situations or on how one determines right action in specific or complex situations.

The Virtues Project is another programme that has been recently set up in a small but growing number of English state schools, according to Nancy Thompson, writing as a concerned parent in *Quaker Voices* (Thompson, 2016). This approach also emphasizes the positive moral influence that a virtues-based programme can have on children and on the life of the whole school. The Virtues Project offers a list of 52 virtues to promote (which, naturally, boil down to a smaller number of clusters such as that around the virtue of love or care). Pedagogically, the programme encourages strategies to reinforce pro-social values and build good character. Broadly speaking, the virtues are treated unproblematically and rarely in relation to circumstances where one virtue is in conflict with another. The project's co-founder, Linda Kavelin-Popov (2000), describes the basis of the approach as spiritual and claims that the virtues at its heart are derived from the major world wisdom traditions and, hence, universal. Considerable emphasis is placed on the quality of the relationship between student and teacher. Courage, honour, justice and compassion are identified as core virtues and the project proposes that teachers should practise 'spiritual companioning' to *get alongside* students and provide an environment that is always caring and supportive. Peer mediation for the resolution of disputes is advocated, as is restorative practice for students who infringe school rules.[10] This project has much in common with character education projects at the conservative, uncritical end of the spectrum, which are more common in the USA than in the UK (Stengel and Tom, 2006: 16).

At the time of writing, the most influential programme of this kind in the UK is probably Values-based Education (VbE), founded by Neil Hawkes, a former primary head and local authority inspector. This is a whole-school approach whose aim is to instil in students a respectful awareness of the importance of what Hawkes calls 'universal human values'. These values are drawn from religious, classical and humanistic traditions, while Hawkes also brings recent work in positive psychology and brain science to support his focus and methodology.

Pedagogically, the VbE movement emphasizes the value of reinforcing a small number of core values, once these have been locally agreed by staff in partnership with students and parents (thus avoiding any charge of 'indoctrination'). These values might typically include: cooperation, happiness, responsibility, simplicity, freedom, unity, peace, respect, love, tolerance, honesty and humility (Hawkes, 2003). These 12 values become the focus of pupils' attention by rotation on a monthly basis (variations include 11 values, omitting August when schools are closed, or identifying 22 values to provide a two-year cycle). They are promoted in school assemblies and teachers reinforce them in various ways through work in class, which often includes a weekly discussion of a moral issue relating to that month's value. Behaviourally, these values become the building blocks of the school's ethos. Students are commended and rewarded for behaviour that is in line with the values, and poor behaviour is discouraged as being against the agreed collective ethos of the school. Hawkes (2013: 82) asserts that 'there is no doubt that ... traditional forms of discipline may control children's behaviour, but there is scant evidence that they help them to act from a code of ethics rather than from the fear of punishment'. (Fear of punishment is stage 1 in Kohlberg's hierarchy of reasons to behave well.) I note that, absent from Hawkes's typical list of values quoted here, is justice, which, arguably, is a key moral concept and one that has been prominent in the Judaeo-Christian and classical traditions. I believe this absence is unfortunate, especially in view of the centrality of the justice concept to the citizenship curriculum.

Crucially, according to Hawkes, teachers must be willing to examine their own values and act as role models and he argues that staff should make use of inward reflection and stillness as a means of personal spiritual development, thus achieving a greater level of moral authenticity and consistency. Teachers then encourage their students to use moments of reflective stillness to become more self-aware and hence more understanding of others. These meditative practices are encouraged for students of all ages. Hawkes (2013: 103) recalls how, as a headteacher, he had 'noticed that people who appeared to be reflective seemed to be more self-aware and have a greater capacity for wisdom'. In terms that echo, albeit implicitly, moral development theory, he believes that personal reflection aids the internalization of the school's values.

It is claimed that several thousand schools in the UK are now values-based schools. The VbE movement holds that effective values education improves school ethos, creates a better learning environment and, hence, raises academic achievement. Support for such claims has come from an Australian federal roll-out, which was evaluated on a large scale by the University of Newcastle, New South Wales (Lovat *et al.*, 2009).

b) *Rights-based approaches*

Morally speaking, programmes that focus on personal virtues draw inspiration from traditions going back to Aristotle in the classical tradition and from the major world religions, in which individuals aspire to act in accordance with the values of their faith. From this perspective, right action (or good behaviour) is regarded as an expression of the good character of the person (hence the term *virtue* ethics). But I would argue that the morality that emerged with the Enlightenment, drawing on the concept of rights, is equally important in places such as schools. In the event of people's failure to show kindness or respect to others spontaneously in the school setting, it becomes necessary to inhibit anti-social behaviour, to protect the rights of others as part of the school's duty to safeguard *all* members of its community.

The Rights, Responsibility and Respect (RRR) project was developed as a rights-based approach to behaviour management, based on the pioneering Canadian research of Katherine Covell and Brian Howe (2001). These researchers found that, when children of any age were made aware of their rights, they simultaneously became more sensitive to the rights of others. At the heart of this approach is the United Nations Convention on the Rights of the Child (UNCRC). It adopts a democratic, participative pedagogy and emphasizes the importance of participation in all aspects of school life, which must have regard for the physical and social as well as cognitive development of all its students. All school policies should be in line with the UNCRC, and teaching strategies about rights must be developmentally appropriate. Positive relationships are encouraged between all members of the school.

Covell and Howe have carried out a considerable amount of evaluation of the Rights, Responsibility and Respect approach, both in North America and in the UK. One major evaluation was conducted in Hampshire, offering training to primary and secondary schools right across the county (Covell and Howe, 2011). When implemented effectively across the whole school, the approach reportedly resulted in confident usage of rights language by children of all ages, with commensurate improvements in respectful behaviour. Improved learning also followed, and children perceived the school to be a safer and more caring environment. This values-rich approach explicitly puts the values of equality, dignity, respect, non-violence, non-discrimination and participation at its heart. The emphasis on the *duty* to respect other people based on their rights is in contrast to virtues-based approaches, which regard positive behaviour as spontaneously offered to others, as if it were a gift.

The United Nations Children's Fund in the UK (UNICEF UK) also promotes this approach under the banner 'Rights Respecting Schools' through its own curriculum resources and a whole-school award. UNICEF UK has introduced a national set of awards based on two levels of accreditation. The four-year accreditation process depends on the collection of evidence to show that four standards have been met, initially at Level 1 and, fully, at Level 2. Take-up of the programme is growing strongly at present and nearly 5,000 schools in the UK are now registered.[11]

An empirical evaluation of this programme was carried out by the Universities of Sussex and of Brighton. Their findings mirrored those of Covell and Howe, in that there were improved relationships between staff and pupils and schools experienced an internal climate that was more conducive to learning and improved levels of attainment. Many of the findings in terms of school climate were similar to the findings of the research into Values-based Education.

c) *The use of silence and silent reflection in schools*
One other recent values-rich phenomenon is worthy of mention at this stage: increasingly, it seems, arguments are being made in favour of promoting silent reflection in schools – arguments that, I believe, Friends ought to find intrinsically of value, given that their predominant mode of worship is deep

Whose values? Which values?

silence. Quakers will naturally understand the power of silent reflection in the process of personal development.

Anthony Seldon (2013) of Wellington College (an independent boarding school) described the revolution that began when he transformed the ethos of his school, and which ended in very significant improvements in academic achievement. Seldon wrote:

> Quiet listening is fundamental. Periods of 'stillness' increasingly punctuate the school day. I regularly ask all 1200 in school assembly to close their eyes and be totally still. I begin each weekly staff meeting on Monday break with a period of silence which allows everyone to collect themselves and let go of the baggage. Mindfulness is key to all we do.
>
> (Seldon, 2013)

It is noteworthy that, recently, we have seen the more widespread use of the term *mindfulness in schools* now that, in the Western imagination, this term has become sufficiently detached from any underpinning metaphysical belief structures so as to render it culturally non-threatening. In her recent book *Silence in Schools,* Helen Lees (2012) argues that silence is increasingly being used to promote individual well-being as well as whole-school harmony. Like Hawkes and Seldon, she sees both psychological and spiritual value in such approaches, including those adopted in Quaker independent schools in the UK. Lees points out that some forms of silence in schools are technique-less, while others are based on well-established techniques for stilling the mind. Some programmes are offered to all students and, in some schools, older students can opt to go further into developing personal meditative practices.

Katherine Weare has studied the impact of a number of mindfulness projects with both students and staff in state-maintained schools, although such studies are still in their infancy, particularly for young people. For students, Weare (2013) found that, when well taught and practised regularly, mindfulness was capable of improving mental health and well-being, mood, self-esteem, self-regulation, positive behaviour and academic learning. Among staff, Weare (2014) found early indications of benefits, not only in terms of stress reduction but also 'increased kindness and compassion to others, including greater empathy, tolerance, forgiveness and patience, and less anger and hostility'. Some Quakers have also begun to use mindful breathing in classes, as reported by the Peaceful Schools Project coordinator of Mid Wales Area Quaker meeting:

> Much of the work is done with circle time. We use a mixture of talking, sharing, exercises and games. We use quiet periods and mindful breathing to give pupils the skills to handle their own stresses, and stories to focus attention on particular issues.
>
> (Peaceful Schools Project, n.d.)

This work is part of six-week peace education programmes offered by the Peaceful Schools Project to primary schools in parts of North Wales. Many such initiatives are designed to help students become more self-aware, more self-controlled, more empathic and tolerant, more respectful of the rights of others, more pro-social and engaged in the community. I believe my own work on promoting the moral development of students through critical group analysis of moral issues is entirely consistent with, and complementary to, such programmes. I have been successful to a degree in encouraging teachers to undertake this work under the banner of citizenship or values education, but I remain frustrated in my personal ambition to see 'moral education' accepted as a recognized and explicit element of the mainstream curriculum. The analysis of moral issues as presented in stories reflecting real-life situations that students recognize as familiar has the advantage of replicating the thought processes required of every individual facing situations which can be understood at a moral level. Thus, a circle session based on an apparently simple chain of events can yield, on examination, complex interactions of rights, obligations, justice, care and so on.

There seems to be a regrettable degree of fragmentation across the various values-based initiatives that I have described, with some schools claiming to be 'virtues-based' and others 'rights-based'. I see no justification for this division. Morality embraces *both* virtuous behaviour *and* respect for the rights of others and requires individuals ideally to have a mastery of moral concepts and forms of thought and to be mature in their personal judgements. I believe a more holistic approach, underpinned by a grasp of moral philosophy and moral development theory, would result in more coherent and holistic practices in schools. I believe such developments would be entirely in line with the aspiration of Friends regarding education for peace and justice.

Quakers and education

I have presented evidence that, despite official pressures intensifying the need for schools to meet top-down assessment criteria, many educationists are attaching importance to values-based practices and teaching, and they list a wide range of values and virtues they deem important in the education of young people. For many years, the Religious Society of Friends has characterized its educational work as promoting peace, but peace is just one of Quakerism's core values. Friends also espouse equality, justice, truth, integrity, simplicity and concern for the environment. In addition, though not in the testimonies, Quakers place great value on love and care, following Jesus's treatment of the downtrodden and forgotten of society and George Fox's exhortation to recognize 'that of God' in everyone. This was a theme underlined by the Quaker teacher Francis Pollard (1932) in his Swarthmore Lecture entitled *Education and the Spirit of Man*. In speaking of the duty of the Quaker (and the Christian) educator, he speaks of the importance of combating 'ignorance and prejudice which are the enemy of humanity and the denial of the claims of the good' (ibid.: 71) and states that 'ethical judgement and the forward-looking mind are of the essence of the right educative attitude' (ibid.: 73).

It is arguable that all of the above could be included under the umbrella of peace education by Quakers attached to the label as a descriptor of what they do. But I question whether it is rich enough a term for the purpose. For example, justice cannot be divorced from our thinking about peace, as we have seen. It is a concept central to moral thought and it has the added advantage of having more purchase in the curriculum than peace, as a key concept of the citizenship curriculum. I agree with John Rawls (1972: 3) that there is no higher social value than justice and that 'justice is the first virtue of social institutions, as truth is of systems of thought'. Thus, a key question that all democratic citizens should learn to ask is: 'Is this practice or situation or law (for example) fair?' In the same way, Quakers qualify what kind of peace they espouse, namely a *just* peace, not peace achieved through strength, as Ian Harris and Mary Lee Morrison (2003) put it. And in the same way, in 2011, the World Council of Churches issued *An Ecumenical Call to Just Peace* – not merely to peace (WCC, 2011).

I wonder if, because of our habituation to the term, Friends sometimes use the word 'peace' uncritically. We need to distinguish peace as a state (which all Friends would aspire to) from peace or non-violence as a process. Very many Christians, including many Quakers, see themselves as committed peace-builders but are not equally convinced that a just peace can *always* be achieved or maintained without resorting to force. Witness to this are those early Quakers, including George Fox and Isaac Pennington in the seventeenth century (*QF&P*, 24.21; Valentine, 2013), who were willing to accept the necessity that, on occasions, the state needs to exert force to maintain peace and protect the weak, and those Friends who, more recently, were willing to fight against Nazism in the Second World War

(Rubinstein, 2016). David Rubinstein argues that Friends were divided about fighting what many were arguing was a just war and, having wrestled with their consciences, came to conflicting conclusions. But he stresses that, while divided on this point, what united them as Quakers was 'the principle of the Inner Light guiding the individual conscience' (ibid.: 107).

Jasper Ungoed-Thomas (1997), a former Inspector of Schools and member of the Lifeline Moral Education project, wrote a book called *Vision of a School: The good school in the good society,* in which he argued that the following values, or virtues, are intrinsic to any school that claims to promote the good. As he puts it:

- Respect for persons is the first virtue of the personal school.
- Truth is the first virtue of the whole school curriculum.
- Justice is the first virtue of the school as an institution.
- Responsibility is the first virtue of the school as a community.

(Ungoed-Thomas, 1997: 5)

For myself, I think this conception of the ideal school has much to commend it – it is multi-layered and complex and more immediately actionable than the term 'peaceful'. And although I think it is arguable that 'care' should be regarded as the first virtue of a community (rather than responsibility), I suspect this is quite close to Ungoed-Thomas's intention here. Added together, this conception of the school as an ethical community (as Graham Haydon, 2006, describes it) would indeed be peaceful, but is it not of value for us, as Quakers, to follow Ungoed-Thomas in configuring our aims for education so as to *explicitly* include truth, care (love), responsibility and justice as well as peace? It would be, to my way of thinking, a more holistic, rich, inclusive and less ambiguous definition.

Perhaps this is controversial – it proposes a reframing of Quaker corporate work, not necessarily abandoning its more narrow focus in practical terms. However, some work already embraces multiple forms of 'peace education' – witness to this is the recent publication by Friends of a Peace Week curriculum (Religious Society of Friends, n.d.) that embraces traditional conflict resolution work, human rights activities, moral reasoning, exercises to encourage inner stillness – and much more. Certainly, a broader explicit focus would, to my mind, make sense of the fact that, in the following chapters, besides peace and conflict education, there are Quakers promoting 'just schools', those working on inequality, or arguing for various forms of care in education. There is clearly a distinction to be made between the work of individual Quaker teachers and our corporate activities, which, in practice, have been more concentrated and less diverse

– they are not the same and, hence, I argue that our understanding of, and discourse about, the Quaker mission in education needs to be broad, holistic, inclusive and true to all our Quaker testimonies.

Whatever term we favour, this review of values-rich practices as currently encountered in English schools is surely encouraging – despite the very strong government emphasis on education for economic survival in a global world. The scene is obviously a dynamic one with much that Quakers would wish to support and, dare I suggest, even learn from. It is encouraging that there is much research and strong anecdotal evidence to support the view that the Quaker approaches and government ambitions to promote academic achievement are not entirely inimical.

Notes

[1] Mercer shows that children go through stages of expertise in discussion – disputational, accumulative and, finally, exploratory, in which they offer and accept each other's ideas to advance to new understandings.

[2] For more about this important grassroots critical thinking movement, see the website of SAPERE: www.sapere.org.uk.

[3] To see the method in use, see Part 1 of the video, 'Introducing Citizenship', available online from www.youtube.com/watch?v=exrsdE876zY.

[4] This discussion can be seen in the video cited above, see Section 2 entitled *Weighing the Evidence*.

[5] This lesson can be found in the Council of Europe publication *Living in Democracy*, Unit 3, Lesson 1 (Gollob and Krapf, 2008).

[6] Besides Kohlberg's moral dilemma discussions, these include Peter McPhail's empathy-based *Lifeline* series (McPhail *et al.*, 1972) and John Wilson's approach to teaching 'moral philosophy' (Wilson, 1990).

[7] For a more detailed discussion of this challenge, see Crombie and Rowe (2009).

[8] Another very significant and active 'education' of a slightly different order is the *Philosophy for Children* movement, promoting critical, reflective and exploratory thinking at the same time as encouraging the development of tolerant and respectful debating and discussion skills.

[9] *Ways and Means*, a conflict resolution pack produced by Kingston Friends (1985), and the West Midlands Quaker Peace Education Project (*Peacemakers*) established in 1987 (see Anna Gregory's chapter in this volume).

[10] The project website is www.virtuesproject.com.

[11] For more information go to: www.unicef.org.uk/rights-respecting-schools/ (UNICEF UK, 2018).

References

Bickmore, K. (2013) 'Peacebuilding through circle dialogue processes in primary classrooms: Locations for restorative and educative work'. In Sellman, E., Cremin, H. and McCluskey, G. (eds) *Restorative Approaches to Conflict in Schools: Interdisciplinary perspectives on whole school approaches to managing relationships*. London: Routledge, 175–91.

Brantmeier, E.J., Lin, J. and Miller, J.P. (eds) (2010) *Spirituality, Religion, and Peace Education*. Charlotte, NC: Information Age Publishing.

Carr, D. and Harrison, T. (2015) *Educating Character Through Stories*. Exeter: Imprint Academic.

Chalke, S. (2016) *Radical: Exploring the rise of extremism and the pathway to peace*. London: Oasis Books.

Cohen, R. (1995) *Students Resolving Conflict: Peer mediation in schools*. Glenview, IL: Good Year Books.

Covell, K. and Howe, R.B. (2001) 'Moral education through the 3 Rs: Rights, respect and responsibility'. *Journal of Moral Education*, 30 (1), 29–41.

Covell, K. and Howe, R.B. (2011) *Rights, Respect and Responsibility in Hampshire County: RRR and resilience report*. Sydney, NS: Cape Breton University Children's Rights Centre.

Cremin, H. (2007) *Peer Mediation: Citizenship and social inclusion revisited*. Maidenhead: Open University Press.

Cremin, H. and Bevington, T. (2017) *Positive Peace in Schools: Tackling conflict and creating a culture of peace in the classroom*. London: Routledge.

Crombie, B. and Rowe, D. (2009) *Dealing with the British National Party and Other Radical Groups: Guidance for schools*. London: Citizenship Foundation. Online. www.youngcitizens.org/dealing-with-the-bnp-and-other-radical-groups-in-schools (accessed 12 November 2017).

Davies, I. and Chong, E.K.M. (2016) 'Current challenges for citizenship education in England'. *Asian Education and Development Studies*, 5 (1), 20–36.

DfE (Department for Education) (2014) *Promoting Fundamental British Values as Part of SMSC in Schools: Departmental advice for maintained schools*. London: Department for Education.

Dill, V.S. (1998) *A Peaceable School: Cultivating a culture of nonviolence*. Bloomington, IN: Phi Delta Kappa Educational Foundation.

Drew, N. (1999) *The Peaceful Classroom in Action: A K-6 activity guide on how to create one and how to keep it!* Torrance, CA: Jalmar Press.

Dunn, J. (1988) *The Beginnings of Social Understanding*. Oxford: Blackwell.

Fielding, M. and Bragg, S. (2003) *Students as Researchers: Making a difference*. Cambridge: Pearson Publishing.

Galtung, J. (1969) 'Violence, peace, and peace research'. *Journal of Peace Research*, 6 (3), 167–91.

Gibbs, J.C., Basinger, K.S. and Fuller, D. (1992) *Moral Maturity: Measuring the development of sociomoral reflection*. Hillsdale, NJ: Lawrence Erlbaum Associates.

Gilligan, C. (1982) *In a Different Voice: Psychological theory and women's development*. Cambridge, MA: Harvard University Press.

Gollob, R. and Krapf, P. (eds) (2008) *Living in Democracy: EDC/HRE lesson plans for lower secondary level* (Education for Democratic Citizenship and Human Rights in School Practice 3). Strasbourg: Council of Europe Publishing. Online. https://rm.coe.int/16802f7304 (accessed 5 February 2018).

Harlock, C. (2013) 'The evolution of modern peace education in UK schools'. *Teaching Citizenship*, 37, 8–11.

Harlock, C. (2014) 'The Development and Evolution of Peace Education in English Secondary Schools from Post World War 1–2010'. Unpublished MPhil thesis, Coventry University. Online. https://core.ac.uk/download/pdf/30618034.pdf (accessed 12 November 2017).

Harris, I.M. and Morrison, M.L. (2003) *Peace Education*. 2nd ed. Jefferson, NC: McFarland and Co.

Hawkes, N. (2003) *How To Inspire and Develop Positive Values in Your Classroom*. Cambridge: LDA.

Hawkes, N. (2013) *From My Heart: Transforming lives through values*. Carmarthen: Independent Thinking Press.

Haydon, G. (2006) *Education, Philosophy and the Ethical Environment*. London: Routledge.

Hirst, P.H. (1974) *Knowledge and the Curriculum: A collection of philosophical papers*. London: Routledge and Kegan Paul.

Hopkins, B. (2004) *Just Schools: A whole school approach to restorative justice*. London: Jessica Kingsley Publishers.

Huddleston, T. and Rowe, D. (2001) *Good Thinking: Education for citizenship and moral responsibility*. London: Evans Education.

Huddleston, T. and Rowe, D. (2015) 'Discussion in citizenship'. In Gearon, L. (ed.) *Learning To Teach Citizenship in the Secondary School: A companion to school experience*. 3rd ed. London: Routledge, 94–103.

Jubilee Centre for Character and Virtues (n.d.) 'About the Jubilee Centre'. Online. www.jubileecentre.ac.uk/355/about (accessed 7 December 2017).

Kavelin-Popov, L. (2000) *The Virtues Project: Educator's guide*. Austin, TX: Pro-Ed.

Kingston Friends (1989) *Ways and Means*. Kingston, UK: Kingston Friends Workshop Group.

Kohlberg, L. (1984) *The Psychology of Moral Development: The nature and validity of moral stages* (Essays on Moral Development 2). San Francisco: Harper and Row.

Lapsley, D.K. (2008) 'Moral self-identity as the aim of education'. In Nucci, L.P. and Narvaez, D. (eds) *Handbook of Moral and Character Education*. New York: Routledge, 30–52.

Lees, H.E. (2012) *Silence in Schools*. Stoke-on-Trent: Trentham Books.

Lovat, T., Toomey, R., Dally, K. and Clement, N. (2009) *Project to Test and Measure the Impact of Values Education on Student Effects and School Ambience: Final report for the Australian Government Department of Education, Employment and Workplace Relations*. Newcastle, NSW: University of Newcastle. Online. www.curriculum.edu.au/verve/_resources/Project_to_Test_and_Measure_the_Impact_of_Values_Education.pdf (accessed 5 February 2018).

McPhail, P., Ungoed-Thomas, J.R. and Chapman, H. (1972) *Moral Education in the Secondary School* (Lifeline). London: Longman.

Mercer, N. (1995) *The Guided Construction of Knowledge: Talk amongst teachers and learners*. Clevedon: Multilingual Matters.

Mosley, J. (1996) *Quality Circle Time in the Primary Classroom: Your essential guide to enhancing self-esteem, self-discipline and positive relationships*. Cambridge: LDA.

Mosley, J. and Tew, M. (2014) *Quality Circle Time in the Secondary School: A handbook of good practice*. 2nd ed. London: Routledge.

Noddings, N. (2008) 'Caring and moral education'. In Nucci, L.P. and Narvaez, D. (eds) *Handbook of Moral and Character Education*. New York: Routledge, 161–74.

Peaceful Schools Project (n.d.) 'Peace Edu: The Peaceful Schools Project'. Online. https://quakersmidwales.org/peace-education (accessed 7 December 2017).

Peck, R.F., Havighurst, R.J., Cooper, R., Lilienthal, J. and More, D. (1960) *The Psychology of Character Development*. New York: John Wiley and Sons.

Piaget, J. (1932) *The Moral Judgment of the Child*. Trans. Gabain, M. Glencoe, IL: Free Press.

Pollard, F.E. (1932) *Education and the Spirit of Man* (Swarthmore Lecture). London: Allen and Unwin.

Power, F.C. and Higgins-D'Alessandro, A. (2008) 'The just community approach to moral education and the moral atmosphere of the school'. In Nucci, L.P. and Narvaez, D. (eds) *Handbook of Moral and Character Education*. New York: Routledge, 230–47.

Rawls, J. (1972) *A Theory of Justice*. Oxford: Clarendon Press.

Religious Society of Friends (n.d.) 'Peace Week'. Online. www.quaker.org.uk/resources/free-resources/peace-week-resources (accessed 25 January 2018).

Rest, J.R., Narvaez, D., Thoma, S.J. and Bebeau, M.J. (2000) 'A neo-Kohlbergian approach to morality research'. *Journal of Moral Education*, 29 (4), 381–95.

Rowe, D. (2000) 'Common schools, good citizens: Towards a public discourse model of moral education'. In Best, R. (ed.) *Education for Spiritual, Moral, Social and Cultural Development*. London: Continuum, 68–79.

Rowe, D. (2001) *The Sand Tray*. London: A&C Black.

Rowe, D. (2006) 'Taking responsibility: School behaviour policies in England, moral development and implications for citizenship education'. *Journal of Moral Education*, 35 (4), 519–31.

Rowe, D. (2010) *Under the Skin: An enquiry based approach to identity, race and nationality*. London: Citizenship Foundation.

Rowe, D. (2014) *Scaffolding Moral Talk in the Classroom: A professional development unit*. Birmingham: The Jubilee Centre for Character & Virtues. Online. www.jubileecentre.ac.uk/userfiles/jubileecentre/pdf/My%20Character%20PDFs/Rowe%20-Scaffolding%20Moral%20Talk.pdf (accessed 11 March 2018).

Rowe, D. and Dickson, A. (2006) *Smart Thinking: Helping young people develop moral reasoning and thinking skills about offending and anti-social behaviour*. Lyme Regis: Russell House Publishing.

Rowe, D. and Newton, J. (eds) (1994) *You, Me, Us! Social and moral responsibility for primary schools*. London: Home Office. Online. www.tes.com/teaching-resource/you-me-us-6144159 (accessed 11 March 2018).

Rowe, D. and Thorpe, T. (eds) (2002) *Your Rights and Responsibilities: Understanding the role of law in society*. London: Evans Brothers.

Rubinstein, D. (2016) *Essays in Quaker History*. York: Quacks Books.

Schrumpf, F., Crawford, D.K. and Bodine, R.J. (1997) *Peer Mediation: Conflict resolution in schools*. Rev. ed. Champaign, IL: Research Press.

Seldon, A. (2013) 'Why the development of good character matters more than the passing of exams'. Priestley Lecture, Jubilee Centre for Character and Values, University of Birmingham, 23 January 2013. Online. www.birmingham.ac.uk/Documents/college-social-sciences/education/events/priestley-2013-anthony-seldon.pdf (accessed 7 December 2017).

Sellman, E., Cremin, H. and McCluskey, G. (eds) (2013) *Restorative Approaches to Conflict in Schools: Interdisciplinary perspectives on whole school approaches to managing relationships*. London: Routledge.

Stengel, B.S. and Tom, A.R. (2006) *Moral Matters: Five ways to develop the moral life of schools*. New York: Teachers College Press.

Thompson, N. (2016) 'The Virtues Project'. *Quaker Voices*, 7 (2), 23–9.

Tyrrell, J. (1995) *The Quaker Peace Education Project 1988–1994: Developing untried strategies*. Coleraine: Centre for the Study of Conflict.

Ungoed-Thomas, J. (1997) *Vision of a School: The good school in the good society*. London: Cassell.

UNICEF UK (2018) 'Rights Respecting Schools Award'. Online. www.unicef.org.uk/rights-respecting-schools/ (accessed 5 February 2018).

Valentine, L. (2013) 'Quakers, war, and peacemaking'. In Angell, S.W. and Dandelion, P. (eds) *The Oxford Handbook of Quaker Studies*. Oxford: Oxford University Press, 363–76.

WCC (World Council of Churches) (2011) *An Ecumenical Call to Just Peace*. Geneva: World Council of Churches.

Weare, K. (2013) 'Developing mindfulness with children and young people: A review of the evidence and policy context'. *Journal of Children's Services*, 8 (2), 141–53.

Weare, K. (2014) *Evidence for Mindfulness: Impacts on the wellbeing and performance of school staff*. Exeter: University of Exeter.

Wikipedia (2017) 'Hannah More'. Online. https://en.wikipedia.org/wiki/Hannah_More (accessed 29 April 2017).

Wikipedia (2018) 'Alternatives to Violence Project'. Online. https://en.wikipedia.org/wiki/Alternatives_to_Violence_Project (accessed 5 February 2018).

Wilson, J. (1990) *A New Introduction to Moral Education*. London: Cassell.

Chapter 3
Relational and restorative practice in educational settings: A values-based, needs-led approach
Belinda Hopkins

This chapter focuses on the development of a new approach to teaching, learning and addressing relationships in schools that I have personally been involved in, and played a significant role in developing, over the last twenty years or so.

The approach, now widely referred to as Restorative Practice, began as a narrowly focused process based on a new initiative being used in the field of youth justice. This process was founded on the philosophy of restorative justice. However, over the course of twenty years, educationists and others have taken this very narrow, functional approach and, based on experience and reflection – with insights and contributions from many other fields, fashioned it into what amounts to a different way of *being* in school. Taken on fully, Restorative Practice affects how the leadership team leads, how teachers teach, how young people learn and how everyone in the school community interacts with each other. These interactions could be in the way they forge new relationships, maintain those already in place or address conflicts and challenges to heal and repair relationships. The school community in this context includes all paid and voluntary staff (from the grounds staff and cleaning team to the senior leadership team and Board of Governors), the students and their parents and carers, all the visiting professionals who support staff and young people, and any other stakeholder involved in the life of the school. No longer an approach inspired by, and based on, criminal justice, which is how some people used to think of it, Restorative Practice now offers a template for developing social justice in schools and, as such, will be an initiative dear to Quakers' hearts.

In this chapter, I explain why a new approach to relationships has been needed in schools, and set out briefly the historical and geographical roots of the approach. I describe my own involvement in, and contribution

Relational and restorative practice in educational settings

to, the rise of Restorative Practice in the UK and how various Friends have supported me and influenced my development for many years. Finally, I reflect on my own personal experience of supporting whole-school change and what I believe is needed for bringing about what, for some people, is a cultural revolution in schools.

School and conflict

Schools are no strangers to conflict. Children and young people are still learning what it is to be social beings, and many mistakes are made getting that right. After all, there are very few places where so many people of more or less the same age are obliged to spend many hours a day in each other's company, engaged in activities they may not have chosen for themselves. Adults and the young people in their care may also find themselves in conflict on a regular basis, in part because adults expect compliance from children and young people with the rules and expectations often laid down by the adults themselves. Do we need a different way of thinking what education is all about? The following piece from *QF&P* was written by Janet Gilbraith (1986) in relation to peace education, but I tend to think it refers to all education:

> I feel peace education is about teaching children to discover that they have power to change things they see are wrong and developing the imagination to find alternative responses to conflict ... If we teach children to feel their own power we must be ready for them to criticize the school itself. In order to survive we must begin to teach them to challenge authority, our own included.
>
> This means there are likely to be conflicts. And conflicts are to be welcomed as opportunities for growth. Too often conflict leads to violence and aggression because we are trapped in a mentality which expects every conflict to be resolved by a victory by one party. But victory for one implies of necessity defeat for the other and therein lies the seed of further conflict.
>
> (Gilbraith, 1986, 62–3: *QF&P*, 23.85)

Staff deal with conflicts and challenges as best they can, but unless they are skilled listeners and mediators, it is likely that someone will feel hard done by, and then they have to deal with appeals and complaints. Traditional approaches to gaining compliance are based on rewards and sanctions and these are still what one mostly finds in schools across the UK, even in

Quaker schools. This is because most teachers have not received training, either at college or on the job, in developing intrinsic motivation and self-regulation (what I call an 'inner moral compass'), nor are they helped much with relationship-building, conflict management and mediation. They often know of no alternative approach, even though they instinctively sense that punishment or threats of punishment are very blunt instruments for gaining compliance and addressing difficulties. If staff rely on a compliance and discipline policy that involves sanctions, then they are likely to have even more conflicts, since punitive threats and responses:

- cause resentment rather than reflection
- discourage empathy, since the wrongdoer tends to think only of the consequences to themselves of any harmful actions they engage in, and not the consequences on those they have affected
- are rarely considered fair
- do not repair relationships between those in conflict and indeed can make them worse
- leave those labelled as wrongdoers feeling bad about themselves, leading to further alienation and conflict
- can often leave the adults expected to act punitively feeling uncomfortable and frustrated – and wishing there were an alternative
- can lead to a climate of deceit and fear, since the likelihood of punishment encourages those who do wrong to avoid discovery and to threaten those who might otherwise report wrongdoing.

When in conflict, people need a chance to tell their side of the story, express their own thoughts and feelings, reflect on their own needs in a situation and on the needs of others, feel understood by the others involved and, if harm has been caused, find ways to put things right, to move on, to feel better about themselves and learn how to do things differently another time.

Approaching any situation with this mindset changes the way people talk, even if it is an exchange lasting minutes – in a playground or a corridor, for example. Dealt with in this way, these conflicts help people repair the damage done to their connections with the others involved or even build connections where there were none previously. People feel fairly treated and respected, since they have been trusted to find solutions for themselves and put things right in their own way. Because they have been listened to, people in conflict are more ready to listen to others' perspectives and emotional responses and so empathy is developed. This can change the choices made in future situations, as mutual respect and consideration develop.

So many schools have come to the conclusion that 'if you do what you've always done, you'll get what you've always got'. Things need to change! They want to reduce the need for sanctions (which often mean exclusions). They want people to feel heard and fairly treated whatever their age or status. They want to raise attendance among staff as well as students! They want some job satisfaction back!

So what can be done? Clearly there is a need to equip school staff with the skills and techniques they have not learnt initially. Some teachers are natural mediators and resolvers of conflict and, for them, coming across Restorative Practice is a joy. At last, they see a structure that recognizes and validates what they have been trying to do all along – but with no system and no consistent framework for their practice. For others, this approach does not come naturally. Rather than joy, instead they can display fear, masked behind anger at being asked to change their practice. So offering training to teachers in schools is not without its challenges. And training alone is not enough. It is only one tiny step towards the whole-school culture transformation that is needed if the Restorative Approach is to be successful. This chapter will talk about one approach that offers a clear, consistent, replicable and teachable model of practice that is helping to transform schools across the UK.

International development of restorative approaches

To set the development of restorative approaches in schools in the UK in context, I will sketch briefly the history of restorative justice *per se*. Every field has its legends and stories, and restorative justice is no different. While tracking restorative approaches to wrongdoing back through history, both in the West and elsewhere, commentators like to refer to four key sources of inspiration for the current wave of interest in restorative justice.

One key part of the story is the development in New Zealand of the Family Group Conferencing (FGC) model for dealing with youth offending, enshrined in the youth justice system since 1989 as the preferred way of dealing with any offence other than the most violent crimes (McCold, 2001). This approach was in response to Maori communities' unhappiness with how their young people were disproportionately finding themselves on the wrong side of the law and being dealt with in a way that went against the Maori custom of involving friends and family in resolving the situation (Consedine, 1995). This model included some community accountability for what might be behind the young person's wayward behaviour and for helping to reintegrate them back into the community. This process involved everyone affected by an incident coming together, sitting in a circle and having the opportunity to share how they had been affected by what happened and then sharing ways forward to repair the harm.

The second story develops from the first, since the New South Wales Police Force in Wagga Wagga developed its work with young offenders (and later other offenders), inspired by the New Zealand model. Sergeant Terry O'Connell, supported by John Macdonald and David Moore, developed what has become known as 'the scripted conferencing model'. They had been influenced by the good reports of what was happening in New Zealand (Moore and O'Connell, 2003). O'Connell's model streamlined the Maori model and, by creating a script, enabled the process to be disseminated widely and quickly among police officers. The process was still based on the key principles of listening to all affected, exploring the impact of what had happened and collaborating to find ways forward, with the emphasis being on repairing harm – on restoration, both materially and also in terms of relationships.

The third strand is the story of Mark Yantzi and Dave Worth, Mennonites working in the criminal justice system in Kitchener, Ontario. In 1974, they dared to do differently when handling the case of two young men who had vandalized the properties of 22 residents in a nearby town. They proposed the idea of arranging for the men to meet their victims, to hear directly from those affected about how what they had done had impacted on their whole family and to agree with each family what they could do to make amends. Unprecedented as this was, the judge administering the sentence made this possible. The young men were taken to the houses of each victim and, in almost all cases, there was a positive outcome and reparation was made. The meetings had a dramatic effect on the two men and on the lives of many of the victims, and was the beginning of a Victim Offender Reconciliation Program (VORP) that spread through Canada, to the USA and then to Europe (Peachey, 1989; Zehr, 1990). Later, one of the men recounted how his life had been changed by the meetings and how he had gone on to work as a volunteer for a VORP scheme (Yantzi, private communication, 2004).

The fourth strand comes from Canada, where First Nation communities, especially in the Yukon, developed 'sentencing circles', involving the community in deciding the appropriate sentence and way forward for a young offender, endorsed by the judge who also takes part. Zehr (1990) points out the value of involving the community in dealing with its own problems and the potential this offers to build relationships between people and communities.

It is worth pondering at this point on the difference between these kinds of community-led encounters (with the emphasis on story-sharing, emotional expression and collaborative problem-solving) and the way most schools currently deal with conflicts and difficulties. What challenges to the existing power structures and hierarchies does such a community-led approach present?

Restorative developments in the UK

It is important to recognize that, before terms like 'restorative justice' reached our shores, restorative work had been taking place in the UK for many years under the guise of victim–offender mediation (inspired by the aforementioned VORP programmes) and community mediation.[1] Services offering both were scattered around the country, relying on statutory funding and intermittent government support. Peer mediation was, similarly, being developed in piecemeal ways around the country but was not having a major impact on how schools managed behaviour.

In 1997, a multi-agency meeting was held by the Thames Valley Police to introduce youth justice professionals and educationists to restorative justice for the first time.[2] The Thames Valley is a large area encompassing the three counties of Berkshire, Oxfordshire and Buckinghamshire in the south-east of England. Terry O'Connell, a police officer from New South Wales Police Force, had been invited over to the UK by Charles Pollard, the then Chief Constable of the Thames Valley Police Force. He explained the concept of restorative conferencing and how a restorative conference (meeting) worked; how, with careful preparation, the victim of a crime is given the opportunity to sit down in a circle with the offender (the person responsible for the crime) in the company of members of their respective communities, usually close family members; how each person in turn has the chance to tell their own story about what has happened and how they have been affected; how the offender also tells their story and is able to answer the victim's unanswered questions; how there comes a moment in the meeting when deep remorse and shame are experienced, often by many people in the room, and how from this there comes a tipping point when the focus shifts towards repair and healing; and finally how, after a discussion in which all present find ways forward, with an agreement written down and signed by all, there is a symbolic breaking of bread – a chance to share refreshments and talk more informally.

Listening to O'Connell describe the potential of restorative conferencing for addressing youth offending, many people present at his talk saw the links between school settings and youth justice settings. It seemed likely that restorative approaches could also address issues such as disruption, aggressive behaviour, bullying, petty crime and disaffection. It was possible that they may hold the key to reducing the need for exclusions or, at least, make re-integration meetings post-exclusion more meaningful.

How O'Connell's talk changed the course of my life

As a classroom teacher, I had been using what I would now term relational and restorative practices on a daily basis throughout the 1980s and early 1990s. Such terms did not exist at that time, and it was many years before they became more widely known. As a trainee teacher, I had been influenced by the writings of John Holt (1964), Ivan Illich (1971), Everett Reimer (1971), Neil Postman and Charles Weingartner (1971), all of whom were critical of mainstream educational ideas and of the suppression of children's creativity, autonomy and voice. A move to Bristol in 1983 brought me in touch with the Peace Education Network and some of the inspirational publications from the USA, such as *A Manual on Nonviolence and Children* (Judson, 1977) and the work of inspirational Friend Jim Wingate in the UK, whose book *How To Be a Peace-Full Teacher* (1987) is long overdue a revival.

I first came across Quakers in Bristol after a personal tragedy and found the values held by the people I met, and the way this was lived through their daily lives, a real support at a difficult time. I was encouraged to get more involved working with the young people there, especially by Marian Liebmann, who has been a friend and a mentor since those days.

By 1990, I had two very young children and we had moved to Reading. After a few years at home I returned to teaching in the local comprehensive school which happened to be for girls only. The school was a mix of white working-class girls who lived locally, in a very socially deprived area of South Reading, and Muslim girls from families around the city who valued single-sex education. Behaviour was sometimes challenging, but what distressed me most was the level of unpleasantness between students, the put-downs and sparring, mostly verbal. Like the vast majority of teachers, I had received little, if any, training in so-called 'behaviour management' or relationship management. I sought help in further training. The course 'Playing with Fire' at Leap Confronting Conflict, founded by Quakers, was a road-to-Damascus experience for me. It was exactly what I needed, but not just for my immediate experience in the school. What I learnt on the course helped me to identify, for the first time, what I really wanted to do in my life – namely, to share the skills of community-building, conflict resolution and mediation with as many schools as possible. In effect, I wanted to help transform schools and make them happier, safer and more harmonious places where effective teaching and learning can take place, where adults and young people respect each other and learn from each other.

Initially, I offered to run circle time for my colleagues during their tutor group sessions and also to mediate when some of the students found themselves in conflict. The school was not ready to introduce peer mediation at the time and I was a long way from realizing that it might be possible to transform a whole-school behaviour management system. However, I did experience the power of regular circle work on the relationships and dynamics of class groups. Circle work helped to bridge the cultural and ethnic divide in the classes. It also developed emotional literacy and gave everyone in the circle a voice and an opportunity to share their thoughts, feelings and needs. I saw how it empowered children to be problem-solvers and build empathy and compassion. I saw evidence of how behavioural issues and conflicts between class members were much diminished by having regular circle experiences with each other. I began to teach more and more of my modern language classes using the circle time format, with very positive results both academically and socially among the students. And I knew that I wanted to share all these discoveries more widely than in one school.

I became involved in Reading's mediation service, founded and largely run by a group of volunteers based at Reading Friends' meeting house. I soon became not only a volunteer neighbourhood mediator but also a trainer of mediators, and helped to set up several new mediation services in Berkshire and North Hampshire. With a huge leap of faith, and much encouragement from Reading Quaker meeting and tremendous support from my husband, by 1994 I had left the classroom, established myself as a freelance conflict resolution trainer and founded my company Transforming Conflict.

It was then that I met Hilary Cremin, when I attended one of her courses for people delivering peer mediation training. At the time, Hilary was running her own peer mediation company, Catalyst, having initially worked for the West Midlands Peace Education Project, now Peacemakers (see Anna Gregory's chapter). She is now a Reader at the University of Cambridge Faculty of Education and a leading researcher in the field of peace education and restorative practice in education. To this day, Hilary remains an important source of support and encouragement to me.

And so it was that, in the mid-1990s, I was in the right place at the right time when the Thames Valley Police began to take an interest in restorative justice. Initially, I was not aware of what this was, but was lucky enough to be funded by them to introduce a peer mediation service into a primary school. The service, in Geoffrey Field Junior School in South Reading, is still running today and is among the longest-running peer mediation projects in the UK.

This early involvement was probably why I was invited to hear Terry O'Connell speak to multi-agency staff on one of his early visits over from Australia. These visits led to training being arranged for key police personnel and then later for multi-agency staff, and gradually policy began to develop, driven by Charles Pollard. In the Thames Valley, a restorative justice consultancy was established to roll out training, principally to police officers in the first instance. At that time, various educational initiatives were being developed, which began to make links between schools and restorative justice.

Initial restorative work in schools

I was invited to be trained as a restorative justice facilitator and join a national team of trainers to deliver this practice to police officers around the country. Committees were set up to explore the potential of restorative justice in school settings (and I was thrilled to be on these). A series of public events were organized to raise awareness of its potential not only for schools but also for prisons (Preston, 2002). A pilot project began in Banbury, Oxfordshire, in 1998, in which a police officer, Graham Waddington, was placed full time in Drayton School to work restoratively with young people and support the school in dealing with challenging behaviour. This would be the school where I ran one of the first ever whole-school training courses for teachers a few years later. The then headteacher, Graham Robb, has since become a leading light in the field of restorative justice and youth justice.

As an educationalist, my interest in restorative approaches was, from the outset, driven by their transformative potential and their contribution to creating safer, more respectful, more caring communities and to help develop the relationship and citizenship skills of young people. For me the word 'justice' in the term 'restorative justice' was closer to my notion of *social* justice than *criminal* justice. I was not alone in these views, but the focus of police interest was more on the potential of restorative approaches to reduce reoffending and to lower the number of school-age young people on the streets by reducing exclusions.

What excited me was that I saw the relationship between work I had been doing in schools for many years and the potential of a restorative justice philosophy to provide an overarching framework for this work. I had suspected for a long time that working with children on short-term projects addressing violence, bullying, peace-making and so on – or even establishing circle time, school councils, peer mentoring schemes and peer mediation in schools – would never make a huge difference if adults were still modelling *power over* rather than *power with*. In other words, while that bastion of power, the behaviour management system based on sanctions and rewards, remained in place, adults working in schools were not actually able to model the values and principles of mutual respect and empowerment that were fundamental to so many of the aforementioned projects and initiatives. I, like many teachers, had found myself under pressure to assert my own authority, impose my own (and the school's) expectations on my classes and use the sanctioning system available to me if students did not comply. My own internal conflict made me very uncomfortable, and many teachers have told me since how reassuring it is to at last find a system that realigns their practice with the values and beliefs that first took them into teaching. As Friend John Guest writes:

> When I taught my children how to do many things I ensured that they would have skills to give them abilities, enjoyment and health. What I think I chiefly taught them was that I was right and they were wrong. When I hear them teaching their friends how to play games I realise just how much I bossed them around. In seeking to pass on our values to our children I think we largely waste our time. They will pick up our values from us by the way we live and the assumptions that underpin our own lives.
>
> (*QF&P*, 23.82)

I began to write about the connections between the restorative response to conflict and challenge as opposed to the traditional retributive one. I made links between proactive circle time and responsive, interpersonal resolution, mediation and restorative conferencing, urging people to consider restorative justice more as a whole-school approach than a discrete intervention (Hopkins, 1999a, 1999b, 2002, 2003). I did not realize at the time that, simultaneously, in other countries, others were making similar calls (Cameron and Thorsborne, 2001; Claassen, 2000a, 2000b; Morrison, 2001; Riestenberg, 2000).

Developing the model for transforming practice and culture

A great opportunity came when the Thames Valley Police commissioned me to adapt their conferencing training for use with teachers in schools. Prior to this, I was being commissioned to work in schools but was used to developing bespoke training courses for wherever I was working, drawing on some tried-and-tested materials that I had gathered, adapted or invented, inspired by books I had read or courses I had been on. My involvement as a volunteer for the Alternatives to Violence Project (AVP) for several years, a project that many Friends have been involved in, gave me many good ideas and a love of experiential, participative learning. This style of training is what I still love best.

Around this time, again encouraged by Friends from my Quaker meeting, I had begun my doctoral research into the narrated experiences of teachers who had received training in restorative conferencing. The feedback I was getting was that, although they appreciated the power of the restorative conference, they wanted a wider range of skills – especially to help them with day-to-day occurrences in classrooms, corridors and playgrounds. This was the spur I needed to make a bold choice. Rather than simply adapting the Thames Valley Police training course (itself adapted from Terry O'Connell's training),[3] I drew on all my influences over the previous ten years or more and developed, for the first time, a training course specially designed for educationalists. The early course incorporated proactive techniques such as circle time to build community in classrooms, lots of Jim Wingate's (1987) ideas for developing young people's ability to take responsibility for their own learning, interpersonal conflict resolution, face-to-face mediation, and the more formal restorative conferencing process for when things had gone badly wrong and parents and carers needed to be involved.

At the time, this course was commissioned by Thames Valley Police, who had developed a partnership with a company called Real Justice, now better known as the International Institute of Restorative Practice (IIRP). My contention that mediation was a restorative practice did not go down well, and I was asked to remove all references to mediation from the course. The view that mediation and restorative justice conferencing are very different was held by several other practitioners at that time (and indeed is still held by some today). However, the course was built up, step by step, incorporating all the values, principles and core micro-skills of mediation into the larger restorative conferencing practice (as opposed to a script-based approach). It was like being asked to pull the skeleton from a body, or the foundations from a building. I took the bold step of retrieving the course from the metaphorical dustbin to which it had been consigned.

The words from Quaker Advices and Queries offer great support when asked to do something that feels wrong: 'If pressure is brought upon you to lower your standard of integrity, are you prepared to resist it? ... Do not let the desire to be sociable, or the fear of seeming peculiar, determine your decision.' (QF&P, 1.02, 38). Fortunately, I had retained copyright of the course, so although it was not suitable for Real Justice, I still owned it and had the right to start offering it independently – which is what I have now been doing for over 15 years.

Change-agency

Since the original course was developed, the field has greatly evolved. 'Restorative approaches', as I first termed them in schools and care homes, have now more widely become known as restorative practice. Internationally, there is a growing consensus, backed by research (Kane et al., 2007), that for the approach to make a real difference in any environment it needs to involve systemic change. The senior team need to be not just on board, but *modelling* the practice; this process of cultural transformation can take between three and five years, and will need constant nurturing and developing after that (Hopkins, 2011; 2013; Thorsborne and Blood, 2013).

When I first began offering training courses in a range of restorative processes, I had no idea about how to manage organizational change, nor that it would be necessary. It swiftly became clear that, for teachers to take on board a restorative approach in their school, what was required was a complete transformation in the way people handled their relationships, managed conflicts and challenges, and delivered the curriculum. Systems, policies, procedures and protocols needed to be in place, as did timetabling that freed up people to use their restorative skills. Evaluation, monitoring and recording procedures needed to be congruent with intended outcomes. A restorative approach offered a systematic way to build, maintain and repair these relationships, but, to be successful, what was required was for everyone in the school community to adopt the same approach and be supported by, and indeed led by, management in doing so.

Winning hearts and minds

As I intimated earlier, the restorative approach can pose challenges to teachers who are used to expecting compliance and, like so many people, believe that when someone has done something wrong they need to be punished (despite the lack of evidence that this actually does change behaviour or develop self-regulation). Also, there is often resistance to dedicating time to developing strong classroom communities and having pro-social goals for one's lessons as well as academic ones. When the pressure is on to achieve outstanding academic results, the links between happy, well-balanced, mentally stable young people who feel safe and valued, on the one hand, and their academic success, on the other, are so readily forgotten.

The challenge for someone keen to introduce teachers to the restorative approach is to acknowledge the deep-seated beliefs associated with wrongdoing. The more traditional authoritarian mindset might typically begin with the person in authority asking themselves:

- What happened (with the focus on fact-finding and gathering witness statements)?
- Who started it? Who is to blame? Who is the guilty party?
- What is the appropriate response to deter and possibly punish those at fault, so they will not do the same thing again?

It can be seen that the emphasis on gathering evidence, taking down witness statements, identifying the culprits and then assigning the appropriate punishment all have much in common with the criminal justice system. But why do educationalists take their model from the 'name, blame, shame and punish' model? Instead, an adult more versed in the restorative perspective would ask themselves:

- What's happened (with the focus on hearing different perspectives)?
- Who has been affected and how?
- What do those affected need?
- How can those involved find a way forward together and put things right?
- How can everyone do things differently in the future?

Within this paradigm shift in thinking lie the keys to culture change and to winning hearts and minds. Underpinning the request that everyone share their different perspectives is the implicit belief that everyone has a unique and valuable voice that is worth hearing – and indeed needing to be heard. Expressed in this way, most people agree that this is something worth striving for – as an adult in the school who wants to feel valued and also as an educator who wants to bring up children to feel valued. What are the implications for a whole institution of creating the kind of place where everyone's voice is heard? The question can be reflected on without feeling threatened – although there are deep-seated implications for striving for such an environment.

Asking how people have been affected by a given situation implies attention to their felt experiences and their innermost thoughts, which in turn impact on their emotions. It implies that there is an interest in the impact of our actions on others – and points to an environment where there is consideration, respect and empathy for those around us. When seen from this perspective, again teachers can generally agree that developing these qualities in every young person is a goal worthy of taking action towards. So what are the implications for an institution where these issues are in the forefront? What is often not appreciated at first is that the traditional behaviour management systems neither give an equal voice to all ages when something goes wrong, nor encourage consideration, respect and empathy.

Asking what everyone affected by a situation needs – and perhaps what the unmet needs had been that had led them to behave as they did – also implies a freedom from judgement and, instead, a focus on empathy and understanding. What can be done to create an institution where this kind of deep understanding is part of everyday thinking? Once again, seen in this way, teachers are often willing to explore how this might be possible.

Asking how those most affected can be supported to find ways forward implies a belief that it is those most affected by a situation who are best placed to find ways forward for themselves – a belief in collaboration and empowerment. How can an institution become a place where shared problem-solving is the norm – for whole staff groups, smaller teams, classes, parents and staff? Surely this must be an aspiration for all educators – to develop the ability of young people to think independently and learn how to face up to, and resolve, problems for themselves.

Five core beliefs

By asking these questions, I came to develop my own particular model of whole-school restorative change (and, indeed, the model can be applied to any institution, organization or workplace), which I believe links very closely to values Quakers hold dear – respect, equality, empathy and social justice.

First, I identified five core beliefs with which I invite school staff, and readers of this chapter, to align themselves:

Core Belief 1: *Restorative practitioners believe that everyone has their own unique perspective on a situation or event and needs an opportunity to express this and feel heard.*

In this regard, it is not appropriate for any one person to impose their own view on others without there being a chance for everyone to have their say. The respect accorded to everyone's individual perspective also has implications in environments where some people have greater power and authority than others.

Core Belief 2: *Restorative practitioners believe that what people think at any given moment influences how they feel at that moment and these feelings inform how they behave.*

Thoughts and feelings are often hidden beneath the surface and yet are key to understanding why people behave the way they do. 'Lowering the waterline' and sharing what is going on inside can lead to much greater mutual understanding and authentic connection.

Core Belief 3: *Restorative practitioners believe that our actions and deeds impact on those around us. It can be helpful to reflect on the wider ripple effects of any given action or incident.*

Anticipating such ripple effects and seeking to minimize any harm in advance are essential to maintaining good relationships with others. When there are conflicts or disagreements, harm can result – in the form of negative emotions such as anger, hurt, fear, frustration and confusion and in terms of damaged relationships and connections between people. Taking time to think about the ripple effects with empathy can help move the situation forward.

Core Belief 4: *Restorative practitioners believe that when our needs are met we can function at our best and that all our actions are strategies we have chosen to meet our needs at the time.*

To make decisions or solve problems, it helps to identify the needs of all concerned first, and then it is easier to identify appropriate strategies to address these needs. Unmet needs can be the underlying cause for harmful behaviour. Whether someone has caused harm or been on the receiving end of it, they are likely to have similar needs. Until these needs are met, the harm may not be repaired and relationships can remain damaged. These need exploring to help people break the cycle of inappropriate behaviour. Identifying what people need precedes identifying strategies to meet these needs. My understanding of needs has been inspired by my long-term study of Nonviolent Communication (Rosenberg, 2001).

Core Belief 5: *Restorative practitioners believe that it is those who are affected by an issue or problem who are the people best placed to find ways forward – in collaboration with each other.*

People value being consulted and involved in decision-making in matters that concern them. Conversely, people tend to resist and resent decisions imposed on them.

This ownership of decision-making and problem-solving demonstrates respect and trust, develops pro-social skills and confidence, strengthens connections and helps to develop an inner moral compass (what Don Rowe refers to as 'moral maturity' – see his chapter in this volume).

Five-step framework
Next, I set out a framework for interacting with others that is based on these five core beliefs. I offer five questions people can use when engaging with others in a conflict scenario:

1. 'What's happened?'
   Variations of this can be used depending on the situation: What's happening? What's going on? What's up? What's troubling you? – and so on.
2. 'What were you thinking when … ? And so how were you feeling inside?'
   This question can be used several times at various stages of the account, since we have countless thoughts and related feelings in the course of minutes, hours and days; variations might include: What was going through your mind? What were you telling yourself?
3. 'Who do you think has been affected by what has happened, and how? What are the ripple effects?'
   Future-focused discussion variations might include: Who may be affected if you do this?
4. 'What do you need to be able to move forward and for things to be put right?'
5. 'What do you think needs to happen next to put things right/to move forward?'
   (if appropriate: What could you do to put things right?)

Learning to use this five-step framework is as much about avoiding other habituated responses to conflict and misbehaviour and simply learning to listen. It can require huge restraint from some people to avoid:

- judgement
- giving advice
- reprimands
- expressions of surprise/shock/anger/disapproval
- taking sides
- assuming that any side has the monopoly on truth
- thinking you know what's going on!

Five applications
Once the basic framework has been learnt, there are daily opportunities to use it:

- As a *five-step self-reflection process* before ever engaging with anyone or opening one's mouth, asking oneself each question.
- *One-to-one, listening to another person – restorative enquiry –* in supervision or when counselling, offering a supportive listening ear, listening before saying anything if someone has done something you do not like, or undertaking private individual preparation for a face-to-face meeting.
- In *face-to-face meetings* as a five-step framework for mediating between two people in conflict. In a school, this might be between two students, a student and an adult, two adults on the staff, or a parent and a member of staff.
- In *group problem-solving meetings* when everyone has the opportunity to reflect on each question in turn, sitting in circle, perhaps with a facilitator posing the questions. This can be used for classroom problem-solving, in team and staff meetings and for governor meetings, parent groups and so on. Everyone gets used to using a talking piece[4] and passing it around the circle with no interruptions and no breaking the flow or pulling rank as it goes around.
- In *formal restorative conferences* with a facilitator and probably involving students with their family or carers in the event of serious incidents. Such meetings would always be preceded by private preparation, using the restorative enquiry model.

In my five-day training course, everyone learns how to use the five-step framework in these five scenarios. The next step is to practise as much as possible and, then, share the successes.

Implementation

There are some excellent resources out there now to help schools with implementing whole-school cultural change (for example, Thorsborne and Blood, 2013). The steps I have outlined are my preliminary ones for at least getting a school started. From there, people can begin to think about what they need to do to bring existing policies and procedures for addressing challenges into line with the restorative ethos.

Thought needs to be given to how to help people transition from one way of doing things to another and to offer support when things go wrong. Not everyone is up for this new approach. Some schools like to introduce different elements of an approach one by one.

One secondary school I am working with chose to introduce weekly 45-minute circle time sessions for all tutor groups from Year 7 to Year 13.

There have been some initial teething problems as not all staff felt comfortable in the role of circle time facilitator and not all students appreciated the benefits. (Other schools have chosen to introduce the process class by class, beginning with Year 7.) However, all the senior leadership team have been trained in circle facilitation and have been supporting any staff experiencing problems by, for example, forming smaller, safer circles for students who have found it difficult to engage without sabotaging.

The leaders are also using circle processes for their own meetings and staff meetings generally, using a talking piece and ensuring everyone in turn has the chance to contribute. At the same time, this school has had non-teaching Year Heads and behaviour support staff trained in a range of restorative interventions so that, when young people are in conflict with a member of staff, someone is on hand to help. Meanwhile, all teaching staff are being familiarized with the five-step questioning framework and encouraged to use it as appropriate when addressing classroom challenges.

Another secondary school I have been working with for many years began with the training in restorative conversations and mediation. Now, all their Progress Leaders (Year Heads) are able to respond when students are in trouble. This school actually came across restorative approaches, via my book *Just Schools* (Hopkins, 2004), when they were in the process of reviewing their policies on teaching and learning. They wanted young people to take more responsibility for their learning and for the development of social and meta-cognition skills, and found their old behaviour management system was at odds with this. They discovered what John Dewey was writing about many years ago:

> If you have the end in view of ... children learning certain set lessons, to be recited to a teacher, your discipline must be devoted to securing that result. But if the end in view is the development of a spirit of social co-operation and community life, discipline must grow out of and be relative to that aim.
>
> (Dewey, 1907: 3)

The school now integrates the five-step questioning framework into lesson delivery, encouraging students to reflect more deeply on what they are learning, how and why – what they are personally thinking, feeling and needing in their studies – but also, when appropriate, to reflect on the thoughts, feelings and needs of literary characters, historical figures and people in the worlds of social science and politics. In other words, they deepen the learning by engaging in the affective domain. This is another school where the circle process is a regular part of classroom and staffroom practice. Restorative practice is woven into everything they do and hence takes no more time than traditional, more authoritarian, styles of teaching and behaviour management. It is a completely different paradigm and not a bolt-on for which extra time needs to be found. In fact, staff would say they spend much less time on behavioural issues, as they arise less often. The school has now gained a national award for being a restorative school and has monitored the impact of the approach on a range of performance indicators. In 2016, they were proud to share the following statistics about positive changes during the six years we had been working together:

- Exclusions were down by 93 per cent.
- The school no longer used detentions or merit awards as external behaviour control mechanisms and, instead, young people were encouraged to develop internal self-regulation and skills such as sensitivity and consideration for others.
- Beyond-the-school-gates referrals to the local Youth Offending Service were down 78 per cent and anti-social behaviour attributable to young people in the town was down by 48 per cent.
- Attendance was at its highest level ever – 94 per cent and rising.
- Staff absenteeism with a stress-related tag was down by 60 per cent – a saving of over £60,000 and a testament to how beneficial the restorative approach can be for staff health and well-being.
- In 2017, the school achieved its best-ever GCSE and A-Level results, and was the most-improved school in England and Wales.

These successes have been attributed in large measure to its restorative ethos, which nurtures staff as well as students so that everyone feels supported to go that extra mile.

Conclusion

Implementing a restorative culture in any school makes sense for both the children and young people and the adults who work in the school. The approach offers the perfect way to ensure that peace, truth, equality and social justice are modelled and upheld – values that Quakers hold dear. Who could object to places of learning that are safe, happy, respectful and productive?

Recently, at a meeting of the senior leadership team of a school in Denmark, I asked them what struck them most about their visit to a number of English restorative schools. 'Everyone was happy, friendly and smiling' was the answer. And that is what they want for their own school, a school where every student is either a refugee or an immigrant, and that is located in a place with a reputation for being violent and ghettoized. I am optimistic that their wish will come true. As I write, the team I trained in the full range of restorative processes has returned to Denmark eager to begin instituting regular circle time into all their classes. Around their necks they wear a lanyard with a series of cards attached, reminding them of the five-step questioning framework they can use whatever occurs, instead of the previous reprimands or punishments. They are going to live adventurously – and they are going to make a difference.

Notes

[1] Marian Liebmann from Redland Meeting in Bristol has played a huge role in developing both Victim–Offender Mediation and also Community Mediation in the UK. She helped to found the Forum for Initiatives in Reparation and Mediation (FIRM) in 1984, which later became Mediation UK, under her directorship.

[2] Several years before, Mark Umbreit from Minnesota had spoken on this topic at a conference organized by Mediation UK, and Victim–Offender Mediation was already quite widely established around the UK. But links between these areas and education were not being made explicitly, except perhaps through peer mediation projects, where interpersonal conflict and wrongdoer/wronged issues were dealt with in similar ways.

[3] To be fair to Terry, his own involvement in schools in New South Wales led him also into very varied and different ways of engaging staff and young people, and he was very supportive of my work and willing to share his experiences generously.

[4] The talking piece is an object that is passed round the circle, indicating whose turn it is to talk.

References

Cameron, L. and Thorsborne, M. (2001) 'Restorative justice and school discipline: Mutually exclusive?'. In Strang, H. and Braithwaite, J. (eds) *Restorative Justice and Civil Society*. Cambridge: Cambridge University Press, 180–94.

Claassen, R. (2000a) 'Holistic discipline'. *Conciliation Quarterly*, 19 (2), 2–3.

Claassen, R. (2000b) 'From principles to practice'. *Conciliation Quarterly*, 19 (2), 4–5.

Consedine, J. (1995) *Restorative Justice: Healing the effects of crime*. Lyttelton, NZ: Ploughshares Publications.

Dewey, J. (1907) *The School and Society: Being three lectures by John Dewey, supplemented by a statement of the University Elementary School*. Chicago: University of Chicago Press.

Gilbraith, J. (1986) 'Hope and imagination'. In *Learners All: Quaker experiences in education*. London: Quaker Home Service.

Holt, J. (1964) *How Children Fail*. London: Pitman.

Hopkins, B. (1999a) 'Restorative approaches in the community'. *Mediation*, 15 (3), 3–4.

Hopkins, B. (1999b) 'Restorative justice in schools'. In *Restoring the Balance: A handbook of restorative approaches in community safety*. Chilton: Thames Valley Partnership, 93–101.

Hopkins, B. (2002) 'Restorative justice in schools'. *Support for Learning*, 17 (3), 144–9.

Hopkins, B. (2003) 'Restorative justice in schools'. *Mediation in Practice*, 1 (April), 4–9.

Hopkins, B. (2004) *Just Schools: A whole school approach to restorative justice.* London: Jessica Kingsley Publishers.

Hopkins, B. (2011) *The Restorative Classroom: Using restorative approaches to foster effective learning.* London: Optimus Education.

Hopkins, B. (2013) *Improving Behaviour with Restorative Approaches: Develop a learning ethos and positive relationships across your school.* London: Optimus Education.

Illich, I. (1971) *Deschooling Society.* Harmondsworth: Penguin.

Judson, S. (ed.) (1977) *A Manual on Nonviolence and Children.* Philadelphia: New Society Publishers.

Kane, J., Lloyd, G., McCluskey, G., Riddell, S., Stead, J., Weedon, E., Maguire, R. and Hendry, R. (2007) *Restorative Practices in Three Scottish Councils: Final report of the evaluation of the first two years of the pilot projects 2004–2006.* Edinburgh: Scottish Executive. Online. www.gov.scot/Resource/Doc/196078/0052553.pdf (accessed 5 February 2018).

McCold, P. (2001) 'Primary restorative justice practices'. In Morris, A. and Maxwell, G. (eds) *Restorative Justice for Juveniles: Conferencing, mediation and circles.* Oxford: Hart Publishing, 41–58.

Moore, D.B. and O'Connell, T.A. (2003) 'Family conferencing in Wagga Wagga: A communitarian model'. In Johnstone, G. (ed.) *A Restorative Justice Reader: Texts, sources, context.* Cullompton: Willan Publishing, 212–24.

Morrison, B. (2001) 'The school system: Developing its capacity in the regulation of a civil society'. In Strang, H. and Braithwaite, J. (eds) *Restorative Justice and Civil Society.* Cambridge: Cambridge University Press, 195–210.

Peachey, D.E. (1989) 'The Kitchener Experiment'. In Wright, M. and Galaway, B. (eds) *Mediation and Criminal Justice: Victims, offenders and community.* London: SAGE Publications, 14–26.

Postman, N. and Weingartner, C. (1971) *Teaching as a Subversive Activity.* Harmondsworth: Penguin.

Preston, N. (2002) *Restorative Justice: A new school of thought?* Chilton: Thames Valley Partnership.

Reimer, E. (1971) *School is Dead: An essay on alternatives in education.* Harmondsworth: Penguin.

Riestenberg, N. (2000) 'Restorative schools'. *Conciliation Quarterly*, 19 (2), 6–7.

Rosenberg, M.B. (2001) *Nonviolent Communication: A language of compassion.* Encinitas, CA: PuddleDancer Press.

Thorsborne, M. and Blood, P. (2013) *Implementing Restorative Practices in Schools: A practical guide to transforming school communities.* London: Jessica Kingsley Publishers.

Wingate, J. (1987) *How To Be a Peace-Full Teacher.* Canterbury: Pilgrims Publications.

Zehr, H. (1990) *Changing Lenses: A new focus for crime and justice.* Scottdale, PA: Herald Press.

Chapter 4
Building, maintaining and repairing a peaceful culture in school
Anna Gregory

The West Midlands Quaker Peace Education Project (WMQPEP) (more commonly known as 'Peacemakers') has been working in schools since 1987. It delivers peace education via practical workshops and experiences that develop social and emotional learning, and furthers understanding of how to resolve conflict creatively.[1] In this approach, peace education is the explicit teaching of the values, skills and knowledge required to help people in schools operate more harmoniously with each other. WMQPEP educates *for* peace, not *about* peace, in that it promotes the foundational skills needed for peace, such as communication, inclusion, dialogue and conflict transformation. The work is informed by the Quaker testimony of peace. *QF&P* gives this advice in relation to peace:

> The places to begin acquiring the skills and maturity and generosity to avoid or to resolve conflicts are in our own homes, our personal relationships, our schools, our workplaces and wherever decisions are made.
>
> We do not have a blueprint for peace that spells out every stepping-stone towards the goal that we share. In any particular situation, a variety of personal decisions could be made with integrity.
>
> (*QF&P*, 24.10)

The peace testimony is put into practice in the work of Peacemakers through the use of games, activities, drama and stories. Working as part of a group, having fun together, creating peace within ourselves and then extending this to develop interpersonal peace is at the centre of the work. Many of the children who have taken part in our workshops self-identify as peacemakers. They appropriate the word and become the peacemakers for their school.

School culture

Until 2010, we – the Peacemakers team – worked by delivering termly peace education workshops to a single cohort per school. These workshops would run for up to two hours a week for ten weeks. Separately, we also offered peer mediation training for both pupils and staff, plus one-off peace education workshops. However, we began to feel this method of working, good though it was, achieved only limited impact across the whole school. We wanted to explore how to join up the separate elements of peace education, including the practice and theory of mediation and alternatives to violence, along with whole-staff training. So, in 2011, we conceived the Whole-School Approach Project to help schools to create a more holistic peaceful culture.

The culture of a school is hard to define. Often, there is a feeling as you walk through the door at reception that gives a clear indication of how the school operates. This feeling makes a far greater impact on school life than the posters and displays identifying the school mission statement or core values. The relationships between people (how the receptionist greets you or talks on the phone to parents), or the relationships between people and their environment (what the building looks like in terms of its displays and so on, plus how it is used) are an embodiment of the school culture.

Relationships in a restorative approach

The whole-school approach was designed to be a cultural change programme that develops the school's capacity to build, maintain and repair relationships and foster a more peaceful community that, at the same time, supports teaching and learning. It includes a wide variety of training options for both adults and children, alongside the development of the seen and unseen systems that make up a school's culture. The development of this project was informed by a restorative approach (see Hopkins, 2004;[2] Wright, 1999; and Belinda Hopkins's chapter in this book). A restorative approach puts the repairing of relationships over and above the need for assigning blame and dispensing punishment. In a school setting, a restorative approach is a departure from seeing a wrongdoing as a breaking of the school rules to understanding it as a form of harm experienced by a person or persons. It is a move away from establishing blame or guilt (Who did what? What do they deserve by way of punishment?) to exploring what happened (Who needs what? What feelings do people have? And how are people going to move forward?). Importantly, in a school, it is a departure from the imposition of a punishment towards a joint process where the goal is for all parties to

Building, maintaining and repairing a peaceful culture in school

be responsible for, and involved in, a reconciliation process and to consider future accountability by putting things right.

Typically, relationships are the focal point of a restorative approach. A relationship can be between people, between a person and their environment, and/or between a person and their learning, and/or between a person and their role. How we feel, what we think and who is affected by our actions all impact on these relationships. Therefore, central to a restorative approach is the understanding that relationships are not static or fixed but that they need *building* up, they need *maintaining* to stay healthy and, when things go wrong, they need support to *repair* them. These many interconnecting relationships, shown in Figure 4.1, make up the culture of the school, a culture that is built on shared values.

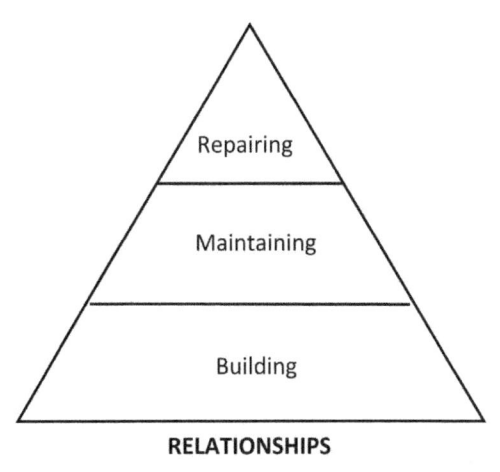

Figure 4.1: The Relationship Triangle
Source: Abridged from Vaandering (2014a), adapted from Morrison (2007) and Hopkins (2011)

For Peacemakers, the starting point is clarity around the term 'peace', which we interpret as *positive* peace (following Galtung, 1969). For Johan Galtung, negative peace is the absence of violence, such as a ceasefire. It is negative because something undesirable has stopped happening, though the violence may only be repressed at this stage – or it may persist in structural form, as in a system or an institution. Positive peace, on the other hand, is an active process whereby the building of relationships and the creation of social systems that serve the needs of the community are the focus. Positive peace includes the use of non-violent processes of managing conflict. It emphasizes the presence of justice, systems that are equal and fair, and the development of a shared ethos across an organization or community.

In schools, we can work towards achieving these characteristics by using restorative practices such as circles, checking in with each other (building), peer mediation (maintaining) and more formal restorative conferences (repairing).

To be clear, a peaceful culture, whether in a school, a town or within a family, is not about doing away with conflict. Conflicts are an important and unavoidable part of being a social human being. What is important is how we deal with them:

> Conflicts are inevitable and must not be repressed or ignored but worked through painfully and carefully. We must develop the skills of being sensitive to oppression and grievances, sharing power in decision-making, creating consensus, and making reparation.
>
> (*QF&P*, 24.10)

The whole-school approach

The Peacemakers' Whole-School Approach Project was piloted in three Birmingham state primary schools from 2011 to 2014. From 2014, we made it part of our core offer and it now operates in between one and three schools per year. Although the schools receive comparable input, each interprets and adapts the work differently. There is no one-size-fits-all approach. Indeed, the project explicitly takes into account the changing landscapes in which schools are operating, including, but not limited to: increased intake of children with special educational needs, the departure of a senior leader, increasing complexity around social media, a change in government or even a change in curriculum. We quickly learnt that if we were to operate as agents of change within a school, we needed to remain adaptable and confident that the final outcomes would be positive, albeit different in each case. We have built on the groundwork laid by those before us (Boyes-Watson and Pranis, 2015; Hopkins, 2004, 2011; Vaandering, 2014a, 2014b; Zehr, 1990) to offer a diverse, needs-focused, tiered package that works with schools at a pace that suits them. The Peacemakers' Whole-School Approach Project has responded to Dorothy Vaandering's call to create a comprehensive approach:

> ... in which 'reactive' post-incident conflict resolution strategies to repair harm are bracketed by 'proactive' democratic peace-building engagement of the adults in the school and the 'proactive'

infusion of democratic peace-building pedagogies in classrooms such as class meetings and cooperative learning.

(Vaandering, 2014b: 511)

As such, the Peacemakers' philosophy understands the term *whole-school approach* to mean that the employment of restorative practices – designed to build, maintain and repair relationships – affects all aspects of the school. It is hoped that these practices can be used to their full potential by both adults and children within the school. Peacemakers also extends this understanding of the term to include the variety of physical spaces within the school (classrooms, lunch hall, playground, corridors, offices) and the content and the delivery of the curriculum. This chapter is therefore largely organized around the themes of building, maintaining and repairing relationships.

Level one: Building a peaceful culture
The circle
Much has been written about the value of circle work (Bickmore, 2013; Boyes-Watson and Pranis, 2015; Hopkins, 2004; Stuart and Pranis, 2006), which I do not want to repeat here except to share a few methods that have worked for me. All Peacemaker sessions, with children and adults, are conducted in a circle. Working in circles helps me not only to demonstrate practice and theory together but also to develop trust with people in the school.

The circle must be even and round, not a 'squircle' (an approximation that does not give everyone an equal place). Everybody should be able to see each other comfortably. There should be chairs (I do not personally conduct circles sitting on the floor) and the gaps between the chairs should be even. Many of the games demand an identifiable space. Some schools working with very young children use mats or carpet spots to indicate a space and this is fine. I personally like chairs, as they help to start conversations about personal space. The chairs should ideally be the same colour and height. I much prefer the teacher not to sit on a chair that is more (or less) comfortable, or higher or lower, than the others, to ensure equal status within the circle.[3] I will ask the group what they notice about this particular arrangement. Common responses include: 'It's the only time in class we get to see each other, most of the time I'm looking at the back of someone's head' and 'The chairs make it fair, we won't be racing to sit in the best one'. I might have to prompt with questions such as: 'Why are all the chairs the same?' or 'Why is it important that we can all see each other?'

I will have some form of talking piece. This is usually a bean bag or a Koosh ball (a toy ball made of rubber strings attached to a soft rubber core) – something that feels nice to hold, can be thrown and caught easily, does not roll away if dropped and won't hurt anyone if misaimed. The children are trained in how to request the talking piece (they gently cup two hands together loosely in the lap) and how to share the talking piece by either passing it around, or throwing it across the circle. When we throw the talking piece, we make sure we are throwing it to someone who wants it, we make eye contact with the person and we say his or her name before we throw it. With this technique alone, children (and adults) practise valuable social skills.

The circle and talking piece establish peaceful values such as respect, positive listening and equality. This is not to say Peacemaker circles are always quiet! They are often very noisy with a lot of action. A successful session will have a balance of high-energy group games, focused group work and thoughtful circle dialogue where each person is given the opportunity to listen, think, speak and be heard.

Peppered throughout the session are games designed to mix up the group. These are often high-energy and can involve some risk-taking, such as being left alone in the middle of the circle. After a 'mixer' game, people often find that they are sitting next to someone new. A fun paired activity then takes place. I want them to experience working with someone new positively, so the activity is usually designed to be achievable in a short amount of time. No one has to bear the burden of working with just one other person for the duration of a session. These mixer games help to break down barriers within a class, reducing prejudice, stereotypes or cliques. After a time, I might ask the participants why they think I am mixing them up so often. The usual response is: 'So we get to meet and work with people we don't know so well'. The response is rarely a revelation to the class. In asking this question, the method and its outcome are made explicit – not by me, but by members of the class. In my experience, there then follows a feeling of acceptance that it is ultimately more positive to work with someone than against them.

This fast-paced approach needs some slower, quieter moments to lend balance to the session. On occasions this can happen without planning for it. For example, someone may have asked for the talking piece but a pause indicates that they might not yet have found the words they want to say. During these moments, I hope to have fostered an attitude of respect in the circle, a sense of trust that the individual should be granted the time and the space to find what they want to express. In this situation, the circle momentum slows right down. We all have to learn to be comfortable enough in the silence that is taking place. This can be critical. There is an art to discerning how the children react to someone taking their time; how the observing teacher copes with it; and how long I feel I can hold the space before moving on. I often feel that I am more comfortable sustaining this uncertainty than the teachers are. After all, I am not in a hurry to get an answer out of a child and move on to the next prescribed learning outcome, as so often happens in normal lessons. We can go with the flow in circle and if something crops up that needs further enquiry, that's the direction we take.

The content of the sessions really depends on how comfortable the group is in a circle. My aim is to spend a few weeks developing positive listening, respectful dialogue, a sense of inclusion, the skills of giving and receiving affirmation and so on. From here, we can move on to the more complex topics that might include how to work with others, how to manage and express our emotions, how conflict escalates and how to de-escalate it. After a time, both teachers and pupils can inform the content of the sessions. For example, the teacher might have noticed that some children are quick to blame each other when something goes wrong. A circle session on 'blame' then follows.

A session focusing on blame might start with some games in which people are 'out' quite quickly. From here, we can process how it feels for individuals to be out of a game or activity they are enjoying. The range of responses (which includes anger, frustration, relief, nonchalance and more) helps me to start a discussion around feelings and to gauge a) how emotionally literate the children are and b) how confident they are at talking about their feelings in the circle. I then ask the children about blame, what it is, how it feels to be blamed for things, what words we might hear and so on. This can be revealing for the adults, as the children often describe situations in which adults don't fully listen to children's version of events and assign blame over-hastily. With the teacher, I will model an activity called the 'blame game', based on a set of cards that are printed, folded and laminated to use in sessions. Using a red card (see Figure 4.2) with 'It's ... fault because ...' written on it, the teacher and I pass the card (blame) back and forth and elaborate mutual accusations of the form 'It's your fault because ...'. Our responses to each other escalate in terms of volume and emotion. This often causes a lot of laughter as the children enjoy seeing their teacher acting. I then ask the children what they noticed about our bodies and our voices. The responses might include 'You were jabbing your fingers at each other' and 'Your voice got so high and loud like you were shouting'. They are then asked to comment on the content of our blame game and what we said to each other. The responses typically include 'You stopped making sense, you just wanted to win the argument' and 'You brought in things from the past that had nothing to do with it'. It would appear that everyone, regardless of age, has experience of playing the blame game for real and so can recognize the nuances and strategies used to succeed.

It is now the children's turn to have a go at the blame game. This activity is time-limited to less than 20 seconds, just enough time to experience the emotion, language and physicality associated with blame. Now the teacher and I model an alternative. Using a green card that has written on it 'It's *partly* my fault because ...', we pass the card back and forth as before. Again, the children are asked to comment on what they have seen and heard. This time, they will say things like: 'You were calmer, you had an actual conversation' and 'It slowed right down' and 'You were looking at each other'. Again, the children have a go at experiencing what it feels like to accept some of the responsibility. They are not being asked to accept *all* of the responsibility, just to take what steps they think they can to accept their part in the incident. This activity quickly highlights for the children and the adults that, given the opportunity and the right structures, they can transform conflict into something much more positive. We then debrief to facilitate the children's learning about their own experiences. I believe that everyone (supported if need be) can make sound, respectful, non-violent, perceptive judgements and decisions about what to do the next time they encounter blame.

Blame game - side 1	Blame game - side 2
It's .... fault because	It's partly my fault because ....

Figure 4.2: The 'blame game' card
   Source: Reproduced by kind permission of Peacemakers (more resources online at: http://lifeworldslearning.co.uk/lfp/index.html)

These circle experiences are not limited to the classroom. I insist that staff training sessions are also held in a circle, that a talking piece is used and that some relationship-building activity is built into the session. It is down to the skill of the trainer to make this experience authentic, valuable

Building, maintaining and repairing a peaceful culture in school

and inclusive. Some adults' perceptions of a professional development session are quite clearly fixed on the idea that the training should be led by a person with seniority, ideally with a slide presentation, and be about school policy. Interestingly, these perceptions can often mirror how these people feel children should be taught – by an expert, with children seated behind desks and according to staged curricula. Peacemakers' adult training involves: games and small group work; people mixing with others outside their professional and/or preferred peer groups; throwing a Koosh ball across quite a large circle; and sometimes sharing personal information and reflections. To be clear, I use the same methods as I use in a class but the content is different. For example, when playing a large circle game designed to find commonalities and connections such as 'The sun shines on all the people who ...', children might say, 'The sun shines on all the people who have a rabbit', and all the children who have a rabbit swap places. In an adult training session, people might share information that relates to the session ('The sun shines on everyone who has carried out a restorative chat this week') or share more personal or reflective information ('The sun shines on everyone who has had a tough time with Year 5 this week').

Often, the staff team is delighted to have a break from the norm, and experience something they can apply in their classrooms, delivered in a dynamic way (the sessions can be quite rowdy). But for some, it can also be confusing and uncomfortable, as it does not align with their conception of professional development. As a result, they may opt out of activities, openly challenge me or display some other form of negative behaviour. Interestingly, as we are all in a circle, everyone's behaviour and communications are seen by everyone else in the circle. It is my responsibility to spot people who may be feeling excluded, to approach them at the appropriate time (often outside the session) and gently enquire what they need to feel more comfortable. I might then ask them if they can think of any children they work with who might also feel anxious about circle activities. They usually can. I can then remind them of the pass rule, which allows anyone to skip his or her go and pass the Koosh ball straight on to the next person. Interestingly, the pass rule is shared at the outset of any training but people can forget, or get wrapped up in the moment or don't feel empowered enough to use it. The circle is not owned by me. Therefore I must find ways to keep people engaged so that they might be more able to contribute in their own way to its working.

Finding ways to listen to people and support them in communicating their thoughts is a key component of my role. I am consciously forming meaningful relationships with a variety of stakeholders while trying not to appear partisan. I need to be equally able to work with a group of children and/or lunchtime supervisors and/or senior leaders at any given point. The development of all these relationships is based on trust. The formation of trust is multi-layered. I must demonstrate, among other qualities, friendliness, professionalism, competence, reliability and integrity. People must feel safe with me. I attend meetings prepared and punctually. I spend time listening to people. I am open and transparent about what I do. I model appropriate behaviours and attitudes to both adults and children, and endeavour always to be authentic in my interactions. I model the restorative toolkit inherent in the project. This means facilitating circles for up to eight weeks with classes, demonstrating materials and techniques for the staff in the circle. But it also means exposing myself to the possibility of things going 'wrong'. When this happens, I look to develop trust with the circle (adults and children included) by talking through what happened, what didn't work so well that time and asking for suggestions on what might be improved next time. I also talk through events with the teacher after the session, to hear from them what they saw and how they felt about it. As one teacher put it:

> The whole idea of restorative works on that idea. You're building a mutually trusting relationship. That's what I am now able to have with the children. It's a mindset that you need to 'get'.
> (Early Years Foundation Stage teacher, Birmingham school)

The language of judgement and blame is often a part of school culture, emanating from the top – through school inspection, senior leadership assessing teaching quality and performance-related pay, to judgements about colleagues, children and their families. Peacemakers works within this existing culture to set new internal norms. Common responses to something going wrong in a session or a class might be to ignore the issue, to hide it from others or to pass the blame on to the children, the supply teacher or the parents and so on. Ultimately, I am trying to work towards an acceptance that we all get it wrong sometimes but that we can help each other to learn, grow and develop. This humanization underpins principles common to restorative practice: restoration or repair, dignity, fairness, trust and safety. In my experience, the schools appreciate this in-situ training working directly with students, which, it seems, not all trainers are prepared to deliver:

> We ask other trainers to do [training] with our kids too. They say 'it's not their job'. They'll tell us how to do it but they won't come in and show us.
>
> (Deputy Head, Birmingham school)

Building healthy relationships is also an investment in building social capital for people. The more heavily a school can invest in banking goodwill, strong relationships and good feeling among its stakeholders, the better the return on the investment of time. Sooner or later some relationships will wobble and will need support to maintain them.

The use of the circle is essential in restorative practice and to the building of a peaceful school culture. The circle is the foundation on which future culture-building, maintenance and repair work in the school can be carried out. The ceremonial aspect of a circle lends gravitas and humanity to a process. The opening rituals (checking-in) and use of a talking piece make equity and fairness explicit. From this base, the use of 'circles [can] present a radical shift in how we respond to hurts and create social order' (Pranis *et al.*, 2003: 10). Pranis *et al.* help us to see the paradigm shift from a dependence on the state/teacher/authority to self-reliance within a community – a response to wrongdoing that moves from coercion to healing, from individual to collective healing and, finally, from seeing justice as getting even to justice as getting well.

Level two: Maintaining a peaceful culture

Lynn Duckworth *et al.* (2012) contend that the factors that contribute to a school-wide culture of peace include:

- adults modelling non-violent communication[4]
- a peer mediation scheme available to students
- the use of restorative justice approaches to student offences
- a curriculum that integrates the themes of non-violence, social justice, diversity and peace throughout the disciplines.

Peacemakers offers training in all of these features and also goes a stage further via a personalized mix of coaching, training and modelling for some people, where appropriate. The whole-school approach generally starts with setting up a peer mediation service at lunchtime. This underlines the importance of relationship maintenance. It empowers young people and, at the same time, releases adults from having to control, repair or manage much of the low-level conflict that can arise between pupils.

Peer mediation is the practice of young people helping their peers to find solutions to a range of conflicts. I know of no better ambassadors for this way of working than a group of well-trained, well-supported and respected children who help their community maintain relationships, work together as a team, demonstrate active listening and reframing techniques, and offer a non-judgemental approach to problem-solving. A peer mediation service is one way for the whole school to give prominence to the maintenance of child-to-child relationships, problem-solving and non-violent communication. (For more on peer mediation, see, for example, Cremin and Bevington, 2017, and Schrumpf et al., 1997.) There is also an important role for staff contracted to cover the lunch period; devolution of power from the senior leadership can help during this time. At the very least, lunchtime supervisors are there to ensure children's safety. At best, members of this midday team are engaged with the pastoral work of the school, know the pupils and staff by name, are permitted and empowered to play games with the children, act as appropriate adult role models and offer assistance to children who need it. They also have a role in sorting out problems.

Lunchtime supervisors are sometimes undervalued in the school. The lunchtime team maintains order over the most chaotic point in the school day, yet are afforded the least time to develop relationships with others. They are paid by the hour, which leaves little 'wiggle room' for them to stay longer and help sort out disputes or facilitate a conversation with the children to put things right. Similarly, the incentive to attend extra or after-hours training can be tricky to negotiate. In our project, we advise a minimum of two lunchtime supervisor training sessions, but this impacts on their hours and can therefore be a structural impediment. I ask the senior leader commissioning the training if the lunchtime team will be paid for attending the training, or offered time off in lieu, or given other incentives to attend. My aim is to move the perception of their role from that of a body in the playground (marshal, peacekeeper, referee or judge) to that of a trusted and respected team member.

Valuable knowledge-sharing can happen when lunchtime staff are invited to take part in training with other staff or with the children. In one project school, the peer mediators introduced the lunchtime team to an emoji[5] display board that they had been using in their mediations to help younger children identify feelings and emotions. The supervisors saw the benefit of this tool and copied the mediators, who were delighted to have it recognized as useful. As the headteacher observed:

Building, maintaining and repairing a peaceful culture in school

> We had a core group of people who became involved. It was important to have the Deputy Head Teacher, Teachers and Teaching Assistants and the lunchtime team actively involved because they're on the shop floor ... We also got the Governors involved. We got children involved who received extra training and led on the development of new ideas out in their classrooms ... It had to be a whole team.
>
> (Headteacher, Birmingham school)

Where the majority of adults and pupils are familiar with the restorative approach, and pupils are able to resolve their own conflicts creatively, then schools report fewer recurring or escalating conflicts.

Exclusion and inclusion

Fostering a sense of welcome and inclusion is integral to the maintenance of a peaceful school culture, but it can be difficult to achieve. Despite 'inclusion' often being stated as a school value, it is not uncommon for a number of exclusionary practices to exist. A set of social practices has been developed that rely on impersonal criteria to increase management efficiency in the classroom. Often wall charts with exclusion policy guidelines are displayed in classrooms, listing what a teacher will do in response to various behaviours: from a verbal warning, through to writing the child's name on the board (visual warning), to removing the child from the classroom and putting them in another class for a period of time. Typically, someone is on call to pick up excluded children and take them to a designated space for a set period of time. Rarely do the teachers have time to respond to such situations in enquiring, curious, meaningful, supportive or personalized ways.

A Peacemaker approach attempts to reimagine these exclusionary practices so that they become inclusive. We evaluate behaviour that can lead to exclusion through a series of activities that can become practices, and then policy, highlighting children's need to be embraced inclusively into a community of care, attention and support. This is not to say the response needs to be 'pink and fluffy'. No one is allowed to get away with anything. A restorative approach is high in care and support as well as being robust and structured. To work inclusively is to work *with* people, not to ignore either them or the issue, or to do things *for* them or *to* them. We must constantly ask young people how we can involve them in the processes of decision-making that ultimately affect them.

Sometimes children will need to exclude themselves temporarily from what is happening. Ideally, the first restorative message to this child should be: 'It is OK to leave but we will always have a discussion about it. You are part of a community of people who have expectations of you. If you have to leave, you will be welcomed back.' This statement allows for negotiation of learning and social expectations. Always, the expectation of us, the community, is to welcome someone back after absence. This needn't be a big deal; it can be a smile, a nod and a prepared, agreed space for the child to sit in.

Ideally, prior to a child leaving a classroom, a conversation elicits suggestions of what will happen next: Who will accompany them? How will the time be negotiated? Who gets to decide? How will each party check in on each other? ... and so on. All that is needed is a quick chat between the teacher and the pupil to decide on a mutually agreeable procedure. With young children this can be signified with an object (a teddy bear, a cushion) that will be brought back later; with older children it can be a card with agreed information on it. On their return, the child is welcomed back in the manner they have agreed (a thumbs up, a smile, a 'here is your work and your pen, Sam'). What I am trying to show here is that relationships wobble; people, young and older, can have 'off days'. What we need to do is humanize our relationships and create effective ways to maintain them. The child who has been excluded from the class should not have to bear the burden of having their name displayed on the 'sad side' of the whiteboard all day, or be further shamed by being made to sit on the floor or being labelled the 'naughty child' for their entire time at school. Through acknowledgement of the issue and taking responsibility for putting it right, we all have the option to start over.

Level three: Repairing a peaceful culture

In our efforts to create a peaceful school culture, we focus resources on the building and the maintaining of relationships in school. No less important is the repair of relationships when they break down. If the foundations of the whole-school approach have been well built and well maintained, then the reparations when things do go wrong are minor and achievable. This is quite different to how some school systems work, in that the majority of resources and energy (staffing, time, processes, outside agencies and so on) are invested in tackling situations of conflict that have already happened. Less focus and training time are given to this element of the Peacemakers project because it is less necessary than in some other settings. For example, in the criminal justice context, matters are rather more starkly delineated (the work of Edward Sellman *et al.*, 2013, provides some useful insights

Building, maintaining and repairing a peaceful culture in school

here). Elsewhere, Hilary Cremin and colleagues (2012) describe restorative justice (often known as rj)[6] as a process used in:

> ... criminal and youth justice sectors, and more informally in schools and looked-after settings where harm has been caused. It involves an impartial third party facilitating a process whereby an offender (or wrong-doer) is held accountable and makes some form of reparation to his or her victim. The victim is placed at the centre of the process, and is given the opportunity to express the ways in which s/he has been affected and to ask questions about the offence.
>
> (Cremin *et al.*, 2012: 422)

This does not show the complexity involved in applying a restorative way of working in education. Moreover, it uses binary or oppositional language (victim/offender), which may be accepted (indeed necessary) in criminal justice settings, but to label children as victims or offenders during their time in school is not as helpful as talking about their behaviour, the underlying thoughts, feelings and unmet needs. Of course, there are acts that are wrong – bullying and stealing, for example – but it is also important to explore the *context* of the behaviour (Sellman *et al.*, 2013: 3).

Harm and consequences

For some working in rj settings, there needs to be an acknowledgement that harm has happened from those responsible for the harm. In schools, the reality is often more nuanced. A specific moment of harm may be identified, but there has often been a lot going on prior to the incident that could also count as harmful. Indeed, there can be multiple harms happening for multiple parties. For example, two girls can be causing harm to each other on social media (unbeknownst to the school) long before one decides to take action and shout at/kick/punch the other at playtime. To focus solely on the physical harm and not take into account the multiple factors that led to the outburst is not useful. Within education, there needs to be a conscious shift away from a dualistic restorative way of working towards one that accepts multiple views, stories and histories and is more supportive, relational and ultimately more educational.

The development of restorative approaches over the past thirty or so years reflects the adaptations people have made to the rj process of transforming conflicts in a variety of settings including schools and communities. The use of language changes as we move from rj to a restorative approach and the terms 'victim' and 'offender' become 'person(s) harmed' and 'person who has caused harm'. A process involving a facilitator asking a set of questions is still at the heart of the work (see also Belinda Hopkins's five-step framework in Chapter 3), and these questions may be asked of everyone involved:

- What happened?
- What were you thinking and feeling at the time?
- What have you been thinking/feeling since?
- Who else has been affected? / Who else got hurt?
- What needs to happen to put things right?

The questions illustrate a move away from focusing purely on the event, the perpetrator and the punishment, towards a recognition of incidents that lead up to the event, the different actors affected by the event and different responses to the harm caused. The non-adversarial process is given precedence and (often) allowed to guide the outcome.

So, we shift the focus from one that views misconduct as school-rule-breaking, and therefore as a violation against the institution, towards one that acknowledges and supports social engagement, with an emphasis on relationship maintenance. Schools wishing to create a peaceful school culture along these lines need to examine their structures and processes and, perhaps more importantly, the views of everyone involved, before deciding how – or even whether – to move forward. In my view, merely transplanting a set of restorative processes onto an existing punitive, authoritarian system is unlikely to work. Even so, making the move away from a traditional, authoritarian approach can be very challenging.

Behaviour management and behaviour development

Before adopting a restorative way of working, schools need to reflect on the differences between behaviour *management* and behaviour *development*. I ask staff to consider if they perceive misbehaviour as a barrier to teaching or as an opportunity for learning. The former mindset is likely to have been informed by behaviourist theories in which adults consider it their responsibility to manage the behaviour of the pupils; they want to make pupils comply with the rules and are likely to use control methods such as rewards and punishments or hierarchical sanction systems, and perhaps have a zero-tolerance attitude to wrongdoing. Some of the Peacemakers schools have recognized that the use of control measures only serves to limit behaviour and moral development. Once a school identifies the number of external control measures it has in place (such as behaviour boards; stickers to reward work and behaviour; standing children in lines until they are silent and so on) we can start to explore how to develop the internal controls children need to function in, and beyond, school.

Take lining up before entering a classroom as one example. First, I respect both the desire and statutory requirement to keep people safe around school and to provide routine and structure. But I explore with staff the idea that children have a lot of experience of travelling safely around buildings other than school without having to line up in silence. We explore how to involve the children in considering alternative ways to entering the building safely. Exciting options reveal themselves. In one school, adults are situated on stairwells and outside the classrooms. The children enter the building and are smiled at and greeted by name at each junction point in the school. Their walk from the playground to the classroom changes in dynamic as they smile back, engage, slow their pace and ultimately learn to self-regulate. In another school, the older children walk with the younger ones to their classrooms to help settle them in. No lines, no pushing, fewer adults shouting and less stress for everyone.

Those who consider their role to be that of behaviour-developer in schools are more informed by humanistic psychology and moral development theory. These people see it as part of their job to help pupils to develop and learn appropriate behaviours through explicit teaching, modelling, dialogue and collaborative problem-solving. Helping young people to see how their actions have harmed others, and giving them opportunities to make amends, is morally nurturing and develops empathy, which is a key element of becoming morally mature and self-directing.

Restorative approach or restorative justice?

The use of the word 'approach' as opposed to 'justice' is one way to start a conversation about how people view a restorative way of working. Do they see it as a way of being, a lived approach based on values and behaviours that continuously infuse all interactions, or a moment in time in which justice is meted out? Is a restorative intervention only utilized when a school rule has been broken and justice needs serving? Or is it the norm to use circles and mediation to actively develop the emotional vocabulary of both children and adults? This latter philosophy resonates with Quakerism as a way of being in the world rather than a specific religious dogma.

Dan Van Ness describes the term 'restorative' as a contested concept in that, in practice, people's interpretations and applications of it have developed differently. It is a concept 'around which there is general agreement about meaning but little if any likelihood of consensus forming around a precise definition' (Van Ness, 2013: 33). The concept of rj has equally manifested itself differently over time and with experience. Van Ness describes three separate but overlapping understandings of rj on which institutions and practitioners place varying emphases. For some, the focus is on restorative encounters (or meetings), while others attend more to the reparative outcomes (repairing the harm) and others (such as Peacemakers) are concerned with the transformative aspect. Those with a focus on encounters are likely to suggest that they be used even when no particular crime or offence has been committed, such as when two neighbours are in an ongoing conflict that needs to be resolved (in a school, this might be two students who have fallen out). Van Ness (ibid.) cites 'victim offender mediation, conferencing and peacemaking circles as programmatic examples' of encounter. Those who favour the second conception, of rj as reparation, are likely to want to ensure that there is reparation even in situations where there is no encounter, such as when the offender (or the person who has caused harm) refuses to participate or cannot be found.

In isolation, these are not sufficient to achieve what Van Ness describes as a 'transformative' level of implementation. As he puts it, 'restorative approaches to schools must include all three conceptions of restorative justice: repair of harm, encounter of the affected parties and transformation of relationship and culture' (ibid.: 38).

The transformative conception of restorative practice goes beyond both the encounter and the reparation, and ultimately offers something more than the sum of these parts: 'It offers a perspective that changes how we view ourselves, others around us, and the structures that influence and constrain us' (ibid.: 33). This perspective invites deeper thought about the relationships involved, the impact on the community, and consideration of the wider, systemic injustices that may have contributed. A structured, intentional consideration of underlying injustices can lead to positive changes to a system that go beyond the initial event. One such example from a school in Birmingham is the development of an induction video created by children who had previously felt isolated to welcome those new to the school.

The ideal is to embrace all three conceptions but, in reality, they often operate separately. There may be an encounter where reparation is neither possible nor appropriate; a response designed to repair can fail to transform; and transformation can happen without an encounter (Van Ness, 2013). The transformative conception holds the most potential for genuine and lasting change. Within the whole-school approach, we support the school community in valuing the transformative conception, as this is where change ultimately lies: change for individuals, the system and school culture.

Conclusion

Is it possible to create a fully peaceful school? In truth, the goal is never achieved. Peace is a process, a practice, and must be continually attended to. We are not trying to eradicate conflict or to force our views on people. We have no fixed blueprint for peace in schools, only a model that shifts and changes with each interaction with each person in each school. Ironically, the nature of change in the project can be upsetting, disruptive and conflictual. Fundamentally, the Peacemakers' Whole-School Approach Project holds a different view of the world to that held by some schools. This divergence in perspective can present itself early and may sometimes be too wide to achieve any kind of change. However, even where a school requires punishments to remain part of its culture, it is still possible to build a worldview within the school that is based on peacebuilding through the teaching of social and emotional skills, empathy, effective listening, the establishing and maintaining of relationships, self-worth and compassion for others.

Notes

[1] For more information and resources, see www.peacemakers.org.uk and http://lifeworldslearning.co.uk/lfp/ (West Midlands Quaker Peace Education Project, 2016).

[2] It is important to make clear that much of the project's early framework was informed by the work of Belinda Hopkins, who generously shared her experience and knowledge.

[3] Necessary adaptations are made to include wheelchair users as part of the circle.

[4] Non-violent communication (NVC) is considered to be both a spiritual practice and a set of skills from which people learn to listen more deeply to themselves and others. To communicate non-violently is to communicate authentically, with compassion and from the heart.

[5] An emoji board has a range of faces showing various facial expressions to help children identify with an emotion.

[6] The terms restorative justice and restorative approaches are often shortened to RJ and RA. Dorothy Vaandering consciously uses the lower case to abbreviate restorative justice to *rj*, arguing that treating it as a proper noun risks it being seen as 'a particular approach, practice or strategy instead of a more general way of being' (Vaandering, 2013: 311). Out of respect for Vaandering and Quakers, who consider Quakerism 'a way of being' rather than a thing, I refer to restorative approaches and restorative justice using lower case.

References

Bickmore, K. (2013) 'Peacebuilding through circle dialogue processes in primary classrooms: Locations for restorative and educative work'. In Sellman, E., Cremin, H. and McCluskey, G. (eds) *Restorative Approaches to Conflict in Schools: Interdisciplinary perspectives on whole school approaches to managing relationships*. London: Routledge, 175–91.

Boyes-Watson, C. and Pranis, K. (2015) *Circle Forward: Building a restorative school community*. St Paul, MN: Living Justice Press.

Cremin, H. and Bevington, T. (2017) *Positive Peace in Schools: Tackling conflict and creating a culture of peace in the classroom*. London: Routledge.

Cremin, H., Sellman, E. and McCluskey, G. (2012) 'Interdisciplinary perspectives on restorative justice: Developing insights for education'. *British Journal of Educational Studies*, 60 (4), 421–37.

Duckworth, C.L., Allen, B. and Williams, T.T. (2012) 'What do students learn when we teach peace? A qualitative assessment of a theater peace program'. *Journal of Peace Education*, 9 (1), 81–99.

Galtung, J. (1969) 'Violence, peace, and peace research'. *Journal of Peace Research*, 6 (3), 167–91.

Hopkins, B. (2004) *Just Schools: A whole school approach to restorative justice*. London: Jessica Kingsley Publishers.

Hopkins, B. (2011) *The Restorative Classroom: Using restorative approaches to foster effective learning*. London: Optimus Education.

Morrison, B. (2007) *Restoring Safe School Communities: A whole school response to bullying, violence and alienation*. Annandale, Aus: Federation Press.

Pranis, K., Stuart, B. and Wedge, M. (2003) *Peacemaking Circles: From crime to community*. St Paul, MN: Living Justice Press.

Schrumpf, F., Crawford, D.K. and Bodine, R.J. (1997) *Peer Mediation: Conflict resolution in schools*. Rev ed. Champaign, IL: Research Press.

Sellman, E., Cremin, H. and McCluskey, G. (eds) (2013) *Restorative Approaches to Conflict in Schools: Interdisciplinary perspectives on whole school approaches to managing relationships*. London: Routledge.

Stuart, B. and Pranis, K. (2006) 'Peacemaking circles: Reflections on principal features and primary outcomes'. In Sullivan, D. and Tifft, L. (eds) *Handbook of Restorative Justice: A global perspective*. London: Routledge, 121–33.

Wright, M. (1999) *Restoring Respect for Justice: A symposium*. Winchester: Waterside Press.

Vaandering, D. (2013) 'A window on relationships: Reflecting critically on a current restorative justice theory'. *Restorative Justice*, 1 (3), 311–33.

Vaandering, D. (2014a) 'Implementing restorative justice practice in schools: What pedagogy reveals'. *Journal of Peace Education*, 11 (1), 64–80.

Vaandering, D. (2014b) 'Relational restorative justice pedagogy in educator professional development'. *Curriculum Inquiry*, 44 (4), 508–30.

Van Ness, D.W. (2013) 'Restorative justice as world view'. In Sellman, E., Cremin, H. and McCluskey, G. (eds) *Restorative Approaches to Conflict in Schools: Interdisciplinary perspectives on whole school approaches to managing relationships*. London: Routledge, 32–9.

West Midlands Quaker Peace Education Project (2016) *Learning for Peace: A guide to developing outstanding SMSC in your primary school.* Birmingham: West Midlands Quaker Peace Education Project. Online. http://lifeworldslearning.co.uk/lfp/ (accessed 5 February 2018).

Zehr, H. (1990) *Changing Lenses: A new focus for crime and justice.* Scottdale, PA: Herald Press.

Chapter 5
Learning for emancipation
Tim Small

When I was a headteacher, I remember telling people, perhaps a little sanctimoniously, that I was not much interested in holding the power invested in me for any other purpose than to bestow it on young people. The philosophy behind the sentiment was sincerely held. A liberal upbringing, a formative teaching practice term at Dartington Hall School (see Curry, 1947) and becoming acquainted with Carl Rogers's *Freedom to Learn* books (Rogers, 1969, 1983), all important influences, had kindled a professional passion for enabling people to become the authors of their own lives. This also, however, put me on a collision course with the apparatus of an education system that too often appeared to diminish, label, corral, impose on and 'tick off' its principal users.

Later, at a time of turbulence, when both my headship and my marriage were approaching their endings, joining a Quaker meeting felt like a homecoming. The values that I can now name and advocate were more subtly expressed and experienced at first, in the way people spoke, behaved and treated one another. First, there was an alert recognition of each person's unique spirit and agency, echoing the testimony that there is 'that of God' in everyone. Then I felt welcomed into a fellowship of seekers, full of curiosity, open to challenge and enquiry, many of whom were still travelling rather than seeming to have arrived at their truth. There was a generous abundance of John Keats's 'negative capability', which I loved: being 'capable of being in uncertainties, mysteries, doubts, without any irritable reaching after fact and reason' (Gittings, 1970: 43).

As I went on to become a member of the Society, never having been much of a joiner of things, my sense of belonging deepened, along with my appreciation of Quaker values of community and cooperation. I found others who had been wounded and discovered relationships with healing properties. We seemed to grow ever-more whole together in our own unique ways.

I have come to associate the most intellectually challenging and enriching of these values with the Quaker peace testimony, and was profoundly influenced by Parker J. Palmer's (1998, 2000, 2004) writings on education and personal growth. I began to see how reconciliation may depend on our capacity to hold conflicting ideas in creative tension. This would involve embracing uncertainty and doubt, welcoming ambiguity and perplexity – not recoiling from them. This offered the promise of finding, in the discomfiture of *not* knowing, the essential energy to learn, let go, resolve differences and integrate diversity. We might then make sense of the world as it unfolds. It is this energy that I aspire to for our children and young people to flourish in the twenty-first century, because it enables them to take responsibility for the meaning and purpose of their own lives.

Two years after ending my full-time employment in the education service, I was introduced, as a relatively inexperienced consultant, to the research team of the Learning Power project at the University of Bristol. It was another homecoming.

This chapter is a personal account of how this research, and the field-testing of it that I was privileged to lead, became a rich source of empirical and narrative evidence of how these values can be engendered and expressed in action, in practical and achievable ways. The work would take me into schools and other learning communities as far afield as Australia and Malaysia, as well as across the UK, and as diverse as infant schools, young offenders' institutions and universities. Using an apparently simple self-report survey as a catalyst, I was to spend the next dozen or so years supporting and recording stories of profound personal and educational transformation, with a common theme of renewing and releasing the energy to learn. I end with a call to action for these values to re-energize our current education system.

The original Learning Power research

In about the year 2000, two professors at the University of Bristol had a conversation that went something like this: 'Wouldn't it be interesting if we could identify the characteristics of really effective lifelong learners? Once we could name these qualities, we could devise an instrument to assess them. In these assessment-obsessed times, people might start attending to what young people need to get better at, to be ready for the twenty-first century.' One was Professor Guy Claxton, already well known for his advocacy of 'learning to learn' and 'learning power' (Claxton, 2002). The other was Professor Patricia Broadfoot, a leading figure in the Assessment Reform Group, whose research was soon to report on the negative impact of assessment and testing on motivation to learn (Assessment Reform Group, 2002). With funding from the Lifelong Learning Foundation, Dr Ruth Deakin Crick was appointed to undertake the research. Now a Professor at both the University of Technology, Sydney, and the University of Bristol, she continues to lead the Learning Power research, applying it to an increasingly broad range of system design and problem-solving needs, in contexts of high complexity, including governmental and corporate programmes as well as schools and universities.

Following an exhaustive review of the literature and wide, systematic consultation, the Effective Lifelong Learning Inventory, or ELLI as it became known, emerged. It originally consisted of seven dimensions, or constructs, each representing a continuum between a positive and a negative pole, identified by factor analysis as having a significant impact on people's power to learn (Deakin Crick *et al.*, 2004). The dimensions are explored in more detail further ahead in this chapter.

By means of a simple, online survey, originally consisting of 72 items (since reduced to 49), learners reflect and answer straightforward questions about how they think, feel and behave in everyday learning situations. They receive instant feedback in the form of a spider-diagram depicting their strengths and areas for development in all the Learning Power dimensions (see Figure 5.1).

ELLI offered users a snapshot of their current learning identity, best used with skilful facilitation, as a starting point for potentially transformative coaching or mentoring conversations. As well as acquiring a new learning identity, learners would see and commit to an agenda for personal change. Following these and other pedagogical interventions, the inventory would provide learners with new feedback, if retaken, to show how their learning power had grown or changed.

The construction of the instrument and the rationale behind it were strongly influenced by the theories of Jurgen Habermas, who argued that the elevation of scientific or technical knowledge above other kinds needed rebalancing by appreciation of 'practical' and 'emancipatory' knowledge (Habermas, 1984). This valuing of knowledge acquired through experience and reflection, best understood as changed consciousness or 'perspective transformation', was to become a feature of both the learning stimulated by the inventory and the action research through which we gathered evidence of its impact. I believe this underpinning of the work by an emancipatory rationality is the key to its appeal among educators and others wanting to move beyond a reductionist worldview. This worldview, characterized by over-reliance on authority, predictability and control, was prevalent through much of the twentieth century but has arguably been rendered non-viable by post-modernism (Gillman, 2007: ch. 5) and the pace of change in the twenty-first.

Self-assessing learning power: The CLARA profile

In 2013, the data from around 70,000 cases (past users of ELLI) were subjected to a rigorous meta-analysis, sharpening understanding of how the constructs in the original ELLI related to each other and what they signified. This enabled the research team to reduce the length of the survey while increasing its validity and to reformulate the feedback, renaming some constructs to reflect more faithfully what the data were saying. The publication of these findings (Deakin Crick *et al.*, 2015) was also licensed *Creative Commons*, removing legal and commercial barriers to researchers and practitioners harnessing the ideas for educational purposes. To avoid confusion, I'll refer from here on to the up-to-date version, known as CLARA: the Crick Learning for Resilient Agency profile.

The simplest way to understand CLARA is by looking at the feedback it generates for an individual learner. You will see in Figure 5.1 that seven (of eight) dimensions are represented by a spider-gram, where the stronger a learner reports herself, the fuller the shaded area. From an early stage, it was clear that this visual representation often had significant impact on individuals' understanding of themselves as learners and how they learnt. At a glance, they could see relative strengths, weaknesses and potential for self-improvement. John Scott, the CEO of a large polytechnic in the Middle East and also a professional artist fascinated by the effect of shapes on the brain, made a valuable observation about this visual representation. When he saw the spider-gram, he remarked that our brains have a strong, subliminal desire to make round what looks as if it *should* be round. The shape itself, he believed, would have a motivational effect on its owner.

The eighth dimension, *Openness to Learning*, represents one of the most significant changes in the evolution of ELLI into CLARA. There is a good reason why it no longer fits within the spider-gram, which I shall explain when we come to it. It is worth taking a few moments to look at the shape and potential impact on a young learner of the spider-gram in Figure 5.1 before we consider each of the constructs in turn and the values inherent in them.

Tim Small

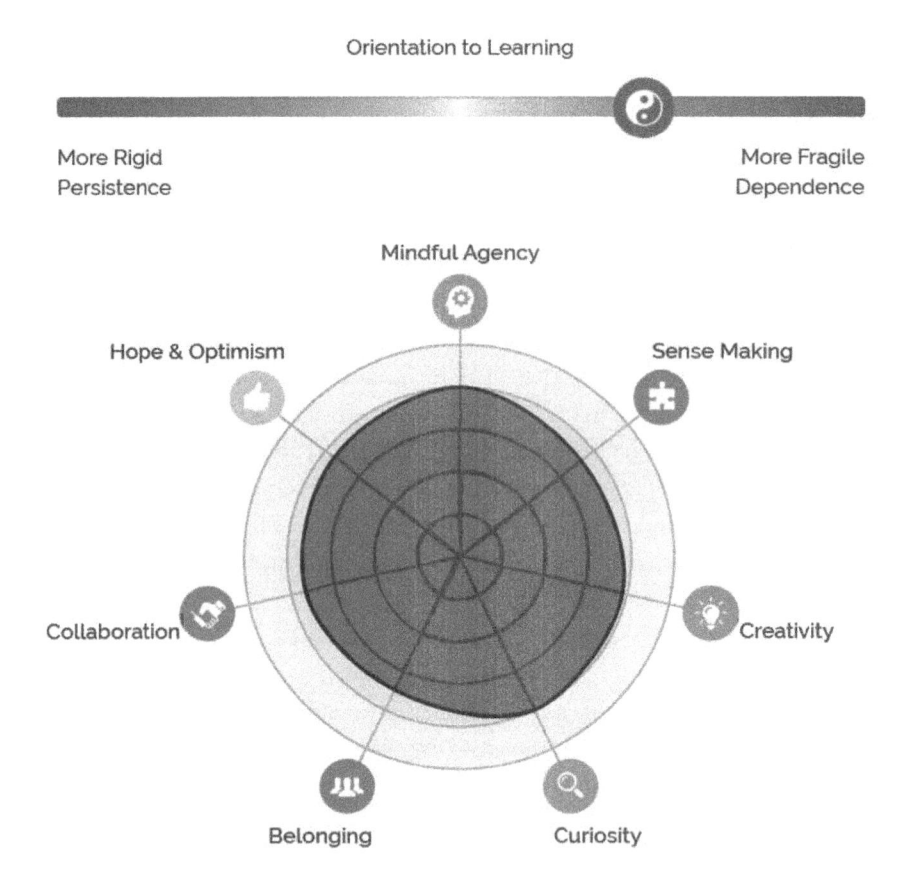

Figure 5.1: A CLARA profile

Source: www.learningemergence.com

The eight dimensions and their inherent values

The reason they are called dimensions is that, originally, as each construct emerged from the factor analysis it was named according to keywords strongly represented in the data. This is known as the 'emergent pole'. Drawing on George Kelly's construct theory from the 1950s (Kelly, 2003), a 'contrast pole' was then named to represent the conceptual opposite, creating a continuum, or dimension, along which the self-report data would sit. All the dimensions include both internal, or intra-psychic, elements and environmental or contextual factors and they all relate to thinking, feeling and doing, so they are holistic. They are also interconnected parts of a complex whole and, perhaps most importantly, they are plastic, changing over time, unlike aspects of personality or temperament assessed by some other psychometric tools.

I find it sobering that, for all our advances, such a notion of learning was being proposed over sixty years ago:

> ... a notion about how man [sic] may launch out from a position of admitted ignorance, and how he may aspire from one day to the next to transcend his own dogmatisms ... a theory of man's personal inquiry – a psychology of human quest.
> (Kelly, 2003: 3)

Kelly's notion of 'a personal inquiry – a psychology of human quest' is uncannily well suited to post-modern needs and in keeping with our theme of an individual taking full responsibility for constructing her own meaning from life's phenomena. I am also reminded of Janet Gilbraith's words on education for peace (1986):

> The two qualities which are most important to children today are hope and imagination. Hope to believe they can change the world they live in and imagination to find ways to do so.
> (Gilbraith, 1986, 62–63: QF&P, 23.85)

As I describe the constructs in the CLARA profiling tool in more detail (Deakin Crick *et al.*, 2015), I hope their resonance with the values under discussion will be noticeable. The original theorization of the *Hope and Optimism* dimension drew significantly on Carol Dweck's research and her notion of the 'growth mindset', as opposed to the 'fixed mindset' (Dweck, 2000). Having a sense of history and hope, the learner strong in this dimension is familiar enough with growing and changing to feel confident in overcoming obstacles and coping with the ups and downs of learning. The contrast pole is being stuck and static in our self-concept as a learner. There is something important in how this dimension enables open-mindedness, which relates to the values of courage, tolerance and embracing of diversity. With hope and optimism, a new, unfamiliar person or idea is welcomed as an opportunity for learning and discovery, rather than regarded as a threat or a problem.

The *Mindful Agency* dimension is about being able to relate immediate learning tasks to a bigger picture and wider purpose, estimating how long they might take, being strategic as well as focused. It includes taking responsibility for our own learning journeys and managing the feelings that come with them. The contrast pole is being robotic or reactive: so unaware or dismissive of the direction of travel that collisions with reality, such as deadlines and setbacks, are almost inevitable. Sometimes iconized as an owl or eagle who can both spot the prey and survey the prairie, this dimension has a leadership quality. People strong in mindful agency can be relied upon to clerk or chair meetings ably, keep goals in view and in perspective and remember why and in what direction everyone is heading. It carries a personal and spiritual awareness.

Sense Making is part of our normal, cognitive functioning: making connections between what we encounter and what we already know, to make meaning out of the world we live in. It relates closely to the synaptic connections we make in our brains. When primary schoolchildren do a show-and-tell session, they are relating new learning to their lived experience, which helps assimilation. The contrast pole is experienced as fragmentation: learning seen as the collecting and storing of disparate, irrelevant pieces of information, possibly for regurgitation in test conditions. It is not only cognitive, however. Learning matters to those strong in *Sense Making*, because it is personal to them. This dimension has a quality of understanding and acceptance, an accommodating frame of reference, with the wisdom of seeing how everything fits and works together, including heart and head.

Creativity has different meanings in different contexts. Here, it is about using imagination and intuition in learning, being playful, allowing ourselves to dream and have hunches, letting right-brain and even subconscious functions have their say. The contrast pole is being rule-bound or procedural in our learning: thinking there is always a right way to do it – someone else's way. Schools can be rule-bound places and sometimes for good reason. Fostering creativity in learning does mean creating safe spaces to be different, quirky, willing to think aloud, stand out from the crowd and, perhaps, come up with moments of inspiration that might never have arrived if conventions had been more strictly followed. I think of Quaker meetings as safe spaces for creativity.

Curiosity speaks for itself. It is like the fuel that drives us to go on learning. People high in curiosity are unsatisfied by simple answers to complex problems. Unlikely to take slogans, headlines or propositions at face value, they want to dig deeper, get beneath the surface, find out more. (We might feel, as voters, that our democracy would benefit from more of this.) The contrast pole is *passivity*, when we metaphorically fold our arms, shrug our shoulders and expect learning to be done *to* us. It brings to mind an image of reluctant teenage learners turned off school, often because their natural curiosity has been dampened by 'Gradgrinds' and transmission of 'facts' (Dickens, 1998). I referred at the beginning to how glad I was to join a community of seekers, reflecting a kind of collective curiosity.

Belonging, in the original model, was in a dimension called 'learning relationships' (Deakin Crick *et al.*, 2004). The meta-analysis indicated that this aspect of relating to others was important enough to become a dimension in its own right. Feeling supported by a community of fellow learners, teachers, friends, family members and other helpers, who create an atmosphere in which 'it feels OK to be me' is highly significant to our success in learning, which can seem like an uphill struggle without it. The contrast pole is feeling misunderstood, out of place, neglected and left to fail. This is about a reciprocal connection between the emotional and psychological needs of any individual and the social qualities of the context designed to optimize their learning.

The other, perhaps more obvious, component of 'learning relationships' is *Collaboration*. As well as being able to manage on our own, we need to learn with, from, through and alongside others. Effective learning is usually, though not exclusively, interactive. Formulating my understanding through dialogue, for instance, helps to concretize my learning: 'How do I know what I think till I hear what I say?' This involves mutuality, where listening is well practised. The contrast pole is self-isolation or withdrawal due to feeling unwelcome or out of place. We should not underestimate the part played by attentiveness to, and concern for, one another in people's capacity to learn.

The reason the last dimension, *Orientation to Learning*, is configured differently from the others merits explanation. In the original model, 'Fragility and Dependence' was the single negative emergent pole. Assuming highly effective learning to be completely free of this, the team named the contrast pole 'resilience'. Through experience and meta-analysis, however, it became clear that the survey items for this dimension were not measuring something whose contrast pole was wholly desirable. Anecdotally, five out of a sample of 37 young offenders had profiles with exceptionally high levels of resilience. They happened to be those locked up for the most violent offences (Deakin Crick and Salway, 2006). A hypothesis emerged, later supported by meta-analysis, that the contrast pole of 'Fragility and Dependence' was better understood as a closed, brittle relentlessness, an unswerving determination to carry out intentions. It is now named 'Rigid Persistence'. That is why this dimension is given a sliding scale, above the spider-gram, allowing the 'score' to appear at a variable point between two extremes, rather than on a negative-to-positive scale within the spider-gram.

The optimal score on this dimension, lying somewhere between the two poles, clearly depends on the challenge being faced. In some situations, it could be better to dig in, be single-minded and do battle, while in others it might be preferable to think again, be adaptable, give way, accept defeat, lose gracefully or find another way. That is why it was renamed *Orientation to Learning*, to reflect how effective learners display grit and perseverance tempered by adaptability and readiness to change.

Learning about learning power: Using CLARA as a research tool

Importantly, measurement is intentionally invisible in the spider-gram, with no numbers or gradations shown. This is because there is no statistical or comparative validity in data generated by a single user. Two identical profiles could tell very different stories.

Nevertheless, the instrument is generating numeric data behind the scenes, and if samples are large enough the aggregated data can be analysed for statistical significance, taking standard deviations into account. One of the first findings from using the tool in research was sobering: levels of learning power appeared to fall significantly through the secondary age range, being at their highest in KS2 (upper primary) and declining progressively through to the end of compulsory schooling (Deakin Crick *et al.*, 2004). We can only hypothesize why secondary schooling appears to reduce learning power. Could it be due to fragmentation of subjects and relationships? Exam stress? Adolescence? A combination of such factors?

The instrument has been used in several university-led projects to investigate patterns of learning power in different populations and its relationship to other key variables. One of the earliest studies, across KS2, 3 and 4 in Bristol schools, analysed pupils' Learning Power data in relation to teachers' National Curriculum assessments in the three core subjects, and data generated by two other validated survey tools: the Assessment of Learner-Centred Practices survey (McCombs and Whisler, 1997) and a School Emotional Environment for Learning survey (Haddon *et al.*, 2005). A strong association was found between these co-variables: pupils who had fuller, more rounded Learning Power profiles tended to (i) gain higher levels in the core subjects, (ii) report their teachers as being more learner-centred and (iii) describe their schools as places where it 'feels emotionally OK to be me'. Hence the title of the paper publishing the results: 'The ecology of learning: Factors contributing to learner-centred classroom cultures' (Deakin Crick *et al.*, 2007).

The fieldwork for this study was conducted in 2003. Already, a picture was emerging of the educational environment offering the most fertile ground for growing learning power: a values-led classroom where feelings and individuals counted, and meta-cognition was an explicit part of learning. Just as significantly, it was clear that this approach was compatible with achieving good levels and grades. It turns out that it is possible to serve the humanity agenda *and* the accountability agenda, to mutual benefit.

A further two-year project, funded by the Bedford Charity, involved working with a group of 14–15-year-olds (823 in total) in three independent schools and two state-maintained comprehensive schools in the Bedford area. The aim was to characterize underachievement and explore how to address it (Ren and Deakin Crick, 2013). Why do some young people fall below expectations? Could we characterize underachievement in terms of learning power? Could interventions reduce it?

In keeping with the emancipatory philosophy, the project used mixed methods research, combining quantitative and qualitative data with narrative enquiry, valuing the perspective of participants as highly as that of researchers. Phase 1 was dedicated to identifying underachievers, using a combination of regression analysis (of prior and recent attainment using national test scores) and teacher nomination. A clear finding emerged: that the 104 underachieving students were significantly weaker than their fellow students in four of the Learning Power dimensions: Mindful Agency, Curiosity, Sense Making, and Hope and Optimism. In other words, they tended to be more static in their view of how they changed and learnt over time, more passive and less curious and less likely to connect things up to make sense of their learning; and they demonstrated less awareness and self-regulation of their own learning processes.

Phase 2 included an intensive mentoring programme, which I undertook with a researcher/observer, involving a sub-sample of 18 underachieving students. As mentors, we used the students' spider-grams as a starting point and focused on helping them understand how to use the dimensions they were stronger in to build their weaker ones, which we knew were associated with underachievement. Fascinating qualitative and narrative data emerged in support of the quantitative data generated by the survey. Three shy 15-year-old girls, for example, confronted by their low Curiosity, contracted to start putting their hands up when they didn't understand something in class, rather than staying quiet out of shame. Their feedback in following weeks was heartening: they reported being taken more seriously by their teachers, finding they understood homework tasks they would previously have left undone, handing them in on time (a new experience) and rarely getting into trouble over school work thereafter.

Several boys connected their relative weakness in Mindful Agency to the frequency with which they forgot books or appointments and kept missing deadlines. Simple personal organization techniques, like making task lists and using planners, which they had previously resisted, now became worthwhile to them because of how they had come to know themselves as learners. Some qualitative findings from this study were potentially transformative:

> The students reported enhanced self-awareness as a learner, taking more responsibility for their own learning. On the whole, they thought that they had made significant progress in their academic achievement ... and many of them felt that they had closed the gap between their achievement and ability potential. Their teachers commented that [the] self-diagnosis tool was effective in stimulating the learning agency of underachieving students and re-engaging them in the school learning process.
> (Ren and Deakin Crick, 2013: 248)

The narrative enquiry in the project also unearthed the important and unexpected finding that underachieving teenagers often find it difficult to construct their identities through telling their life stories, possibly because their stories do not seem to connect with what they encounter in the classroom. One of the conclusions was that:

> ... in addressing the needs of underachievers, serious attention should be given to their learning subjectivities, enabling them to relate school learning to their personal values, attitudes, aspirations and beliefs.
> (ibid.: 235)

The concepts of authenticity, identity and agency were emerging from the research as hallmarks of effective learning systems. This helps to explain why using Learning Power profiles as the basis for learning conversations is such a powerful intervention.

A formal event was staged in Bedford to present the project report to the funders, in the presence of a high-profile academic and industrial audience, where the star performers were the teenage mentees. They spoke proudly of changes they had experienced in their sense of themselves and their new-found confidence as learners. When one of their teachers summed up what it meant for them, he was almost in tears, saying if someone had told him two years earlier that these students would stand up and present themselves so confidently and fluently to such an audience, he would have laughed out loud.

Research and development: Investigating and optimizing the impact of CLARA

Working through a small charitable company established for the purpose in 2004, I accepted responsibility for the research and development programme, consisting of small-scale, user-led action enquiries funded by participants rather than research grants. Initially, these were to field-test the instrument, but they soon became more reciprocal, responding to the interests of practitioners from across the UK and the world, with the aim of optimizing the impact of the ideas on students and learning. The reports are all free to download from the online library of the Learning Emergence Network blog, at: www.learningemergence.net/library/reports/.

Some emergent findings became consistent themes. The way the Learning Power vocabulary becomes an embedded language of learning is one. Another is the power of symbolism, metaphor and imagery in meta-learning, especially with younger or harder-to-reach learners. Stories personifying or iconizing the dimensions were particularly powerful. Perhaps the most memorable of these was 'Taronga Zoo Breakout', a narrative we co-created with a group of indigenous 16-year-olds in New South Wales. They were, thanks to their culture, highly attuned to making meaning by 'dreaming', 'storying' and using the communicative power of imagery, especially of the natural world. The story was a moving account of how a group of learning power 'animals' combined their strengths to escape from captivity, underlining emancipatory values, and included a profound insight from the students about how, to achieve success, 'you need to bring your culture into your learning' (Deakin Crick and Grushka, 2009).

Elsewhere, one large 11–18 comprehensive school in the south of England was pioneering the Opening Minds curriculum in 2006 with the Royal Society of Arts. This was based on five competences: learning to learn, citizenship, relating to people, managing situations and managing information (Candy, 2011). Their research questions were about what happens to the learning power of students treated as 'active agents rather than passive recipients' of a curriculum in which the focus is 'as much on process as outcomes' (Small, 2007b). It was clearly a school whose values echoed those of the CLARA research. Unsurprisingly, perhaps, we found this school had bucked the trend of decline in learning power that we had observed in other secondary schools.

Around the same time, I worked with an independent sixth form college in Malaysia to investigate two matters of interest: (i) how to explain the added value provided by the college's broad, expensive, residential education (when grades were already high) and (ii) how to better prepare its students for the academic demands and very different culture of British universities (Small, 2007a). The students were introduced to their profiles and encouraged to reflect on how they related to their experience and aspirations as learners. As a result, they made their own changes to how they learnt and wrote their own evaluations. Here is an extract from one of the self-evaluations:

> The increase in [my Collaboration] is a result of having improved in my communication and teamwork skills. I have acquired the ability of expressing my thoughts, ideas and opinions while being mindful of what the others think. Contrary to being quite rigid in my learning patterns previously, I [have] a slightly more creative approach. I feel that active participation in class has nurtured my ability to, as it were, think outside the box.
>
> (Small, 2007a: 16)

Their adoption of the project's learning vocabulary was striking, despite English being their second language. Even more striking was the increase in learning power over two years, once the college had addressed what we named a 'fragile high achiever' syndrome (Small, 2007a). These students were academically bright, successful by conventional measures, placing a high value on grades. But they were relatively fragile, probably due to over-dependence on success, positive feedback (including marks), and the attention, guidance and structured support that very able students attract by their diligence and performance. The post-intervention data suggested that bringing this into their awareness, together with a strong emphasis on building self-reliance, had largely succeeded in reducing their Fragility and Dependence in preparation for a much less structured and supportive environment in higher education.

Contrastingly, an 11–16 school in a highly disadvantaged, land-locked former ship-building town in the north-west of England wanted our help to broaden the horizons of its students. They used professional actors to perform characters invented to represent the Learning Power dimensions: the 'Curious Cat', the 'Wise Owl' (for Mindful Agency), the Magical Unicorn (for Creativity), the Bees (for Collaboration) and so on. This may explain why some students responded to their spider-grams proactively, before even discussing them. One of the girls told me that as soon as she had seen she was 'low in Wise Owl' she decided to do her homework on the day it was set, rather than 'leave it to some other time'. The teachers reported positive

Learning for emancipation

developments, both in their own practice and in their students' attitudes to learning. Here is an example of their feedback:

> Using [CLARA] ... is now embedded. They reflect and tell you [about it]. You know, in planning, they spot it going on when you weren't aware of it ... It's 'learning taking the place of teaching!'
> (Small and Deakin Crick, 2008: 21)

The project also had important implications for leadership. Once students became accustomed to this way of learning, where they were encouraged and expected to take decisions, find out for themselves, work in teams, make their own rules and set their own goals, they loved it. They found it harder to adjust to classrooms where they sat in rows and were expected to watch and listen to teachers much of the time.

As well as helping us to investigate the impact of the Learning Power ideas, these enquiries were like a searchlight into existing learning cultures. They would throw into sharp relief the tensions between more conventional teaching and the facilitation of powerful learning. The old pedagogy was script-based, founded on planning and control; this one was design-based, creating conditions for learning that were judiciously scaffolded but much freer and more personal to each learner.

Authentic Enquiry: An optimal environment for personalized learning

The impact of these ideas and practices on learners and learning was remarkable, even in the context of the regular curriculum. However, it was most transforming in the bravest schools – those that adopted a structured, enquiry-based learning format that we called Authentic Enquiry (see http://enquiry.learningemergence.com). One 11–16 school in Greater Manchester devoted eight hours of curriculum time a week, in Years 7 and 8, to a content-free programme called 'My World', with remarkable success in developing learner engagement and autonomy.

A full account of the Authentic Enquiry process and how it was tested and validated – with NEET learners (Not in Education, Employment or Training), young offenders and high-attaining 15-year-olds – is available in both the *Curriculum Journal* article (Deakin Crick, 2009) and the project report *Learning by Accident!* (Millner et al., 2006). It is worth offering here one or two snapshots of learners' reflections on the process to illustrate its value, including the use of Learning Power profiles and dimensions to scaffold it.

Tim Small

Jo (not her real name), one of the NEET learners, reflected on her own life experiences and eventually chose Cheddar Gorge (which she had visited with her mother) as a topic for further research. She recorded her reasons for the choice in her workbook:

> I chose this person and place because it was the time in my life when things were just normal at home and it was just me, my mum and my brother and we were all happy.
>
> (Jo, aged 15)

The deeply personal feelings behind her choice were traceable through her entire project and in her final product, an excellent tourist brochure for Cheddar Gorge, which she created with ICT to satisfy the requirements of her Education to Employment (E2E) course. Jo had targeted two dimensions to work on, based on her original profile: Collaboration, and Fragility and Dependence ('I don't normally stick at things') and, to her as if by magic, these were the two in which she made most significant gains during the eight-week project, clearly visible in the upper and lower-right sectors, in Figure 5.2.

It was in Jo's evaluation that it became clear how much it had meant to her and how much she had learnt, both about herself and Cheddar Gorge. The project came to life for her when, after asking one of her earliest questions ('Did anyone live in the caves before?'), she came across the discovery of 'my cheddar man', an ancient skeleton found in the caves, which became a central feature of her new knowledge.

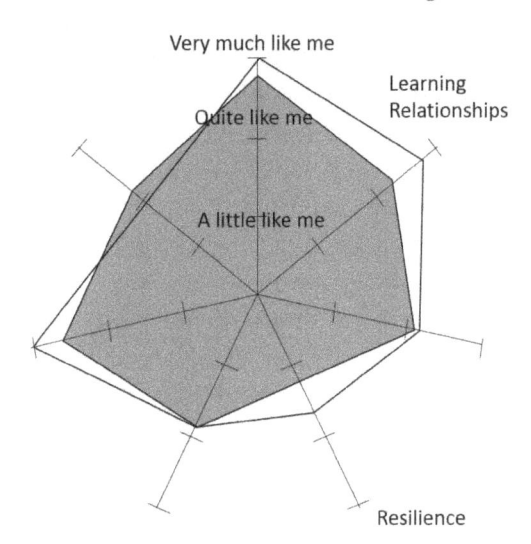

Figure 5.2: Jo's before-and-after CLARA profiles

Source: www.learningemergence.com; author's own

Learning for emancipation

In her final debrief, Jo was enthusiastic about the process. 'It's made me not so scared to learn other things,' she said. 'It was a tiny little project and it spiralled into all these other things that were connected.' For her, it was a key time of attitude change, having dropped out of school as a self-proclaimed failure: 'I didn't think I could learn any more but now I believe [I] can.' The most important moment for her was the group evaluation, when she reflected on 'how deep the project went. It's not just about Cheddar Gorge, it's about life stuff' (Millner *et al.*, 2006: 19).

Those students on the project who were usually high-attaining taught us as much as Jo did. One, Debra (not her real name), said: 'Having limits makes you more creative.' Jeremy (also not a real name), a studious historian who described himself previously as 'bookish', said he had begun 'to think with his feelings'. One of their fellow students, whom I shall call Simon, was quite damning about his experience of syllabus-driven learning in mainstream classrooms:

> I feel doing this project has allowed me to remove myself from the monotony of my usual courses and how they are taught, it gave me an opportunity to almost teach myself and to realize for myself the incorrect manner of doing things, instead of just being told what's wrong. As an alternative of learning how the syllabus dictates I have discovered how to learn as an individual; rather than as the rest of the students in the room are being taught. In a classroom, every student is taught as though they were the same person, outside of it you can choose which ways your mind will best process the task at hand.
>
> (Deakin Crick *et al.*, 2007: 86)

The discussion between these students was enlightening. Reflecting again on the difference between this personalized project and their regular experience of the curriculum, one of them came out with the thought-provoking line: 'We're programmed in such a way that our experience is invisible ...' (ibid.: 85). This suggests that 'normal' learning is experienced as impersonal, by comparison.

One of the NEET learners also made an observation about his experience of mainstream schooling, which might partly explain why he dropped out of it prematurely:

> Students often don't get on with school because every student has to do the same work, you all do one thing. They need more choice in approach – it gives you more freedom to decide instead of depending on what the teacher wants.
>
> (ibid.: 85)

Tim Small

The last word goes to Ollie (not his real name), one of the NEET learners, who had chosen 'outer space' as his place of special interest. He was profoundly dyslexic and had always struggled with school work and learning. The changes to his profile (Figure 5.3) show that, though he remained quite Fragile, he made significant gains in Curiosity and Collaboration (upper left and right), as with Jo, the very dimensions he had targeted.

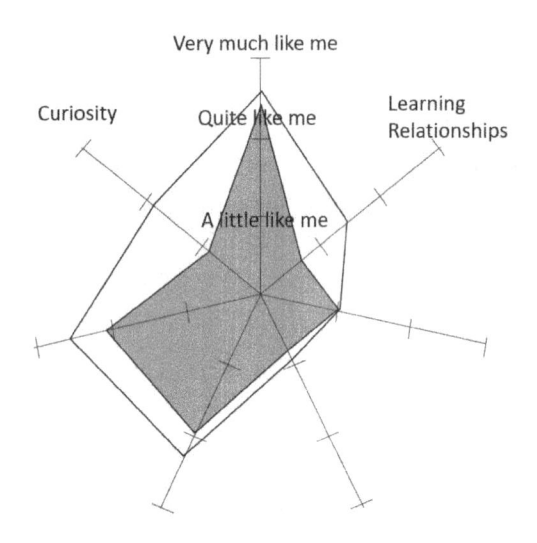

Figure 5.3: Ollie's before-and-after CLARA profiles
Source: www.learningemergence.com; author's own

During Ollie's enquiry, he found an astrophysicist, a former president of the Young Astronomers' Society, in his home town, who welcomed his interest and invited him to his next call-out. It was Ollie who articulated most succinctly the sense of a transformation: 'It's changed what I think I can do!' (Millner *et al.*, 2006: 24).

Conclusion and call to action

Outcomes like these have a similar effect on me as the best moments I experienced in teaching. Evidence that a life has been changed for the better is, surely, what we enter the profession for. I believe we should be concerned, though, about how far the wider system enables professionals to personalize learning and enhance young lives in this way. There are symptoms, in schools, of systemic inertia. Collective fatigue may be the most obvious. National policy, stretched resources, over-prescription of curriculum content, fear of negative judgements, and the compliance mechanisms of an accountability culture can all narrow schools' aspirations, to the extent that they become almost exclusively instruments of state policy. This diminishes the sense that they are also living, human communities with their own values, purposes and direction of travel. It traps them in a status quo that can deprive people of meaning and purpose, deplete their energy and carry a risk of terminal decline. The values of protest and social action, seeking creative alternatives – so much part of the Quaker movement – seem to me an essential counterbalancing force to energize education for emancipation.

A status quo with these negative characteristics can be well defended through the understandable but essentially didactic self-interest of those with most invested in it. What it lacks, I believe, is a proper appreciation of what young people need to flourish in times of accelerating change and uncertainty. They need, surely, to be enabled to become skilled in navigating and mapping unknown territories, not just absorbing and rehearsing what is already owned, determined and prescribed.

Authentic Enquiry challenges the status quo because it is anchored in personal interest rather than didactic intent. It starts with experienced reality, rather than opinion or theory. It creates its own dynamic, rather than following taught routines. It relates and integrates disparate elements, rather than keeping them fragmented. It is reflexive on process, rather than concerned only with outcome. It allows the outcome to be derived authentically from the learning process, rather than predetermining it. It is a fine example of embracing diversity, providing for inspiration and discernment and living adventurously (*QF&P*, 1.01; 1.02, 7, 27). In George Kelly's words:

> It does not say what has been or will be found, but proposes rather how we might go about looking for it.
>
> (Kelly, 2003: 3)

No wonder the status quo is challenged by this; it represents a new paradigm for curriculum and system design, based on a holistic, dynamic and relational view of learning. Contradicting the current experience of most of our school students, this paradigm recognizes the personhood of the learner, her intentionality, authority, relationships and story. It allows these to initiate, shape and motivate the learning process; it includes reflection on process as an essential component of what is learnt and, so, inevitably, involves learning *about* learning; it frees the learner to span and connect with pre-existing forms and stores of knowledge in preparation for the challenge of external or public assessment criteria; thence it allows the learning to achieve a purpose that is of tangible value to the 'accountable' world. It is not only the direct, but also the indirect, outcomes of this process that are so desperately needed. I am thinking of Deakin Crick's definition of 'resilient agency', the collection of dispositions and values measured by CLARA and so well engaged and developed by Authentic Enquiry: 'the capacity to respond profitably to risk, uncertainty and challenge over time' (Deakin Crick *et al.*, 2015: 147). How can we expect anyone to navigate the twenty-first century without it?

Although the need for this paradigm is made more urgent by the times we live in, its principles are not new. They resonate with a rich vein of original thinking, from Bill Curry (1947), Jerome Bruner (1977) and Lev Vygotsky (1978, 1986) to Carl Rogers (1969, 1983) and the wisdom of current thought leaders including Parker J. Palmer (1998), David Hargreaves (2004), Ken Robinson (2010) and Guy Claxton (2002) and enlightened policymakers such as Mick Waters (2007). Ten years ago, national policy reflected these influences. I still wonder what happened to *Personalised Learning* (Miliband, 2004) and *Every Child Matters* (Boateng, 2003) and why education policy in England and Wales has failed to build on the well-documented, break-through successes of Steiner schools (Woods *et al.*, 2005), Opening Minds (Candy, 2011), the International Baccalaureate (Mathews and Hill, 2006), or the Carnegie Foundation (Bryk, 2015).

Our response, surely, cannot be to wait for policy to catch the drift. Practice can, as I think these studies have shown, in time and with collective purpose and clear communication, make an irresistible case for reform. My call to action is for anyone who is inspired, or simply encouraged or reassured, to see how practicable it still is, within existing educational settings, to stimulate profound personal and organizational change. We need to pool the evidence of our efficacy. When our methods and measures are well researched and in alignment with life-enhancing values, it is possible to energize and scaffold the kind of learning that sets young people free to construct their own futures as well as get their grades. As educators, as in all we do, let us live and learn adventurously and enable everyone in our care to do the same.

References

Assessment Reform Group (2002) *Testing, Motivation and Learning*. Cambridge: University of Cambridge Faculty of Education.

Boateng, P. (2003) *Every Child Matters: Presented to Parliament by the Chief Secretary to the Treasury by Command of Her Majesty*. Norwich: The Stationery Office. Online. www.gov.uk/government/uploads/system/uploads/attachment_data/file/272064/5860.pdf (accessed 25 January 2018).

Bruner, J.S. (1977) *The Process of Education*. Cambridge, MA: Harvard University Press.

Bryk, A.S. (2015) '2014 AERA Distinguished Lecture: Accelerating how we learn to improve'. *Educational Researcher*, 44 (9), 467–77.

Candy, S. (2011) 'RSA Opening Minds: A curriculum for the 21st century'. *Forum*, 53 (2), 285–91.

Claxton, G. (2002) *Building Learning Power: Helping young people become better learners*. Bristol: TLO.

Curry, W.B. (1947) *Education for Sanity*. London: Heinemann.

Deakin Crick, R. (2009) 'Inquiry-based learning: Reconciling the personal with the public in a democratic and archaeological pedagogy'. *Curriculum Journal*, 20 (1), 73–92.

Deakin Crick, R., Broadfoot, P. and Claxton, G. (2004) 'Developing an effective lifelong learning inventory: The ELLI Project'. *Assessment in Education*, 11 (3), 247–72.

Deakin Crick, R. and Grushka, K. (2009) 'Signs, symbols and metaphor: Linking self with text in inquiry-based learning'. *Curriculum Journal*, 20 (4), 447–64.

Deakin Crick, R., Huang, S., Ahmed Shafi, A. and Goldspink, C. (2015) 'Developing resilient agency in learning: The internal structure of learning power'. *British Journal of Educational Studies*, 63 (2), 121–60.

Deakin Crick, R., McCombs, B., Haddon, A., Broadfoot, P. and Tew, M. (2007) 'The ecology of learning: Factors contributing to learner-centred classroom cultures'. *Research Papers in Education*, 22 (3), 267–307.

Deakin Crick, R. and Salway, A. (2006) *Locked Up Learning!* (ViTaL Development and Research Programme Report 3b). Bristol: University of Bristol. Online. http://learningemergence.net/wp-content/uploads/2014/02/ViTaL_RDP_Report_03b.pdf (accessed 25 January 2018).

Dickens, C. (1998) *Hard Times*. London: Wordsworth Editions Ltd.

Dweck, C.S. (2000) *Self-Theories: Their role in motivation, personality, and development*. Philadelphia: Psychology Press.

Gilbraith, J. (1986) 'Hope and imagination'. In *Learners All: Quaker experiences in education*. London: Quaker Home Service.

Gillman, H. (2007) *Consider the Blackbird: Reflections on spirituality and language*. London: Quaker Books.

Gittings, R. (1970) *Letters of John Keats: A selection*. Oxford: Oxford University Press.

Habermas, J. (1984) *Reason and the Rationalization of Society*. Trans. McCarthy, T. Boston: Beacon Press. Vol. 1 of *The Theory of Communicative Action*. 2 vols. 1984–7.

Haddon, A., Goodman, H., Park, J. and Deakin Crick, R. (2005) 'Evaluating emotional literacy in schools: The development of the School Emotional Environment for Learning Survey'. *Pastoral Care in Education*, 23 (4), 5–16.

Hargreaves, D.H. (2004) *Learning for Life: The foundations for lifelong learning*. Bristol: Policy Press.

Kelly, G.A. (2003) 'A brief introduction to personal construct theory'. In Fransella, F. (ed.) *International Handbook of Personal Construct Psychology*. Chichester: John Wiley and Sons, 3–20.

Mathews, J. and Hill, I. (2006) *Supertest: How the International Baccalaureate can strengthen our schools*. Chicago: Open Court Publishing.

McCombs, B.L. and Whisler, J.S. (1997) *The Learner-Centered Classroom and School: Strategies for increasing student motivation and achievement*. San Francisco: Jossey-Bass.

Miliband, D. (2004) *Personalised Learning: Building a new relationship with schools*. Speech at North of England Education Conference. London: Department for Education and Skills. Online. https://pdfs.semanticscholar.org/7df7/ceb2d78a797f3b9f2eeb09d36270083c22ac.pdf (accessed 1 March 2018).

Millner, N., Small, T. and Deakin Crick, R. (2006) *Learning by Accident!* (ViTaL Development and Research Programme Report 1). Bristol: University of Bristol. Online. http://learningemergence.net/wp-content/uploads/2014/02/ViTaL_RDP_Report_01.pdf (accessed 25 January 2018).

Palmer, P.J. (1998) *The Courage to Teach: Exploring the inner landscape of a teacher's life*. San Francisco: Jossey-Bass.

Palmer, P.J. (2000) *Let Your Life Speak: Listening for the voice of vocation*. San Francisco: Jossey-Bass.

Palmer, P.J. (2004) *A Hidden Wholeness: The journey toward an undivided life*. San Francisco: Jossey-Bass.

Ren, K. and Deakin Crick, R. (2013) 'Empowering underachieving adolescents: An emancipatory learning perspective on underachievement'. *Pedagogies: An International Journal*, 8 (3), 235–54.

Robinson, K. (2010) 'Changing education paradigms'. RSA Animated TED Talk adaptation. Online. www.ted.com/talks/ken_robinson_changing_education_paradigms (accessed 9 July 2017).

Rogers, C.R. (1969) *Freedom to Learn: A view of what education might become*. Columbus, OH: Merrill Publishing.

Rogers, C.R. (1983) *Freedom to Learn for the 80s*. Columbus, OH: Merrill Publishing.

Small, T. (2007a) *Learning Outside the Box!* (ViTaL Development and Research Programme Report 3). Bristol: University of Bristol. Online. http://learningemergence.net/wp-content/uploads/2014/02/ViTaL_RDP_Report_03.pdf (accessed 25 January 2018).

Small, T. (2007b) *The Learning Agents!* (ViTaL Development and Research Programme Report 4). Bristol: University of Bristol. Online. http://learningemergence.net/wp-content/uploads/2014/02/ViTaL_RDP_Report_04.pdf (accessed 25 January 2018).

Small, T. and Deakin Crick, R. (2008) *Learning in the Outdoor Dimension* (ViTaL Development and Research Programme Report 9). Bristol: University of Bristol. Online. http://learningemergence.net/wp-content/uploads/2014/02/ViTaL_RDP_Report_09.pdf (accessed 25 January 2018).

Vygotsky, L.S. (1978) *Mind in Society: The development of higher psychological processes*. Cambridge, MA: Harvard University Press.

Vygotsky, L.S. (1986) *Thought and Language*. Rev. ed. Trans. Kozulin, A. Cambridge, MA: MIT Press.

Waters, M. (2007) *The Big Picture of the Curriculum*. London: Qualifications and Curriculum Authority. Online. www.curriculum.edu.au/verve/_resources/Waters_Australia_paper_1.pdf (accessed 1 March 2018).

Woods, P., Ashley, M. and Woods, G. (2005) *Steiner Schools in England* (Research Report RR645). Nottingham: Department for Education and Skills.

Chapter 6

Equality, truth and love in subject teaching: Cognitive care in the case of mathematics

Anne Watson

In this chapter, I am going to use mathematics as an extreme example of a school subject that is a political battleground and also often a psychological battleground for learners. In 1945, the Guild of Friends in Education (GFE), a group of Quaker educators, wrote that:

> ... nothing helps people so much as to be cared for, and the tutor must be constantly reminding himself [sic] that the fundamental value of man lies not in his ability but in his possibility.
>
> (GFE, 1945: 12)

I will explore whether 'being cared for' can be balanced with pressure to learn, especially where the need to achieve qualifications and/or the need to have access to common cultural knowledge are seen as ways to achieve a more equal society.

When I began teaching in the early 1980s, it was fashionable to talk about how each child should be supported to develop their full potential in school and how this meant different pathways and opportunities to enhance the natural dispositions of children. It was also seen as important that school students should have some agency in decisions about what, when and how they would study. Even so, it was acknowledged that every child should study English and mathematics. This was the case even before school performance was measured in terms of percentages of students who succeeded in these two subjects. There was some opposition to this universal requirement from two directions. One school of thought believed that there were students who were incapable of learning mathematics as a broad subject, and for whom everyday arithmetic was a more suitable area of study or set of skills. Another school of thought argued that the benefits of mathematical study were vastly overrated and it should be an optional subject for those who were progressing towards studying mathematics and related subjects at advanced levels.

Nineteenth-century Quaker writings about the inclusion of mathematics within education were often confined to expressing a need for hitherto uneducated groups to learn useful arithmetic (O'Donnell, 2013). The Friends Educational Society gave detailed guidance on this task (FES, 1841) but veered away from focusing on clerical work, which was fashionable at the time, by suggesting that writing neatly could be a waste of time since practical application of arithmetic was more valuable. In UK Quaker schools, writes John Reader (1979) in his reflections on a Quaker contribution to education, both the arts and the sciences had been taught since the middle of the nineteenth century, but sciences had been included from much earlier to enable the search for truth, whereas arts were a more recent inclusion. Yet there is little evidence to suggest that mathematics, as a full subject discipline, was any different in Quaker schools than in any other schools – that is, taught to a high abstract level only for some, and taught as useful numeracy to others. In 1902, a small national group of Quaker teachers held a discussion about what would be desirable developments in mathematics teaching, and they suggested including applications, estimations and approximations and the use of realistic problems, with a reduced emphasis on formal geometry proofs. They also recommended delaying symbolic notations and deductive reasoning until learners understood the concepts concerned (Graham, 1902). This suggests that teaching methods might have differed between schools, because most practice at the time assumed that pencil-and-paper methods taught formally in class could be applied in working contexts without any difficulty. Subsequent research showed that applying arithmetic in real situations is a separate craft requiring a different kind of learning, and John Graham appears to have been aware of that. The 1902 discussion was advanced for its time and, to this day, it continues internationally and across cultures and policymakers.

When, in the late 1980s, it became enshrined in British law that all students should study mathematics as a broad discipline up to the age of 16, there were attempts to redefine school mathematics to focus on mathematical methods of enquiry, realistic problem-solving and exploration of mathematical phenomena, rather than the traditional diet of methods, examples, theorems and facts. This redefinition led to problem-based and enquiry-led approaches to concepts, as anticipated in the 1902 discussion. Other responses stayed with formal teaching methods but provided different tracks through the common curriculum, so that some students progressed much slower than others. As I write, all students must follow a curriculum that includes learning to use mathematics to solve multi-step problems, undertake mathematical deductive and inductive reasoning, use trigonometry to solve spatial problems, read statistical information critically and have some algebraic and graphical competence. The current expectation, initiated by government, that all shall learn the same mathematics, challenges the temptation to place students on differently paced tracks (which have the effect of limiting access to core knowledge for some), while it still recognizes differences among learners in their end-of-school achievements.

What might Quakers make of these matters? If Quakers can claim to have insights about education, those insights must have something to say about a strand of the core work of educational institutions: providing access to canons of knowledge. I will now explore how Quaker values of equality and truth might relate to subject knowledge in the case of mathematics and use theories of learning as a bridge to think about how love and care might be acted out in the task of educating. I shall end with some examples of practice in mathematics that show care about learners' cognition of the subject.

I am also drawing here on my own experience as a mathematics teacher and educator, a life task I have always regarded as somewhat sacred, both for the way that mathematics harnesses capabilities of the mind that we all have in common and in the task of nurturing young people to be fulfilled citizens. Also, for me, the transcendent properties of mathematics are never far away. In the first Quaker meeting I ever attended, Elsa King, who was my mathematics teacher at the time, observed my presence with some surprise and was moved to minister that she often thought: 'how wonderful it is that there is infinity in the largest thing and also in the smallest thing.' In that moment, my path was set to become a Quaker and a mathematician.

Equality

A national curriculum that includes mathematics can be seen by some as an attempt to treat all children as future economic units rather than as rounded human beings with manifold human potentials. Equality need not imply sameness, but nor can it imply differentiated access to knowledge and experiences that are regarded as important by society, including mathematics, science and languages. If children do not have this initial access at school, or they reject it when young, then how will they know what it is possible to know and do later on? This argument led to a desire for special educational establishments that preserved Quaker knowledge and culture – in Quaker education history we have an extreme example of treating some things as so worth knowing that we are prepared to put effort and resources into ensuring they are taught to all.

Usually in Quaker writing about education, equality is understood as the need to consider the individual needs of children and their different capabilities, urging that both psychological and social needs be met and reasoning that different capabilities are equally valuable (for example Clarke, 1986). Social justice is, in part, delivered by taking account of individuals through education and treating them accordingly. By contrast, a compensatory view of justice would be to distribute educational input inversely according to the advantages of birth, to level children's access to all educational futures (Gewirtz, 1998). This approach ensures that advantages and disadvantages introduced through parental differences are not carried into the next generation. This is an argument that has been used both by the political right (for example Gove, 2012) and also by economists of inequality (for example Atkinson, 2015).

Quakers as a group cannot change the English national education system; we are too few and too individualistic to do so. So Quaker teachers have to consider how to enact testimonies of equality and social justice within their current circumstances. This situation includes national examinations as both highly important individual passports to future social and educational opportunities and as measures of school effectiveness. A compensatory view implies that those who have most difficulty learning in schools should receive the most attentive teaching to have similar access to future opportunities. Indeed, many teachers come to the profession precisely to change children's life chances within the current system, rather than waiting for system change or opting out of the official system for a parallel life in alternative schooling (see Keir Mitchell's chapter in this book).

This is a tough job, but Quakerism is often not easy to put into practice. Quaker discussions about education usually avoid talking about subject teaching and instead focus on pastoral care, peripheral activities, peacefulness, good citizenship, caring personalities, peaceful schools and communities, the value of self-expression, liberal arts and RE teaching (Dalke and Dixson, 2004; Lacey, 1998; O'Reilley, 1993; Perkins, 1989; Quaker Home Service, 1986). These are important, and yet the heart of schools is the teaching and learning of subject knowledge – and it is on that basis that the successes of individuals and schools are currently measured. It is almost as if the qualities of educational experience I have just listed were regarded as necessary to ameliorate the negative effects of formal teaching of knowledge, to produce rounded, happy and thoughtful individuals who nevertheless can also deal with the formal requirements. Thus, the regimentation of classroom behaviour and the expectation that all children will adopt particular ways to think, particular forms of expression and particular formats for the measurement of their success are achievable within a kinder surrounding context. Within that environment, mathematics lessons can lead to tears and fears; there is a phenomenon called 'maths anxiety' that some claim to be a real and measurable mental and physical state (for example Ashcraft et al., 2007). Traditionally taught, it is possible to be wrong many times during a mathematics lesson, without knowing why; it is also possible to be right, but not to know why; it is also possible to have no idea what is going on because of some earlier difficulties. The potential to be wrong is ever-present. Trevor Jaggar, a Quaker who became Inspector of Schools in London, claimed that a main part of the work of teaching was 'dealing with wrong' (1984).

Truth

Another challenge within Quakerism is that truth is developed and understood through experience. Truth, in Quaker writings, usually means what we understand of God, or something Divine, from which we draw belief, strength and action. It also means personal truthfulness. In Quaker educational writings, the idea that knowing truth comes from personal experience and exploration has been extended to learning the subject disciplines of the arts, humanities and science and explorations of truth, according to the modes of enquiry in those subjects (Jaggar, 1984; Lacey, 1998; Smith, 2004). A Quaker approach to subject teaching would encourage questioning and searching about everything. Yet mathematics and some other curriculum subjects are not seen as fallible, debatable, questionable truths 'for now', but as immutable, imposed truth structures. A typical question in this debate is: 'Does 2 plus 2 always make 4?' This question triggers laughter, ridicule, contradictory examples or philosophical argument, and it misses the point.

Truth in mathematics unfolds successive layers of understanding of structural relationships between quantities, spatial properties and their abstractions. Seeking truth involves understanding the various ways these can be represented, applied and verified. The truths of the subject are not the calculation and manipulation methods to get right answers but the structures of which these are manifestations. Access to mathematics (which is necessary for full participation in society) implies access to these layers of mathematical structure and knowing how to enquire within them. This makes it useful. For example, it is important to understand that subtraction reverses the effects of adding; that a percentage wage rise has different real effects for different wage levels; that the meaning of a graph depends on the axes on which it is plotted; or that reasoning based on visual representation or a few cases might lead to unwarranted assumptions. It is also important to experience how our minds make patterns from the information we perceive and to know that these patterns sometimes represent big ideas but can also be misleading. In other words, it is important for children to know that their own perception can be the starting point for thinking and for new knowledge, as well as knowing how some of that knowledge might affect their lives. The Quaker educator Kenneth Barnes asks teachers whether they give their students the end or the beginning (Barnes, 1960: 29). To give starting points enables learners to use what they already think and know to explore new knowledge and seek truths. But as well as that, the knowledge that one *can* learn, and the ability to take the risks involved in learning, are contributions to achieving equality.

To focus only on the technical aspects of a subject would be untruthful. An analogy from English teaching might be coercing children emotionally and socially into writing and analysing poetry by giving them a particular metre and insisting on certain rhyming patterns yet omitting any sense of encapsulating scene, mood and emotion. It might be an exercise children can do and be tested on, but it would not be true to the meaning of poetry. Truthfulness in subject education includes faithfulness to the discipline as it has developed in human endeavour, truthfulness about why and how it is seen as important, and an approach to the subject that values the human qualities of the learner.

So what about love? Before I talk about love, I shall detour a little into some theories of learning so that I can identify a particular kind of love that recognizes disciplinary truth in education.

Theories of learning

To care for individuals who are learning we have to have some idea of how learning happens. The dominant theories in Western culture come from interpretations of the work of Jean Piaget and Lev Vygotsky (Piaget, 1963; Vygotsky, 1986) and their followers. Piaget, whose description of learning influenced teaching in primary schools across the world, believed that new experiences have an impact on the mind, which has already developed knowledge from previous experiences. New experiences that are not recognized may be rejected, or are assimilated into existing structures of knowledge. Eventually the structures evolve to include the new experience, thus achieving equilibration, a state of knowing that remains until a new experience impacts upon it. This model gives rise to the notion of cognitive conflict, which occurs when a new experience challenges the existing structure and some restructuring has to happen as a result. In its extreme form, this theory of learning is characterized as lonely learners frequently finding themselves to be wrong and having to rethink, or even being given trick questions that almost force them to be wrong. In educational literature, learners are described as having misconceptions, and one aspect of good teaching is to address these common misconceptions. In the best teaching hands, misconceptions are understood as the justifiable efforts of learners to make sense of the world. In the worst teaching, they can be treated as silly mistakes made by children who do not listen properly. In either case, they might be treated as states of mind that somehow have to be avoided or cured. In some Eastern cultures, these are more generously understood as valid acts of the mind based on limited information – there is something limiting about the experiences on which the thinking was based. Children who have been told, or notice, that when you multiply by 10 you 'put zero on the end' might write $2.5 \times 10 = 2.50$. They are using their natural inclination to notice patterns of behaviour and copy them, yet the answer ends up being wrong.

But in school, no one needs to learn as a lonely individual. The thinking that results from individual perceptions can be modified by what others do and say, including the teacher and the peer group. Being wrong, being mistaken, could be a very temporary state out of which one can quickly bounce with confidence. It is important to take account of the fact that learning takes place within a talking environment, so that words as well as written representations carry experiences and meaning (Barnes, 1971). The importance of the role of the teacher can become lost in some applications of Piaget's ideas, which stress peer exchanges. The belief that children can be left to engage with tasks together, and therefore learn, leaves the responsibility for developing disciplinary ideas in the hands and mouths of the children who know least. There can be an assumption that natural development leads children into a state of readiness to learn. Those children who are most talkative and articulate are then more likely to be thought ready to learn. Dependency on peer discussion can also deprive some children of the language that might enable them to talk about the world and understand it more deeply.

A simple example is that children learn the distinctions between the meanings of 'bigger', 'taller', 'wider' and 'heavier' through hearing adults, but on their own might only talk about 'bigger' or 'more'. A more sophisticated example is that, without teacher-talk, children might think that *7 = 3x + 1* and *x + (2x + 1) = 3x + 1* are both equations, yet in the first one there is only one value of x that makes it true, whereas the second one is true for all values of *x*. Adult intervention, which does not have to mean telling, is necessary to make the distinction.

In Vygotskian theories of learning, the role of talk is considered central to the social and intellectual development of children. Vygotsky and his followers believed that interaction with adults enables children to learn the products of human intellectual development that they might never meet without such interaction. Education is seen as part of how society brings all children into the prevailing culture. What is more, education in general, and teacher-talk in particular, should *lead* the development of the mind, not wait for it. In action, this means that teachers provide scaffolding in the form of tasks, questions, discussions and prompts by which learners can participate in the relevant subject culture. It is through talk and further tasks that their ideas are brought to match those in the prevailing culture so that adolescents become adults who fully belong. In this theory of learning, so-called 'misconceptions' are usually conceptual difficulties that arose in the historical development of the subject, or ambiguous interpretations of the use of symbols. For example, children who confuse *$2x^2$* with *$(2x)^2$* are not misconceiving but are learning to use a human invented symbol system; university students who think that 'continuous' means 'can be drawn with an unbroken line on paper' are not misconceiving but are engaging in a debate that mathematicians took about two hundred years to sort out.

This may be an over-interpretation of what Lev Vygotsky actually said about schooling, but if so, it is an over-interpretation in the right direction, which is towards the importance of expert talk and action in education. Many interpretations focus only on peer discussion, which again runs the risk of leaving young learners to rediscover key disciplinary ideas for themselves. To some extent, asking a young person to think about, say, 'polygon' brings polygon into the mind as something to be thought about; similarly, asking a young person to think about 'peace' brings peace into the mind as something to be thought about. The difference is only that the word 'peace' is relatively ubiquitous throughout life whereas the word 'polygon' requires some recognition that is only likely to be developed in school. The teacher who cares about students' cognition, and appreciates the negative power of being wrong without knowing why, will therefore work carefully on language. Mary Rose O'Reilley gives one way to do that:

> It requires a long time to take in a few words. On either side of the word we need a patch of white, of silence, like the white space that defines a Chinese painting, or the rests in music that permit the notes to be heard.
>
> (O'Reilley, 1993: 105)

Another theory of learning that I find useful is not about how the mind constructs meaning, but what a person perceives – not how new experiences become knowledge, but what is noticed in these new experiences. This is the idea that we notice contrasts between what varies and what is invariant; as observers we learn about the sea by looking at waves, at the light playing on its surface, at the borderline of colour and texture between it and the sky or the shore. As swimmers we learn other things about the sea because we perceive different varied aspects of it. The idea that the interplay of variation and invariance influences our learning is sometimes called Variation Theory and is due to Ference Marton (2015), who does not attempt to explain the work of the mind, but looks at its inputs and outputs. I add to this that what we notice changes when we know more about how to look at a phenomenon, so someone with expertise or wisdom might make distinctions between, say, different birds sitting on a wire in ways that are not available to a novice. Similarly, a motor mechanic sees the engine of a broken-down car differently from the perception of a non-mechanic driver; the mechanic looks directly for specific things and symptoms of their failure. This approach gives clues about teaching in ways that harness our propensity to see differences and similarities, and also points towards the development of expertise as a knowledge-based way of discerning differences and similarities.

One problem with much of the writing about learning is that the examples of concepts authors employ are either concrete objects (Lev Vygotsky uses 'dog' in some of his central texts) or visible qualities used as adjectives for concrete or imaginable objects (Ference Marton uses 'green apple'), whereas for learning mathematics the concepts are abstract (such as number) but available to us through representative objects (such as counters or number lines), or only available through symbols (such as: 3, 4, 5 ...).

In Vygotskian thinking, true concepts are thought-forms that solve a problem from some aspect of human existence and relate a person's own experience of the world to the social history. Education is a way to provide learners with 'scientific concepts', a kind of true concept met through institutions, such as schools, rather than by direct experience. In mathematics, instead of pretending that the mathematics one learns in school is of lasting importance in the 'outside world', it becomes part of learning about mathematical conceptualization. Through this kind of education, bringing conceptual ideas and problem-solving together, the place of mathematics in human culture can be recreated, including the need to continue to seek knowledge and to 'think it possible that you may be mistaken' (*QF&P*, 1.02, 17). We have to understand that this phrase came into Quakerism in a particular historical context not related to learning mathematics in school, but it does remind us of how Quaker testimonies run threadlike through the whole of life and influence our take on knowledge in and of the world.

Love and cognitive care

Taking mathematics as an extreme example, the truths of subject disciplines can be met and considered through forms of teaching that do not create anxiety, but enhance confidence and self-actualization – teaching that cares about the cognitive efforts of different individuals as well as their emotional and social development. I call this cognitive care, and see it as a prompting of love in the work of a subject teacher. Cognitive care can lead to a classroom atmosphere in which individual ways of thinking are understood and valued as steps along the way towards the accepted truths of mathematics.

Very often I see classrooms in which students are cared for emotionally and socially, but when it comes to the workings of the brain they are expected to put aside their own thinking and adopt given methods and truths. It is as if teachers coerce students into the required behaviour of passing the tests through hard work, compliance, obedience, tolerance and resilience (all worthy character traits) rather than through interest and love of learning and the subject. While these aims are all important in cognitive care, they do not generate an honest and sustainable relationship with the truths of mathematics.

It is unloving to put young people into a position where the well-meant products of their thinking are very likely to be labelled as wrong. Similarly, it is uncaring to expect them to tolerate and adapt to a stream of situations that present them with cognitive conflict. It is the educational language that is at fault here rather than the underlying idea. First, it assumes that the mind recognizes conflict, abhors it and desires to resolve it. If a learner's experience of mathematics has been a sequence of apparently disconnected facts and calculations that are sometimes relevant and sometimes not, it is unlikely that any conflict of conceptualization will be recognized. Second, it is possible to sustain simultaneously ideas that are apparently in conflict: Carl Jung believed that this was a seat of personal creativity, and in Quaker life it also is seen as a situation in which new ideas might emerge. For example, a well-known Quaker phrase is: 'Take heed to the promptings of love and truth in your hearts' (*QF&P*, 1.02, 1), while Alison Sharman (1986) says:

> ... these two sometimes seem to be in conflict, but in fact they are inseparable. If we are to know the truth, we must be able to see with unclouded eyes, and then we will love what is real and not what is duty or fancy.
> (Sharman, 1986: 139; *QF&P*, 20.75)

Melissa Rodd (2017) takes a psychoanalytical perspective on mathematical learners who have a range of special needs. She develops the notion of a 'math-care environment'. In such an environment, the child and adult are linked in a mutual flow and the child is 'held' in the relationship of working together on mathematics. She identifies meticulous preparation, willingness to be explicit about the teacher being a learner too, and fluidity of time use as features of one teacher's practice that appear to 'hold' the learner. Much of the development of her ideas applies in one-to-one situations and/or with very young children, but she also extends the idea to classes of learners with or without special needs. Preparing oneself to teach in ways in which uncertainty and 'meticulous preparation' are not in conflict is seen as a professional practice. The fact that uncertainty can be encompassed productively in an environment built on relationships resonates with my Quaker sense of uncertainty, which is the familiar ground for listening to others, questioning experience and thinking it possible that one is mistaken.

If seeing conflict as a seat of creativity is of value in relation to big whole-life concepts such as truth and love, then perhaps the same approach to conflict can be used with less important concepts too. If I think X about a mathematical idea and you think Y, we can talk about it and maybe both learn more through the experience, even imagining there might be a Z.

In the case of mathematics, there is a further problem with the language of conflict, which is that the idea held by the learner is likely to be correct in some limited cases and will only appear wrong when applied outside these. This is sometimes to do with not knowing the characteristics of a new context, like a tennis player waiting for a bounce in badminton, in which case resilience for a novice is a prerequisite; other times it might be to do with not recognizing that the field is different. Both of these states give clues about how to teach with cognitive care. Thus, the task for teachers is to foster the learner's development of the ways of seeing that are relevant for the subject in question, rather than correcting or avoiding misconceptions, and to scaffold the construction of conceptual understanding through experiences and talk. It is also important to engender a willingness to use concepts that do not arise from daily life directly, but that society accepts as 'truths for now' within a subject.

Quakerism also accepts that the ideas and thinking of children have the same value as those of adults. George Fox, the founder of the Movement, himself saw 'the Light in children', where 'Light' was his way of describing Jesus (also *QF&P*, 23.73; 23.78). Thus, a teacher who cares about cognition will listen to students and respond to their efforts to learn. John Macmurray, a philosopher who became a Quaker when he found that it fitted with his beliefs about being a person, wrote extensively about the centrality of mutual relationships with others, and his ideas have been used by significant educational philosophers (Fielding, 2012). The problem for teachers is how to establish and sustain mutual relationships of caring in the classroom. Mutual care depends on forming relationships that, as with any good relationships, are based on a shared goal and a shared journey towards it. Caring is not an individual virtue but a lived relationship. Nel Noddings, who was a mathematics educator before she turned to writing about care, describes the mindset of a truly caring teacher as being that of 'attentive love', so that students recognize the attention and the care for them as individual people who, in turn, have a relationship with the teacher (Noddings, 2005b). This requires a lot from teachers. She says:

> Mathematics teachers, for example, must be able to draw on philosophy, biography, history, fiction, poetry, science, art, music and current events. In doing this competently, teachers help students to make connections between school studies and great existential questions.
>
> (Noddings, 2005a)

Noddings points out that many teachers care, but can turn this caring into a one-sided individual campaign to coerce their students into learning rather than a mutually trusted effort. This is not to decry personal care. I am reminded of a teacher who acts towards her students in a very loving way and provides them with a small piece of putty to play with during examinations to remind them of the calming and supportive atmosphere of her classroom. But her students also have to know the mathematics and to know that they know.

Children need classrooms that are emotionally safe places, where everybody knows their name, where they feel they belong with the whole of themselves. However, within that space, the learner has to change the way they think, challenge what they know, acquire new skills that can be difficult, and cope with being wrong and with not knowing, even when they are thinking hard.

Caring and cognitive challenge

The classroom setting must make it possible for changes to occur in the students' minds with respect to the subject. Characteristics of a helpful climate would include: positive relationships, respect for individuals, avoidance of stereotyping, emotional safety and recognition of effort, success or need for further help. It would include everyone as valued individuals and would also draw on collaboration. It would include opportunities for self-expression, for supported risk-taking and to understand how personal effort is related to learning the subject matter. Teachers who engender this kind of atmosphere in classrooms do not need to be told to 'improve engagement' or 'develop a climate for learning' or 'build resilience' or whatever the latest educational buzz-phrase might be.

At the very least, situations in which one can be wrong many times, or can be right without knowing why (such as completing a long set of practice examples without a full understanding and opportunities for feedback), need to be avoided if they generate anxiety or confusion. At best, teachers who care for cognition need to plan for the small changes in thinking that their students need to make, and think about how to support them to make those changes. For example, rather than launching into quadratics as a new topic without any obvious purpose, teachers might talk about how linear graphs have one x-value that gives zero as the y-value (this is something students can say for themselves), then raise the possibility for enquiry: What might graphs look like if they had two zeroes? This query can lead to student-generated conjectures that can be explored in the classroom, or the teacher might next introduce a situation that has two graphical zeroes.

They might use an example such as the width of a rectangular frame for a picture that measures 10 cm by 6 cm, when the whole frame is going to be covered with a limited number of mosaic tiles so has to be less than, or equal to, 80 cm^2 in area. Answers can be found in many ways and can be compared with the students' own conjectures about a possible graph showing the various alternatives. What could have been the grounding for confusion, abstraction, meaningless manipulation and frustration is instead a place for students' ideas and exploration, to be confirmed later with the teacher in formal ways.

Jim Wingate, following M.K. Ghandi's ideas, suggests engaging students in the process of planning the scheme of work (Wingate, 1985) so that the teacher is a resource rather than the organizer of learning. Even at primary school, children can show unexpected maturity in deciding how to sequence the various tasks they have been given. I have seen this take place effectively in primary classrooms and have used this approach myself within the context of mathematics. However, it is rarely the case that merely completing a given task ensures that the learner has extended or changed the way they think; the core concepts of mathematics are not really learnt by seeking them out on Google, or practising a new technique, or solving a realistic problem without a knowledgeable teacher who can shape or orientate new ways of thinking. In mathematics, such approaches may lead to students being able to do standard questions obediently, or solve realistic problems in an ad hoc way or collect useful facts. But a commitment to the truth of the subject requires more. It requires understanding the underlying structures of the subject, knowing when and how to use them, and seeing them in places that are not immediately obvious. To do this, learners need to be able to see things through mathematical eyes, not through everyday eyes; they have to think in ways that are particularly mathematical. This means that the teacher must not only act as a resource but also has to be a model for seeing the world mathematically and anticipate how everyday ways of seeing might have to be transformed.

As an example, suppose the curriculum says that children have to learn about enlargements of shapes, so they are given a rectangle and asked to enlarge it by the scale factor of 2. There are several attempts produced in a typical classroom shown in Figure 6.1, using different interpretations of 'scale factor of 2'.

Anne Watson

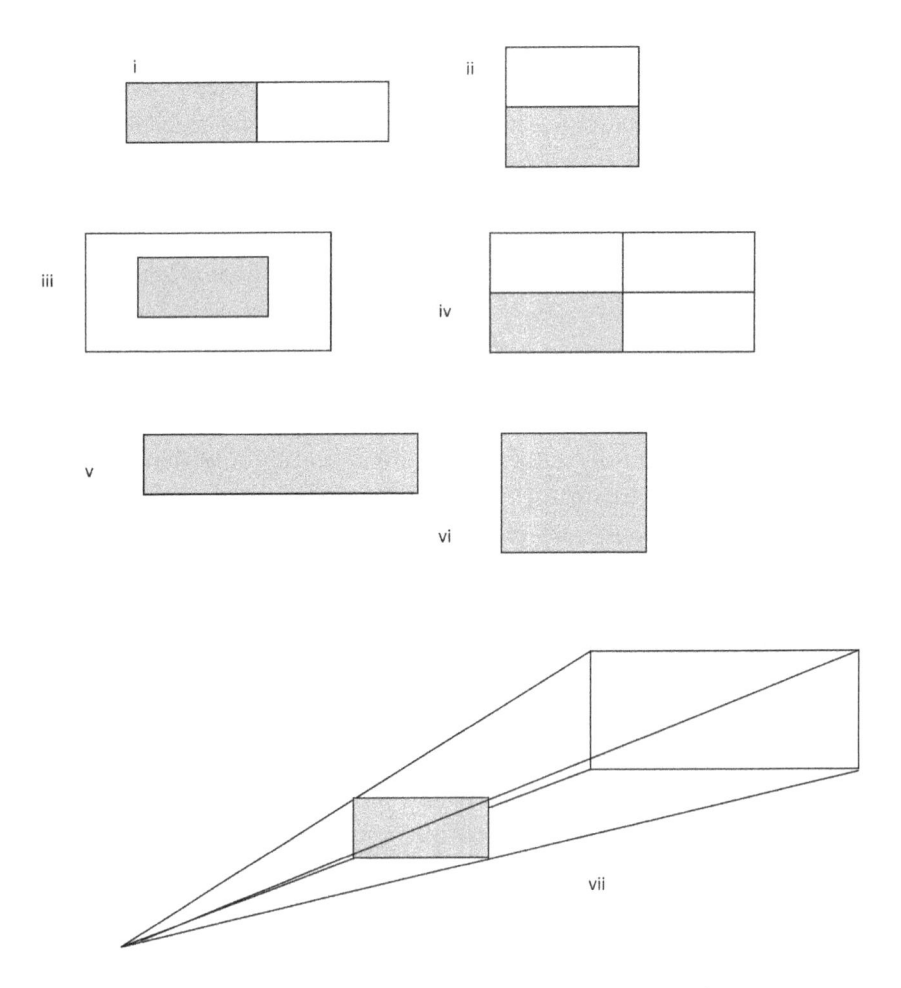

Figure 6.1: Different understandings of 'doubling' a rectangle

In (i) and (ii) of Figure 6.1, the task has been interpreted as reproducing another rectangle so that there are two, or the length or the height has been doubled, either using a ruler or on squared paper. In (iii), there seems to be some understanding that the rectangle has to be made larger by expanding it in some way. From the diagram itself, we would not know whether somebody has merely made it bigger, as one would on a computer screen, or made an effort to double the length and height, or maybe they thought they were doubling the area. In (iv), both the length and height have been doubled, ending up with a rectangle four times the area of the original, while (v) and (vi) are like (i) and (ii) but seem to be based on ideas of stretching rather than 'adding on'. The final diagram, (vii), shows what would normally be regarded as a correct method for enlarging the given rectangle by the scale factor relative to the fixed point. The rectangle they end up with is twice the length and twice the height of the original and therefore four times the area.

All of these possibilities can be seen as various interpretations of the task. All of them are the product of thought and effort. All of them offer material for discussion but, because of the different interpretations, children who produce the first six outcomes are going to be positioned as being wrong while the seventh method is the one that eventually becomes the desirable outcome of the curriculum. A theory of learning that labels the first six as misconceptions makes children become wrong, whereas a theory of learning that sees learning as a response to what is offered, informed by what is known, positions children as thinkers. It is the task and the mathematics that are problematic, not the learners. The task can be interpreted as somehow doubling the rectangle – 'doubling' being an everyday word that is ambiguous and imprecise in mathematics. An approach to teaching that is characterized by cognitive care would lead the teacher to imagine what the students might do when initially choosing or devising tasks and also to decide how to coordinate their efforts towards the mathematical meaning of a scale factor of two. This might include a discussion of what we mean when we say 'double' so that everyone can see the need to be more precise in mathematics if we need to have one answer. I am imagining this discussion to be a genuine one in which the different meanings that children offer can be compared with each other to illustrate the diversity of our understandings. For real discussion, the teacher does not adjudicate what children say by inserting comments such as 'Brilliant!' or 'Would you like to think about that again?' because these are interpreted by children to be alternative ways of being told they are right or wrong. Once the need for precision is agreed, the students can try to phrase precise tasks that might lead to each of the outcomes shown in the diagrams. This puts them in the position of responsibility and control rather than as victims of unfamiliar technical language.

The mathematics curriculum is littered with tripwires such as the one I have just illustrated. The concept lurking in the task is enlargement, scaling or dilation in two dimensions. It is not something that can be recognized and named like 'dog' or 'green apple', so neither visual appearance, nor talk, nor peer discussion nor even a combination of these can on their own lead learners to understand this new concept and use the language correctly. Instead, a cognitive care approach would provide multiple experiences in which learners can act and think about the consequences of their actions, gradually taking control of how, and to what, they apply their actions and why a precise terminology is necessary.

Here is a more elementary example. It is almost universally acknowledged that children need to learn to do calculations, to be able to function in a quantitative society. It is possible to take a different view but currently it remains the responsibility of teachers to help children get to that state. Typically, one sees two heads bowed over a page of calculations: a child and a carer; a child and tutor; a child and learning assistant. The child is stuck and the adult is saying encouraging words such as 'I know you can do it,' 'Take your time,' 'Use your fingers/number line/tables' or 'You did these really well last time I saw you,' and the goal is to get the right answer to one calculation and then move on to the next. A cognitive care approach would not drive a child who has had a miserably slow experience with one calculation to move on to another without turning a negative incident into something more positive by addressing the difficulty the child is having. For example, if they are trying to do a division algorithm but cannot subtract, or do not know how to use the relevant multiplication facts, then instead of continuing to struggle through divisions, some relevant number work could be done to raise confidence. If drawing a good diagram is difficult, someone else can draw the diagram, under instructions from the child, so that the child is free to do some reasoning based on it, rather than being stuck because of poor drawing skills.

Conclusion

The argument for cognitive care applies to students of all ages and all subjects, particularly those in which 'being wrong' is a constant risk. I have tried to show that caring for the mind is as important as caring for the physical, social and emotional atmosphere of school, and is possible while attending to curriculum requirements. My aim is to place the content of the subject at the centre of considerations about a caring school and caring teaching, to challenge the language of 'misconception', 'cognitive conflict' or 'learning from mistakes' in talk about learning. I have also offered some examples where cognitive care can lead to changes of thinking and empowerment for the child, without getting there via situations that depend on some children giving wrong answers to trigger important teaching points. I have placed these ideas within Quaker traditions of care for equality, truth and love, and through respect for children and care for their learning and their thinking, while maintaining integrity with subject disciplines and their modes of enquiry.

References

Ashcraft, M.H., Krause, J.A. and Hopko, D.R. (2007) 'Is math anxiety a mathematical learning disability?'. In Berch, D.B. and Mazzocco, M.M.M. (eds) *Why is Math so Hard for Some Children? The nature and origins of mathematical learning difficulties and disabilities*. Baltimore: Brookes Publishing, 329–48.

Atkinson, A.B. (2015) *Inequality: What can be done?* Cambridge, MA: Harvard University Press.

Barnes, D. (1971) 'Language and learning in the classroom'. *Journal of Curriculum Studies*, 3 (1), 27–38.

Barnes, K.C. (1960) *The Creative Imagination* (Swarthmore Lecture). London: Allen and Unwin.

Clarke, B. (1986) 'To celebrate whatever brings success'. In *Learners All: Quaker experiences in education*. London: Quaker Home Service, 11–12.

Dalke, A. and Dixson, B. (eds) (2004) *Minding the Light: Essays in friendly pedagogy*. New York: Peter Lang Publishing.

FES (Friends Educational Society) (1841) *Report of the Committee of the Friends Educational Society on the Mode of Teaching Arithmetic*. London: Harvey and Darton.

Fielding, M. (2012) 'Education as if people matter: John Macmurray, community and the struggle for democracy'. *Oxford Review of Education*, 38 (6), 675–92.

Gewirtz, S. (1998) 'Conceptualizing social justice in education: Mapping the territory'. *Journal of Education Policy*, 13 (4), 469–84.

GFE (Guild of Friends in Education) (1945) Report, 1 January. Unpublished document in the Friends House Library, London.

Gove, M. (2012) 'Education Secretary Michael Gove's speech to Brighton College'. Online. www.gov.uk/government/speeches/education-secretary-michael-goves-speech-to-brighton-college (accessed 3 August 2017).

Graham, J. (1902) 'Mathematical reform'. Paper presented at the Friends Guild of Teachers, 20–29. Unpublished document in the Friends House Library, London.

Jaggar, T. (1984) 'What should we learn? How should we teach?'. Presidential address of the annual conference of the Guild of Friends in Education. Unpublished document in the Friends House Library, London.

Lacey, P.A. (1998) *Growing into Goodness: Essays on Quaker education*. Wallingford, PA: Pendle Hill Publications.

Marton, F. (2015) *Necessary Conditions of Learning*. New York: Routledge.

Noddings, N. (2005a) 'Caring in education'. In *The Encyclopedia of Informal Education*. London: infed.org. Online. http://infed.org/mobi/caring-in-education/ (accessed 3 August 2017).

Noddings, N. (2005b) *The Challenge to Care in Schools*. 2nd ed. New York: Teachers College Press.

O'Donnell, E.A. (2013) 'Quakers and education'. In Angell, S.W. and Dandelion, P. (eds) *The Oxford Handbook of Quaker Studies*. Oxford: Oxford University Press, 405–19.

O'Reilley, M.R. (1993) *The Peaceable Classroom*. Portsmouth, NH: Boynton/Cook.

Perkins, E.R. (ed.) (1989) *Affirmation, Communication and Co-operation: Papers from the QSRE Conference on Education, July 1988*. London: Quaker Home Service.

Piaget, J. (1963) *The Psychology of Intelligence*. Paterson, NJ: Littlefield, Adams and Co.

Quaker Home Service (1986) *Learners All: Quaker experiences in education*. London: Quaker Home Service.

Reader, J. (1979) *Of Schools and Schoolmasters: Some thoughts on the Quaker contribution to education* (Swarthmore Lecture). London: Quaker Home Service.

Rodd, M. (2017) 'Special needs in mathematics classrooms: Relationships with others'. In Xolocotzin Eligio, U. (ed.) *Understanding Emotions in Mathematical Thinking and Learning*. London: Academic Press, 245–68.

Sharman, A. (1986) 'Women in search of truth'. *The Friend*, 144.

Smith, S. (2004) 'The spiritual roots of Quaker pedagogy'. In Dalke, A. and Dixson, B. (eds) *Minding the Light: Essays in friendly pedagogy*. New York: Peter Lang Publishing, 5–20.

Vygotsky, L.S. (1986) *Thought and Language*. Rev. ed. Trans. Kozulin, A. Cambridge, MA: MIT Press.

Wingate, J. (1985) *How To Be a Peace-Full Teacher*. Waterford: Friendly Press.

Chapter 7
The role and value of the arts in education
Janet Sturge

Recent moves in Britain towards a utilitarian approach to education, in which children are seen in terms of international test results and future economic units, prompt this chapter. The Quaker testimonies of truth, peace, simplicity and equality spring from the religious basis that there is 'that of God in everyone' (*QF&P*, 1.02). This chapter focuses on how these – particularly equality and truth – can be acted upon in education through the arts.

I am very disturbed that current educational thinking, not only by government but also in schools' senior management teams and some public opinion, has taken a step back towards the nineteenth century with a limited focus on academic, verbal/logical and mathematical understandings in the education of children in our state schools. Only literacy and numeracy seem to be treated as essential building blocks for learning. A narrow utilitarian focus is particularly problematic, I believe, during the seminal brain-development years of 13–16, when juvenile concepts are being replaced for many youngsters by more mature perceptions, and many are struggling to find their identity in an adult world that is new to them (Coleman and Hendry, 1999).

This chapter sets out arguments for the arts to be accepted as challenging disciplines, for the educability of aspects of intelligence such as musical, visual/spatial and movement awareness, and for recognition of their common emotional language. I also want to argue for equality of esteem for the varying gifts of students, as well as for arts teachers and the status of their departments. In addition, I address readers who may be unsure about the relevance of the arts to their understanding of spirituality.

Drawing on recent brain research, I argue that, within the brain, there are constant interactions between our analytical, reasoning faculties and the action and decision-making of everyday life, together with aesthetic awareness of sound, sight and movement. These cross-connections develop rapidly during adolescence, the mind and brain changing alongside outward physical alterations. They need to be channelled and stimulated at this

Janet Sturge

critical time to enrich young people's ability to have expansive visions for the future and to think creatively across different subjects with their distinct methods of enquiry.

Quakers' relationship to the arts in the past

At the time of its foundation in the seventeenth century, the Society of Friends (Quakers) resisted what was seen as the profligate lifestyle of the aristocracy, with its excessively decorated clothing, ornamentation, music and leisure activities. It also rejected elaborate forms of worship and church decoration. Hence our ambivalent historical relationship with the arts. In 1906, *Christian Discipline in the Society of Friends* (the book of Quaker discipline and experience, as it was then titled) still included the century-old warning:

> We cannot learn without sorrow of the increasing interest taken by some of our members in musical entertainments – the gratification of sense distracts attention from the duties of religion.
>
> (Religious Society of Friends, 1906: 113)

Early Quaker education, which included girls as well as boys, was limited to reading, especially the Bible, to develop one's own relationship with God, and clerical arithmetic, to act with integrity and probity in the world. Alongside, some practical subjects were imparted. The understanding that a Quaker education should include the arts was slow to develop. Yet William Penn (1644–1718) had warned of the danger of education becoming too formal too early:

> Children had rather be making of Tools and Instruments of Play; Shaping, Drawing, Framing, and Building, &c. than getting some Rules of Propriety of Speech by Heart: And those also would follow with more Judgment, and less Trouble and Time.
>
> (Penn, 2001: 4.8)

Contemporary records show that, in the early part of the nineteenth century, the curriculum in Quaker schools was narrow and utilitarian, though there is mention of how some masters at Ackworth School would give up their own time generously to organize, among other things, drawing, modelling and performances (Vipont, 1959). By the 1840s, many Quaker schools were teaching drawing – albeit, probably, reproductive line drawing. One Ackworth student, Eva Margaret Gilpin, went on to open her own school in 1889, The Hall School in Weybridge, which was commended by inspectors

The role and value of the arts in education

in 1926 for its inclusion of language, history, music, acting, dance, enquiry in biology, writing, drawing and embroidery.[1]

In the 1880s, Mary and May Gripper (my grandmother, who was born in 1869) started at Sidcot School on condition they could continue their piano playing (establishing conditions seems to have been a possibility for fee-paying parents). Their father provided the piano: it was forbidden in the school building but installed in the unheated gardener's cottage down a rough, unlit path – consequently, it was not much used! Similarly, a student at Bootham School is known to have had piano lessons in the 1880s, whereas in 1846 music had been described as a 'temptation' in the Yearly Meeting Epistle (Lovell, 1986: 68).

Twentieth-century Quaker thinking gradually became more accepting of the arts as an important facet of human experience. Even if they could not be incorporated into Friends' silent method of worship, the importance of the relationship between the arts and the spiritual dimensions of existence became widely recognized in the Society. For example, in 1920, John William Graham, a noted Quaker theologian, wrote of John Ruskin:

> The characteristic note he contributed to art criticism was to regard art as a revelation of God and of Man. He was a prophet of Beauty from his birth ... In volume three of *Modern Painters*, John Ruskin [uses] words which throw light upon his special gifts of temperament: although there was no definite religious sentiment mingled with it, there was a continual perception of sanctity in the whole of Nature, from the slightest thing to the vastest; an instinctive awe ...
> (Graham, 1920: 11–12)

Clearly, Graham had studied art through John Ruskin, though like most English people at the time (and many art schools up to the 1950s), he was firmly stuck in the mid-nineteenth century, being more concerned about its relation to spirituality in nature than the value of its underlying principles. Indeed, his lack of understanding of visual art is expressed in his scorn for Impressionism, Cubism and 'other weird follies'. Graham observes with approval that 'Ruskin wrote that conscientiousness in the portrayal of what the artist really sees will not lead him astray' (ibid.: 11). In other words, true representation was seen as valuable, while modernist forms of representation and abstraction were not.

The 1926 book *Christian Life, Faith and Thought* (Religious Society of Friends, 1926) included the understanding that the 'development of the art of seeing is an essential part of true education' since we all have a creative impulse; and in the 1930s, the view of curriculum broadened to embrace social and emotional as well as cognitive purpose. Francis Pollard, a former president of the Friends' Guild of Teachers, spoke eloquently about the need for a child to develop:

> ... ability to use his [sic] gifts effectively, to apply his power of adaptation, curiosity and wonder to the physical universe ... to see a vision of a realm of righteousness and beauty ...
> (Pollard, 1932: 31)

Michael Sadler, the educationist, when opening a new school hall at Saffron Walden Friends' School, claimed to have been influenced by William Penn in his understanding of play, handwork and drawing. Friends' schools, at this time, were also influenced by Maria Montessori, as well as John Dewey, Robert Baden Powell and Alfred North Whitehead. Therefore, they saw their work as educating body, mind and soul together. Michael Sadler imagined that the new school hall would be used for music, singing, activity, poetry recitations and debates and that it would provide space for 'vivacity'. Friends' schools were not about achieving behavioural uniformity but rather were focusing on values, differences, choice, truth-seeking and 'vitality of culture' (Sadler, 1937). Somehow, a change of attitude towards music as a human endeavour took place, as described by Pollard:

> Nor must we omit the claims of music to have a ministry of its own which nothing else can supply. If I don't dwell on this, it is from no lack of appreciation of the contribution that music can make not only to happy resources of life and the expansion and exhilaration of the individual mind, but to the sense of a gathered community in the school.
> (Pollard, 1932: 44)

By the mid- to late-twentieth century, the arts were accepted by Quakers as an important aspect of being human and thus of educational experience. In 1948, during the introduction of state provision of secondary education for all, Quaker discussion minutes about universal secondary education included the comment that methods of teaching that used 'the power of hand and eye' were valuable for all children and therefore should be included in all secondary schools. Then, in 1978, a group appointed by London Yearly Meeting,[2] the national body of Quakerism, reported in *Quaker Involvement in Education* that:

> Friends have, until recently, been slower to see the importance of artistic and aesthetic truth, and the place of imagination in finding and relating to different aspects of the truth. All this is relevant to the concept of an educational community, of teachers and learners, open to a spirit which blows unpredictably.
> (Religious Society of Friends, 1978: 82)

By this time, young people had begun to be obliged to specialize in arts, humanities or sciences from the age of 13 or 14, which was a concern to Friends. They expressed the need for 'creative courses' for 13-year-olds and upwards, alongside technical and commercial subjects and the usual 'bookish' subjects (Quaker Social Responsibility and Education minutes, 1978). And the Guild of Friends in Education (GFE), during a conference on 'A Quaker view of the curriculum in general', minuted: 'Education ought to deal with whole people – with bodies and emotions as well as minds,' and this would include an emphasis on the arts (GFE, 1983). This emphasis on 'the whole person' was in current parlance among progressive educationists at the time (for example Barnes, 1975) and preceded the 1990 National Curriculum, which enshrined a broad and balanced education for all children in state schools up to the age of 16, including arts, humanities, sciences and practical subjects. (In state-funded schools, arts provision had been generally available but access had been haphazard.)

Quakers and the arts today

The current membership of British Quakers includes a vibrant arts network including actors, poets, musicians, composers and novelists of national and international standing. The design of the large meeting hall at our London headquarters ('The Light') was influenced by Quaker artist James Turrell, and hosts art exhibitions from time to time (ArchDaily, 2015). For many years, courses at the Quaker Study Centre, Woodbrooke, have included artwork, crafts, dance and singing, in a wide range of fun, therapeutic and spiritually focused ways. Quaker meeting houses often host art displays, musical and drama events and, until recently, a youth group, The Leaveners, provided thought-provoking entertainment. For example, in 1985 the major oratorio 'The Gates of Greenham', composed by Tony Biggin, was performed by the Leaveners' Orchestra and Chorus at the Royal Festival Hall. This is in striking contrast to the quiet stillness of our meetings for worship[3] and our unadorned places of worship.

And what has been true of the UK is also true of the USA. It has been said that American Quakers deprived themselves of the value of the arts by avoiding music and decoration until the twentieth century and hence have not appreciated 'how God can work through these' (Gray, 1947: 75).

Quaker testimonies and the arts

Despite the preceding heightened awareness of the arts in education and their importance in the development of the whole person, it is not necessarily obvious how the arts help to fulfil Quaker values. Our fundamental position about the divinity to be found in every person is given outward expression in our testimonies: peace, simplicity and sustainability, equality and truth, of which the latter two are most relevant to arts teaching.

Equality

Every youngster, however 'differently gifted', however shaped by environment or genes, deserves equality of esteem as a person. All young people have gifts to offer to society when the whole person – mental, physical, emotional and spiritual – is developed and esteemed. Education, therefore, needs to be hopeful and all-inclusive, enabling us to face life's difficulties in truth and love, based on character-building of the whole child, on valuing what the child has to bring, opening the door to further challenges 'that they may have life and have it abundantly' (John 10:10).

Being open to the potential in children applies especially in arts teaching, where differences due to family background may be very marked, some families encouraging music, others encouraging drama and some not encouraging any arts at all. Discerning an aspect in which a child may flourish and be able to gain satisfaction can require a hard search, and students need to be challenged as well as nourished and encouraged to be the best artists/musicians/dancers they can be. Some children's main experience of the arts may be watching TV programmes based on competitions offering instant stardom and celebrity, so they may well not be aware of the hard work, knowledge and technique lying behind contemporary performances or apparently simple artefacts.

In a creatively taught school arts programme, all can experience the intrinsic pleasures of listening, seeing and especially creating, individually or with others, whether it is encouraged by home background or not. Equality would lead to valuing each student's efforts, giving equal esteem to the exercise of visual, spatial and emotional intelligence besides that of verbal and logical reasoning.

It is, of course, no use pretending that every child is very able, artistically speaking, but this does not mean we should not value him or her. There may well be environmental, social or emotional factors limiting aspiration and self-perception – all the more important, then, for teachers to find a spark that will motivate and to work to make the 'difficult' aspects of engaging in creative acts relevant to the students who struggle. I remember working with a semi-literate, innumerate boy of 11, with the drawing capability of a 6-year-old, who nevertheless had the initiative and intelligence to put a bicycle together from the dump and ride it. This was his form of creative thinking and I am concerned that the current curriculum available for boys like him does not offer many opportunities to use their mechanical skills as a portal to both creative and intellectual forms of learning, maybe at a simple level. In another example, a group of Year 9 youngsters from a Special Needs unit were given the same challenge as their peers: to design a food outlet. They produced a hotdog barrow for the seaside, with the required paperwork – budgeting, recipes, advertising and so on – together with a tasty product, alongside the others' restaurants of varying sophistication. The headmaster was not especially interested, until the head of the design faculty got it into the local paper!

Truth

Truth, for Quakers, is much more than literal fact. It is about authentic human experience that has been through a process of discernment. My take on what truth means to a child is that, if every child is of God, then every child has both a right and a duty to explore and express their own truths. It is in the arts that this exploration can be made without danger and with personal integrity, since the content of the arts is the whole of human life. Genuine differences between truths that have been arrived at with integrity and care can be acknowledged through the arts. These, therefore, provide ways of listening to a young person's truth and helping them to realize who they are in a deep and complex sense. If this is not happening at home, or through voluntary activities, then it must take place through the arts in school. For this to take place for all young people requires that effort, progress and success in music, dance, drama, poetry or visual art be appreciated on a par with language, mathematics, sciences and other more marketable forms of knowledge. A young person is firstly human, and their worth as a future economic unit should not dominate their upbringing and childhood experience.

As well as providing the opportunity to understand the rewards of hard work in the context of personal expression, the areas in which young people can be creative also demand the ability to appraise their own work as it evolves and also to decide when it is finished. They can identify, with help, when the truth of their own vision has been realized, whether visual, musical or in movement. Truth in the arts does not reside in some outside judgement but in the imagination, vision and expression of the creator.

A search for truth through the arts can lead to finding it in observational, expressive and abstract forms, perceiving satisfying relationships and in recognizing the form that best expresses the student's own truth. Discernment, a word that is central to Quaker decision-making, is an effort to identify what is true and of value and what is guided by a deep sense of what is right. The capacity to discern, which should be available to all, can grow through self- and group-assessment in the arts, in choosing what to focus on and also in examining the creative work of others, whether they are famous practitioners or other students in the class.

Development of young people

These testimonies, our witness in the world, have a religious basis that is not necessarily shared across today's society. Our belief that there is 'that of God in every person' is not synonymous with 'every person is always good'; between birth and adolescence, we recognize that the innocence of the newborn will have been challenged and, in many cases, damaged. But it *does* mean that, for us:

- Every child is respected and valued equally, though not identically.
- Every child has a right and a duty to develop truth and integrity.
- Difference must be recognized.
- A simple and sustainable life gives more satisfaction than profligacy.
- Peace, as well as influencing our outlook on world conflict, needs to be nurtured in the home and in school life (see chapters by Belinda Hopkins and Anna Gregory in this volume).

These values lead us to endeavour to:

- listen well to every student, encouraging them to listen to and empathize with others
- provide non-competitive goals and experiences of cooperation
- help students take these into the outside world.

Of course, many of these values are shared by teachers from a wide range of backgrounds and ideals; we do not claim them to be exclusively Quaker.

Nurturing the whole child, according to his or her needs and capabilities, could profitably include a wide range of subjects and areas that have become neglected, including, in my view, home economics, parenting and child development. I would also include the importance of character

The role and value of the arts in education

development. Education, therefore, has a role to play in extending what children think they can do. As Barbara Windle (1988) has said:

> ... we must water the ground of the student's being with faith in that deepest self – to do so constantly, tirelessly, patiently – and to love enough to know what one should demand from the student in response and how and when to ask it.
> (Windle, 1988: QF&P, 23.75)

Many young people are looking for vision and meaning: they want to feel they can make a difference, make their world a better place and, in the process, discover themselves. The arts – creating things, enriching communities through the senses – provide alternatives to individualistic winning or losing. All these contribute to important aspects of students' character development and also reflect how the Quaker peace testimony embraces human diversity and favours cooperation and complementarity.

Mind and brain in adolescence

It is common to talk of left-brain or right-brain as characterizing a preference for someone to be either logical or creative, but Jensen's (2005) review of brain research claims that:

> ... earlier assumptions about the 'left' and 'right' brain – that the left brain is 'logical' and the right brain is 'creative' – are outdated. In general, the left hemisphere tends to process information in parts, in a sequence, and using language and text representations ... Again speaking generally, the right hemisphere tends to process information as a whole, in random order, and within a spatial context. But, like the left-brain tendencies, none of these tendencies guarantees that the right brain will be creative. Creativity can be either more right- or more left-hemisphere dominant.

> ... it's best to avoid the labels of 'left-brain' and 'right-brain' thinking. Clearly, some people do *prefer* linear processing and others do *prefer* randomness. But that's all it is – a preference.
> (Jensen, 2005: 14)

If this is a preference, then it is educable, as Howard Gardner and his colleagues claim (Moran *et al.*, 2006), but no learning takes place solely in any one area of the brain, and currently the phrase 'whole-brain' is widely used to describe interactive engagement of various centres. Nevertheless, current neuroscience, admittedly in its infancy as far as specific brain function is concerned, has revealed a range of centres in the right brain that can jump into action in various artistic contexts (Gute and Gute, 2015): musical, kinetic, bodily and visual/spatial as well as empathetic, emotional and social. Jane Stanley (1986), a Quaker art teacher, uses the left/right brain as a metaphor to draw attention to how young people can get 'lost' in creative work, losing sense of time and bodily needs, following connections, suspending rational judgement and using intuition in contrast with the analysis and reason required for most schoolwork. She describes how she personally can find 'a balanced pattern in a disturbing world' when she is engaged in making something (ibid.: 94).

Lydia Graham expresses powerfully the importance of combining our different faculties:

> ... it must not be thought that Art expresses only emotion and feeling. Art is at its finest when it expresses those subtle gradations and harmonies where intellect and feeling are mingled imperceptibly ... It is the business of pure intellect to measure and weigh and construct an accurate count of things as they are, but intellect unaided by this inner sense achieves very little in the affairs of life. Thought seldom remains purely intellectual: feeling creeps in to help us decide our problems. Art is the expression of emotion guided by intellect, or ... the expression of intellect tempered and warmed by emotion.
>
> (Graham, 1925: 54)

Joseph Southall, a Quaker politician as well as an artist, describes how different kinds of knowledge relate to each other:

> ... we learn to see through our fingers hardly less than through our eyes ... as our fingers work in collaboration with our eyes, do we entirely understand ... The difference between the bookman and the craftsman is that the craftsman's brain extends all down his arms into his fingertips ... the bookman gets his information second hand ... the stone-mason at his work cutting and chipping all day long till the great block of stone is greatly reduced in bulk by his destructive criticism ... behold the shapeless has been shaped ... *I would therefore urge that the training of hand and eye together should form a part of the education of the youth right up to the end of school life.*
>
> (Southall, 1925: 133, my emphasis)

He goes on to say that those who determine what children are supposed to learn in school still seem to look on children as if minds could only be reached 'through their ears'. He sees art as a language of the soul, expressing feelings and ideas that have no parallel expression in words (ibid.: 147, paraphrased).

As a teacher of drawing, painting and sculpture, I have worked on children's visual and spatial intelligence, aspects of development that are not often served by other subjects. I noticed that there could be a marked change in young people's perceptions between the ages of 12 and 16, especially in drawing. For example, young children often draw conceptually, showing a table as a rectangle with four legs splayed out; later, surrounded by photographic images, they may become unsatisfied with their drawings, but do not yet know how to draw what they actually see. Several years may pass before their awareness of what is received on the retina emerges and their drawing skill can develop further. But this is not just an extra skill; this perception will enable them to notice more and differently in general and thus add to their growing awareness of self in relation to the environment. Indeed, Joseph Southall observed that 'seeing is an art to be learned' (ibid.: 132).

Early adolescence is a time when people will give up effort in some contexts, the arts being one of these, yet our knowledge that the brain alters physically during that period of life would suggest that it is an important time to ensure that all possibilities are kept open, rather than closed down. This 'closing down' is not only due to their sense of incapability. Verbal, logical and mathematical thinking are highly valued in our current school system, while spatial and visual capabilities and the enjoyment of making things are not included in measures of school effectiveness, so may be downplayed in schools.

The wider contribution of the arts to schools and beyond

Underlying patterns of school governance vary. A headteacher or governing body may have overriding authority, and governments can exercise control through league tables and academization (see Janet Nicholl's chapter). Alternative models, rarely totally practised, are based on the autonomy of the child or the wishes of a local community. These conflicting ideologies appear to mirror the political structures of society (Murphy *et al.*, 2008: 29–30).

On the surface, a child-centred model would seem to reflect Quaker ideals of the inherent divine presence, but through consideration of Quaker testimonies of equality, truth and peace, together with our tried-and-tested governance based on listening to members' concerns and submitting them to the discernment of the group, a more complex collegiate pattern could be envisaged. Teachers could use their own creativity and also involve children's ideas and initiatives in education.

This has long been the case in the visual arts. Creatively taught, the arts need teacher-led input of skills and concepts and students need to use these imaginatively, whether individually or in groups. Even in the most authoritarian of schools, creative arts provide the context for resourcefulness and lateral thinking, and this openness to developing students' own powers can affect school life and learning beyond a particular art form. The focus on process and reflection, as well as satisfaction in achievement, gives confidence in learning, while social skills are enhanced by working as a team.

Music

In a school curriculum, the educational aim of music is to develop aural awareness, cultural appreciation, specific motor skills, expressive creativity and group activities. The priority is not to produce potential performers, nor is the music lesson a leisure pursuit. There is significant evidence that the study of music aids both language and mathematical development (Hallam, 2010). However, the most positive outcome is the part music plays in the development of the whole person in the language of expression.

The opportunity to lose oneself in music is movingly described in *Children of the Stone* where we meet Ramzi, a boy throwing stones in the Palestinian Intifada, until he is given the opportunity to play the viola. As he wrestles to learn, he realizes he is thinking in music, no longer in violence, and vows to set up a music school for children in the refugee camps of the West Bank. He does just that, and watches how children change from despair and violence to making something good (Tolan, 2015).

Composing – the creative approach – is aided by technology; secondary schools now often have a recording studio and compositional computer software. Links with drama, dance and visual arts give opportunities for the creation of musicals and other composite productions created by students. These help to overcome any divide between the classical repertoire and the world of popular and nascent musical forms which often thrive on developing, blending or mixing different styles that have a variety of cultural roots. Familiarity with a received repertoire helps to exemplify style and construction. Likewise, by composing their own music, students gain a better understanding of received music as well as cultural differences.

Experiencing music through class work, instrumental lessons, bands and choirs illuminates the understanding of music, whether previously composed or improvised. Young people come to be able to identify each element in turn: sound and silence, tempo, rhythm, volume and repetition; timbre, resonance, harmony and dissonance; energy and rest; contrast and similarity; musical shape, direction, climax and resolution; and finally, melodic line as 'conversation'. As well as its practical benefits or the enrichment of learning its history and learning how to listen to music of all genres, music shares with other art forms a language of feeling, action and well-being and can often form part of a young person's identity. Connection with dance and drama is clear, but drawing and painting also have parallel elements, the 'words' with which a language is built up. Performing one's own music or that of others can also boost self-esteem and self-confidence.

Dance

Dance is a fundamental form of expression in all human cultures (Sousa, 2009). The body is as much a vehicle for spiritual experience as our eyes and ears, and dance has a place in all religions. In dance, the discipline can be very demanding, requiring full concentration, practice and intense physical control. Contemporary dance, the form usually practised in schools, is not aimed at producing professional dancers but on creating abstract forms, often fused with expressing mood, emotion or story. It is also a way for young people to feel comfortable about their bodies and physical expression. Street dance and several traditional and classical dance forms also offer these opportunities. Dance may be abstract – the creating of form in time and space – or story-based; for many young people, story and metaphor may be important, both involving relationships, dramatic shape, tension, energy, direction, climax and release. Aims need to be clear: is the primary purpose of this dance to create a beautiful shape in space? Or to respond expressively to an emotional stimulus? Or to heighten awareness of story or theme? Is it to enter into a role (such as a warrior, an animal or a bride) or, using these as symbols, to explore a feeling or situation? How can we communicate these possibilities to, and with, others?

Dance includes several of Gardner's list of multiple intelligences: bodily/kinaesthetic, musical, visual/spatial, interpersonal, intrapersonal and existential intelligence. Its use of rhythm and shape has even been harnessed in the teaching of mathematics, either as a motivating device or to mirror mathematical structures (Watson, 2005). This works better in schools where all students experience dance, so that typical adolescent physical embarrassment does not get in the way of learning.

Notable progress has been made in recent decades in understanding dance as relevant for people with very different physical and learning

Visual and spatial arts

> Beauty has no function, no utility, its value is intrinsic ... It greases no wheels, it bakes no puddings.
> (Jones, 1920, 26: *QF&P*, 26.32)

I need here to distinguish between, on the one hand, the visual and spatial arts (drawing, painting, printmaking, sculpture, textiles and so on) for their own aesthetic and expressive qualities, referred to as 'fine art', and, on the other hand, functional design and craft, where the overriding principle is to fulfil a brief, a need of others. Fine art is also distinct from art therapy; while using the same materials, therapy has the function of relieving distress and often of diagnosing causes of disease; it specifically seeks to express what may lie in the subconscious, as treatment for people suffering mental health problems. However, therapeutic insights, expressive mark-making and use of symbolic forms and colours can also illuminate the language of feeling in an artwork. Lydia Graham observed that an:

> ... inner sense [of Beauty] seems to be at the centre of being. These emotions have expressed themselves since the dawn of man's [sic] self-consciousness in dance and picture, in poem and song, in statue and symphony ... In every individual [it] finds response in the Art of others, but ... must also ... find outlet in its own art.
> (Graham, 1925: 53)

In 'art for art's sake', the elements that are needed in design and the insight of their expressive use in therapy may both play a part, but a work of art does not have to have any utilitarian function. This does not mean that design will play no part in a visual or spatial art course; it is more a case of how the work is read for its dual aspects, aesthetic qualities and function, and how they complement each other.

Using the formal elements of abstract pattern and composition – form, shape, tone, colour, medium to inform observation, design and imaginative work – students begin to form concepts and gain control of their immediate environment, as well as finding a way to express their feelings. While close observation at the right age level is important, representational skill is only one approach and need not exceed the development of perception. For example, different elements may be played with in turn as a means of suggesting reality and one selected to lead on to an expressive form of the student's choosing.

Adolescence is a particularly important time for many youngsters to become more perceptive of the reality of the external world and to redefine their own relationship to it, including their own choice of focus. Exposure to found, contemporary and historic artworks assists an awareness of outer and inner worlds. All ages, at their different levels, are enriched by the world of art and can experience a sense of awe. Students may then use such experiences as stimuli for their own ideas.

Common elements in the arts

Each of the arts has its own language, forged from its material, instruments or medium. However, there are remarkable parallels in the different 'languages' across the arts: all have elements of contrast, complementarity, harmony and dissonance, form, pattern and rhythm, dimensions of space and time, tone, colour and timbre, direction and energies. All use these elements in combination to create a satisfying aesthetic, and/or to express mood, thoughts and states of being. Underlying themes that run through the arts include: expressions of calm and turmoil, love and hate, anger and resolution, loneliness and conviviality, fear and confidence, joy and anguish. The arts provide a safe space to explore these dimensions of the human condition. Such a theme may be transposed from an initial stimulus in one art form, for example musical or poetic, to another – visual or dance (Witkin, 1974). Finding parallel meanings and expressions when studying the works of others, and naming what they experience, enriches the vocabulary for creative writing and can develop emotional literacy and intelligence, including what Robert Witkin calls 'the intelligence of feeling'.

I have considered the separate and shared elements expressed through music, dance and visual arts. Their common language of feeling is a major building block in the development of the whole person and students' further engagement in learning throughout life, as well as their healthy social development. While limitations within educational institutions would call for each area to justify its existence and to define its aims, it may well be efficacious to demonstrate their mutual elements and share themes to achieve more esteem in their school.

Assessment

Assessment methods in the arts are often different from those of other subjects. Far from marking being 'a matter of taste' or of meeting well-defined objectives, young people themselves first need to define what they were hoping to achieve when setting out to create something and what means they have used. Assessment jointly with the teacher can focus on understanding and realization of their initial aims and clarity of expression, choice of materials and instruments, relevant physical skills, completion and presentation, or performance can be discussed. Critical faculties are honed through self- and group-assessment. Learning how to give and receive constructive, acceptable criticism is a life skill. Working with others to aims and standards agreed by the group can increase their ability to make sensible choices and take responsibility. Learning happens at greater depth when a young person puts something of her/himself into the creation of an artistic output, contributing to the development of the whole person while enriching the school and wider community. Students involved in evaluating their own work learn to refine the outcome progressively and use it as a springboard for the next challenge. This attitude is applicable in many other spheres within the school and indeed in subsequent environments, including the workplace.

Educating educators

Throughout this chapter, I have indicated that teaching methods are very important in realizing the possibilities of arts education. Teaching requires creative pedagogy especially in a creative subject. It involves mutual respect. It includes listening to, and valuing, students' contributions, asking questions, discerning the pith of a student's ideas and capabilities, encouraging exploration by helping them think laterally and take artistic risks, living adventurously in a safe environment where being wrong is not possible because the discipline does not depend on facts and categorical truths.[4] Teachers need to be genuine in valuing differences, as a counterweight to the artificial value put on individuals by the prevailing assessment system. This approach implies a school regime where teachers' own creativity is permitted, where subject areas are open to each other in cross-curricular conversations, where most of the staff value all the other subjects and where people are willing to respect and learn from novices as well as from experts and teachers.

All teachers, whatever their subject specialism, need to understand the importance of the arts and their relevance to their own subject, in terms of imagination, decision-making, expression and motivation. It may be difficult for some academics used to dealing in words to understand the nature and value of hands-on subjects. Other teachers and parents alike may well be confused about the visual arts, as in the art world itself there have been constant changes in the very concept of what art is.

What have these aspects to do with Quakerism?
My own experience and belief is that different forms of artistic expression should be seen as important for everyone and that there is a strong link between the arts and spirituality. Mary Fyfe, a Quaker educator, speaks of our spiritual need for openness, awareness, playfulness, flexibility, self-reliance and independence and believes these can be nurtured by studying creative subjects. She says that Quakers 'live with ambiguity. Both creative and spiritual breakthroughs are born out of that discomfort' (Fyfe, 1990: 9).

Arts education addresses Quaker commitment to peace through offering ways to create balance and resolve contrast and dissonance. Students gain experience in appreciating and learning from the work of others rather than competing with them. Young people learn to value things they can make themselves, without the current reliance on external amusement or validation.

Equality can be addressed through the arts. Appraisal of students' abilities could take place across a range of forms of expression; all aspects of the arts can be seen as educable; all disciplines can be recognized as part of essential education in the secondary years. Ignoring students' full range of capabilities may cripple their development as whole people.

Quakers see truth in a different light from many others. In understanding the truth of metaphor, we need to apply this not just to literature and Biblical studies, but also to the arts. Awareness of the personal search for truth and insight could be a way into appreciation of the disciplines of making art, music or dance, as applied in education of the mind. Unlike our Quaker forebears, we are becoming aware of the spiritual in the perception of truth through the senses and can relate this to a true voice within, which is the source of discernment and hence 'come down where we ought to be' (Joseph Brackett, 1797–1882, Shaker dancing song).

A conclusion for current times
A correlation is internationally accepted now between success in core academic subjects and a country's economic growth. Thus, education tends to be seen as a utilitarian economic endeavour with a related curriculum. In the UK, arts subjects are no longer delivered as entitlements for all children. UK society now has academic success so ingrained as a yardstick for children's lives that they are increasingly seen in terms of their test success instead of as people. Far from the vision of the first National Curriculum, which aimed at a rounded multi-faceted education for all, success in the arts is now excluded from the final measures of achievement by which schools

are compared, the league tables at the end of primary and secondary school. But in *The Good Schools Guide*, which gives information about provision of music, dance and drama in all the listed schools, Beth Noakes observes: 'Though large parts of the state system are an artistic desert, there are oases of extraordinary achievement despite cuts in Government funding' (Noakes, 2017).

Selection of children for different educational treatment at secondary level if they have verbal or mathematical acumen is now increasing after three decades of mainly inclusive comprehensive education. While the emphasis on these subjects could be seen as important for digital and technological progress, it is ironic that the UK is a world leader in the arts, music, theatre, fashion and other creative endeavours that contribute to our cultural life and economy. Schools and teachers may have moved from seeing their task as helping all children to develop in a variety of ways to seeing it as ensuring that as many as possible achieve the minimum examination standards to take part in future study and employment. While the arts can add roundedness to the portfolio of a successful student, they can also be seen as a distraction for one who is struggling to get the basic academic grades, rather than as a route to that young person's engagement with learning.

Through the arts, young people can explore deep truths. In Jane Stanley's words, when she talks about 'the unfolding of a miracle' of her students' examination exhibition, all could learn self-knowledge and peace from these processes:

> As each exhibition goes up, the students discover themselves. The forceful passion of gentle probing with which they respond to the world unveils itself, a veritable apocalypse. Might we learn to our advantage more of ourselves ... and demonstrate yet another way of beating spears into pruning hooks?
>
> (Stanley, 1986: 96)

I have pointed out the multiple contributions the arts can make to young people's knowledge, development and well-being. The arts also contribute to character development by increasing the student's control, empathy, management of resources and openings for initiative in whatever field of employment or further study they find themselves.

As I write, it is difficult for many teachers to follow their inner guidance in respect of what should be taught and how. Arts teachers are particularly at a disadvantage when posts are cut, arts timetables curtailed and training grants withdrawn – all signs that policymakers are unaware of the importance of education in the creative arts.

The role and value of the arts in education

Nevertheless, I hope that ways can be found to enable students to go out into the world aware, creative, well balanced, with an understanding of, and respect for, themselves and others. I hope they will carry a sense of meaning and a vision of a better society to which they can contribute with the energy and confidence to take action, as, hopefully, they will have done within the school community. For this, they need to feel that their school has acknowledged their gifts; and, as I have argued, the arts provide a safe place for these to be explored, developed and expressed.

Notes

[1] Eva Gilpin's papers are now held at the National Arts Education Archive.
[2] Now called Britain Yearly Meeting.
[3] Not all Quakers in the world worship in quiet stillness; many have programmed meetings including joyful noise.
[4] Both 'living adventurously' and thinking it 'possible that you may be mistaken' are ideas expressed in *QF&P*, 1.02 (Religious Society of Friends, 2013).

References

ArchDaily (2015) 'Friends House / John McAslan + Partners'. *ArchDaily*, 17 May. Online. www.archdaily.com/630809/friends-house-john-mcaslan-partners (accessed 5 February 2018).

Barnes, K.C. (1975) *A Vast Bundle of Opportunities: An exploration of creativity in personal life and community*. London: Allen and Unwin.

Coleman, J.C. and Hendry, L.B. (1999) *The Nature of Adolescence*. 3rd ed. London: Routledge.

Fyfe, M. (1990) 'Creativity and spirituality'. Jonathan Plummer Lecture presented at the Illinois Yearly Meeting of the Religious Society of Friends, McNabb, Illinois, 4 August. Online. http://iym.quaker.org/plummer/1990.html (accessed 1 October 2017).

Graham, J.W. (1920) *The Harvest of Ruskin*. London: Allen and Unwin.

Graham, L. (1925) 'Art and life'. *Friends' Quarterly Examiner*, 234 (Fourth Month), 52–9.

Gray, E.J. (1947) *Contributions of the Quakers* (Pamphlet 34). Wallingford, PA: Pendle Hill.

GFE (Guild of Friends in Education) (1983). Minutes. Unpublished document in the Friends House Library, London.

Gute, D. and Gute, G. (2015) *How Creativity Works in the Brain: Insights from a Santa Fe Institute working group*. Washington, DC: National Endowment for the Arts. Online. www.arts.gov/sites/default/files/how-creativity-works-in-the-brain-report.pdf (accessed 1 July 2017).

Hallam, S. (2010) 'The power of music: Its impact on the intellectual, social and personal development of children and young people'. *International Journal of Music Education*, 28 (3), 269–89.

Jensen, E. (2005) *Teaching with the Brain in Mind*. 2nd ed. Alexandria, VA: Association for Supervision and Curriculum Development.

Jones, R. (1920) 'Where the wind breaks through'. *The Friend*, 60.

Lovell, P. (1986) 'Friends and music'. *Friends Quarterly*, 24 (2), 65–9.

Moran, S., Kornhaber, M. and Gardner, H. (2006) 'Orchestrating multiple intelligences'. *Educational Leadership*, 64 (1), 22–7.

Murphy, L., Mufti, E. and Kassem, D. (2008) *Education Studies: An Introduction*. Maidenhead: McGraw-Hill.

Noakes, B. (ed.) (2017) *The Good Schools Guide*. 21st ed. London: Lucas Publications.

Penn, W. (2001) *Some Fruits of Solitude* (Harvard Classics). New York: Bartleby.com. Online. www.bartleby.com/1/3/ (accessed 26 November 2017).

Pollard, F.E. (1932) *Education and the Spirit of Man* (Swarthmore Lecture). London: Allen and Unwin.

Quaker Social Responsibility and Education (1978) Minutes. Unpublished document in the Friends House Library, London.

Religious Society of Friends (1906) *Christian Discipline in the Society of Friends*. London: Headley Brothers.

Religious Society of Friends (1926) *Christian Life, Faith and Thought in the Society of Friends*. London: London Yearly Meeting.

Religious Society of Friends (1978) *Friends in Education: The report of the Quaker Involvement in Education Group*. London: London Yearly Meeting.

Religious Society of Friends (2013) *Quaker Faith and Practice: The book of Christian discipline of the Yearly Meeting of the Religious Society of Friends (Quakers) in Britain*. 5th ed. London: Religious Society of Friends. Online. qfp.quaker.org.uk (accessed 13 December 2017).

Sadler, M.E. (1937) 'The new drift in education'. Unpublished document in the Friends House Library, London.

Sousa, D.A. (2009) *How the Gifted Brain Learns*. 2nd ed. Thousand Oaks, CA: Corwin Press.

Southall, J.E. (1925) 'The graphic arts in education'. *Friends' Quarterly Examiner*, 234 (Fourth Month), 130–49.

Stanley, J. (1986) 'A different way of knowing'. *Friends Quarterly*, 24 (2), 92–6.

Tolan, S. (2015) *Children of the Stone: The power of music in a hard land*. London: Bloomsbury Publishing.

Vipont, E. (1959) *Ackworth School: From its foundation in 1779 to the introduction of co-education in 1946*. London: Lutterworth Press.

Watson, A. (2005) 'Dance and mathematics: Engaging senses in learning'. *Australian Senior Mathematics Journal*, 19 (1), 16–23.

Windle, B. (1988) in E. Perkins (ed.) *Affirmation, Communication and Cooperation*. London: Quaker Home Service.

Witkin, R.W. (1974) *The Intelligence of Feeling*. London: Heinemann Educational.

Chapter 8
Early years education and Quaker concerns
Wendy Scott

This chapter reflects on the impact of political decisions on early years and primary education over the past five decades, through the prism of Quaker testimonies. It gives an account of developments in early education in England in the context of our century-old heritage of insightful and principled practice, which responds holistically to children's needs and their potential. This enlightened approach has been established through thoughtful and collaborative development of empirical practice, increasingly endorsed by research, which is closely aligned to Quaker values.

According to George Fox, testimony is to be made through action, and the word 'testimony' is used by Quakers to describe a witness to the living truth within the human heart as it is acted out in everyday life. Mary Lou Leavitt asserts that it is more than a strategy or a political manifesto:

> It is about bearing witness to the truth. It is not a question of opinion or reason or hearsay – what I think, what someone else has told me. It is about affirming our own experience of something as true, as fact, as surely known.
> (Leavitt, 1993: 13)

As Elizabeth O'Donnell points out:

> Quakers have helped to develop educational opportunities for all and new forms of teaching, including an involvement in progressive education, as well as developing resources on peace studies and conflict resolution. Our reputation as significant educators deserves recognition.
> (O'Donnell, 2013: 419)

Jackie Scully links testimonies with ethics:

> The concept of testimony encapsulates the Quaker view of the relationship between spiritual and everyday life. It is ethical inasmuch as it is a statement of how the good life should be lived.
> (Scully, 2013: 541)

Established early years practice in the UK does not explicitly express the relationship between spirituality and daily life, but it can be held up as an example of ethical testimony to truth, integrity and stewardship as well as community and equality. For example, Margaret and Rachel McMillan, driven by their Christian Socialist beliefs, established the Rachel McMillan Open Air Nursery School in Deptford in 1914 because of their concerns about the unsuitable living conditions of local families. Their aim was to improve nutrition and health as well as to stimulate learning, for parents as well as children, and their work laid the foundations for what is now over a century of struggle to establish nursery education for all children. Since then, deep thought has been given to developing practice in ways that I have found entirely compatible with Quaker testimonies (for example, Isaacs, 2013). Eclectic British practice has been influenced by Froebelian ideas, by Steiner and Montessori and, more recently, by work in the USA, New Zealand and Reggio Emilia in Italy. It is now beyond doubt that high-quality provision in the early years can make a significant contribution to improving life chances and narrowing the gap in achievement between the most and least advantaged children (Sylva *et al.*, 2004).

A brief history of early education in England

Although education for under-fives is not compulsory, the significance of nursery schools has been acknowledged by politicians since the pioneering work of the McMillan sisters (Jarvis, 2013). Ramsay MacDonald and Bertrand Russell were members of the Nursery School Association (now the British Association for Early Childhood Education, known as Early Education), which was founded in 1923. The Plowden Report (1967) endorsed the learner-centred pedagogy that typifies the British approach to early years education through the statement: 'At the heart of the education process lies the child.' Education reformer Bridget Plowden recommended that more nursery schools and classes should be set up, especially in deprived areas. Margaret Thatcher, convinced by the contribution to social mobility made by high-quality nursery education, enabled a brief period of expansion in designated priority areas in the 1970s.

Angela Rumbold, advised by early years experts when she was serving as Education Minister, led an enquiry into early years education. Her report (Rumbold, 1990) gave strong support for the expansion of high-quality provision. Its main recommendations remain relevant today:

- Nursery provision needs to be expanded to meet demand.
- All who work with young children should recognize the importance of their educational role.
- Curriculum planners must ensure that no children are denied opportunities on account of their race, sex, social background or special needs.
- Educators should guard against over-concentration on formal teaching and the attainment of a specific set of targets.
- Curriculum planning for the under-fives should be based on the principle that the process of education is as important as its content.
- Children must be given opportunities for playing and talking, and adults with responsibilities for young children must recognize that play is a good deal more than recreation.
- The vital role of parents in their children's learning needs to be fully recognized and acknowledged by parents and teachers.
- Teachers must not lose sight of the child's all-round development in pursuit of detailed information about what children know and can do in the subjects of the curriculum.
- All students training to teach in primary schools should spend some time with children under five.
- While diversity of provision can be healthy, there must be better local coordination of services, with central government setting a national framework within which local development could take place.

In 1994, Christopher Ball, the influential Director of Learning at the Royal Society of Arts, wrote about the importance of early learning (Ball, 1994). He endorsed our enlightened heritage of early years education, which is recognized worldwide. Over the years, many educators have come to Britain from overseas to learn from our child-centred approach to early years and primary education, which is in accord with the Quaker view that each one of us, as a child of God, is unique and precious.

Personal experience

My career, as much as my personal life, has been guided by Quaker testimonies on peace, equality, sustainability, integrity and truth. I have found that they can be expressed at many levels through a commitment to the welfare of children and families, particularly those with special needs or at a disadvantage of any kind. It has been deeply rewarding to find a vocation that has drawn on every aspect of life, making physical, emotional, aesthetic and spiritual as well as intellectual demands, and bringing commensurate rewards. Perhaps because I had been sent to boarding school at the age of 4, some instinct led me to decide to train as an early years teacher at a time when primary teaching was not a graduate profession, rather than to take up a place at Cambridge. It has been very affirming to be awarded an honorary degree over fifty years later, which recognizes the depth and breadth of our initial training at the Froebel Educational Institute. This imbued us as students with strong principles supported by rigorous evidence, high expectations of ourselves, and an understanding of the importance of the practical expression of our ideals. These were coupled with a questioning approach, aligned to the Quaker advice to think it possible one may be mistaken (*QF&P*, 1.02, 17).

I learnt a great deal from the children, families and communities in London's Docklands and the East End where I started teaching in 1961. Conditions were not much better than those faced by the McMillan sisters in Deptford half a century earlier. Children played on unreconstructed bomb sites, and many, including immigrant families, lived in difficult conditions. My college training had not equipped me with necessary knowledge about bed bugs, or prison visiting, so I had a lot to learn. There were 46 children in the reception class I taught, many of whom spoke little English. I was fortunate that the headteacher understood and supported the way I was trying to work, and, over time, parents became strong and sympathetic supporters of the democratic approach I developed.

That experience, together with having children of my own and starting a small private nursery in a rural village, taught me much about the complexity of family life and the uneven nature of child development and learning. In 1974, by then a single parent, I was appointed to open a new nursery class attached to a primary school in an Education Priority Area. The headteacher had little interest in the early years, and I was given a great deal of freedom to develop the provision, which included monthly working parties with parents and close contact with health visitors, social workers and the probation service. Although the places available for children were part time, we were able to offer lunches to needy children (usually only available for those in school full time) thanks to the willingness of colleagues to give up their own breaks.

I consider that my most directly influential role was expressed during five very rewarding years as headteacher of a demonstration nursery school on a university campus. In addition to working with the children and their families, I was directly involved with students, academic colleagues and visitors from around the world as well as a team of dedicated staff. It is perhaps not a coincidence that this was the time when I was accepted into membership of the Society of Friends; I needed to consider and make explicit the rationale that guided my work, and found the deep stillness and reflectiveness within Quakerism, together with refreshing challenges to my thinking, of great help. I learnt to await answers to difficulties rather than rush to decisions, and I continue to believe that the busier I am, the more I should attend meetings for worship to keep a considered balance in life.

We were very fortunate in the setting and staffing of our nursery school and thought carefully about how we could best share our advantages. We built up a specialism in working with children suffering from language delay and difficulty, arranged for a speech therapist to hold her clinic in a tutorial room next to the nursery, and admitted at least 10 per cent of our children on the basis of their need for language support. There was scope for parents and students to learn alongside the staff, and the speech therapist benefited from being able to observe her clients in a natural environment, revealing far more of their communicative abilities than they could show as individuals in a rather daunting clinical setting. Looking back, I would say this illustrated Quaker testimonies of equality, because of the full recognition given to the contributions of all involved and integrity in the informed practical commitment to the best interests of children with special needs. The American Quaker testimony of community was also strongly supported, in terms of the possibility of parental involvement in specialist professional work as well as the way that, in addition to regular meetings, parents spent a whole session with us at least once a month. Because children are more able to work through difficulties and frustrations when they can explain their feelings verbally, our work on signing and expressive language, coupled with an encouraging approach to conflict resolution, made a contribution to peace as well.

There was a one-way window between the classroom and the neighbouring tutorial rooms, which made it possible for observations to take place without disturbing the children's normal activities. This was invaluable for parents and made it possible to welcome visitors from around the world. They included academics, psychologists, and health and social services professionals as well as early years staff. Some of the university students based their Fourth Year research project on work in the nursery; this contributed to the sustainability of early years principles, which we strove to embody explicitly through our daily practice. We were glad to be able to share the UK's globally recognized heritage of high-quality early education and learnt a great deal from these exchanges.

Where they survive, maintained nursery schools continue to make a very effective contribution to social mobility, especially in disadvantaged areas. Many are now combined with Children's Centres and some are recognized as Teaching Schools. It is worth noting that, according to Ofsted (Office for Standards in Education, Children's Services and Skills) in 2017, 68 per cent of these schools were judged to be outstanding and all but 2 per cent are at least good, which is by far the highest proportion for any phase of education. It is of great concern that many have closed over the past twenty years.

Subsequent roles did not allow me to have such an immediate connection with children and families, or with colleagues, because of the change in emphasis from teaching to working through other people. It is more difficult to gauge the impact of less direct influence, although this can be deep and long-lasting, as I recall from personal contact with inspirational lecturers and advisers. In my own career, the move into lecturing at the Froebel Institute in 1986 coincided with increased political interference in approaches to teaching as well as content of the curriculum. The National Curriculum was introduced in 1988 and applied to pupils of statutory school age; some time after it was launched, Desirable Outcomes for Children's Learning (SCAA, 1996) were identified for the end of the reception year, as part of a focus on accountability. They inevitably influenced practice, as schools shaped their teaching to enable children to achieve expected targets. The Labour government introduced specified Literacy and Numeracy Strategies from KS1, along with standard assessment tasks at the end of Year 2, and there was a growing emphasis on measuring achievement.

All this had an impact on initial teacher education as well as continuing professional development. I left lecturing after a year, because externally imposed constraints on the timetable meant that I could only be granted ten hours in a four-year course to teach child development. In addition to being deeply concerned about the future of teacher education, which has too often become limited and restrictive training in how to deliver prescribed content, I was sorry to give up the coordination of a groundbreaking multi-professional Advanced Diploma at Roehampton. This had enabled experienced staff working in different services to think together about their values, to become more objective about the defining culture and priorities of their work, and to shadow a colleague in a different service for a meaningful fortnight, in a way that is no longer possible.

I believe I was the last district inspector to be appointed to the Inner London Education Authority (ILEA), in 1987. Trevor Jaggar, then the chief primary inspector, interviewed me and, although he retired before I started work, his Quakerly influence was evident within the service, and deepened by a wise Quaker colleague who mentored me within the early years team.

The role of inspector was interpreted very positively in the ILEA; it involved providing constructive advice and support for schools rather than the negative culture that regrettably has become the norm under Ofsted.

Although the introduction of learning outcomes and much more specific expectations of young children, coupled with a more explicit early years curriculum, felt constraining to experienced teachers, overall, these developments enabled a more consistent approach. The London boroughs I worked for were proactive in their support for disadvantaged families and invested effectively in early education. It was good to be in a position to mediate access to expert advice and discretionary additional resources designed to counter social, as well as educational, difficulties and to be able to foster and disseminate innovative work. Staff training was a priority and made a notable contribution to equality through accessible translation services and expert teaching for bilingual under-fives, both within schools and in the surrounding catchment areas. I was involved in work on special needs, teaching English as an additional language, gender equality and other social issues, including anti-racism and peaceful conflict resolution, starting with the youngest children in school. My main commitments were to guide and assess newly qualified teachers during their probationary year, to maintain close relationships with the headteachers of a group of nursery and primary schools in four London boroughs, and to identify and address any weaknesses in leadership or governance. There were inevitable misunderstandings and conflicts, but I found that responsive listening was a more effective starting point for achieving a resolution than argument, however well founded. People do need to be heard.

Following the abolition of the ILEA in 1990, I was appointed primary and early years inspector in the Royal Borough of Kensington and Chelsea, where I worked with highly experienced subject specialist colleagues and a dedicated Teacher's Centre leader. The context could hardly have been more different; moving from the largest to one of the smallest Education Authorities in the country provided broad new challenges. The Children Act (1989) had just been enacted and the small size of the borough made it possible to collaborate closely with practitioners in other disciplines. There were two health authorities involved in the borough and it was instructive to experience the very different attitudes taken to joint working, with one paediatrician unwilling to share information or resources and the other open and generous in her approach. Given my wide range of responsibilities, I took the straightforward option of collaborating where possible and used the experience to build up a framework to guide future development, as and when that became feasible.

At that time, local authority inspectors monitored quality and provided support in their particular areas, while Her Majesty's Inspectors (HMI) reported to the Secretary of State on education conditions across the country; they had worked with professional courtesy as well as insight for over a century. All this changed with the introduction of Ofsted in 1992, which led to redundancy for many local authority inspectors, including myself. I was among the first cohort of experienced inspectors to be trained in the use of the Ofsted framework, which was followed by a training inspection in 1993. The HMI who led this insisted that all the school staff and the whole inspection team (eight of us) should meet before the start of the inspection. His final words to the assembled teachers were: 'If you don't feel at the end of next week that you have had the best professional development in your lives for free, we [the inspection team] will have failed.' This positive developmental culture did not last long, partly as a result of changes to the inspection framework and partly due to the employment of inexperienced and inadequately trained inspectors, including some former heads of failing schools. It is telling that when Ofsted brought the inspections back in-house in 2015, having outsourced them for some years, 40 per cent of the inspectors were not retained in their jobs. Inspections now last only a day or two, are rarely moderated, and are focused on data rather than direct evidence. This is leading to serious distortions in practice, especially as it is virtually impossible for schools to change or even challenge Ofsted judgements (Santry, 2017).

Working freelance as an Ofsted registered inspector and early years inspector and trainer enabled me to take on the voluntary role of Chair of Early Education. In that capacity, I was in a position to challenge the approach to early years inspection that Ofsted adopted. It became very obvious that the Chief Inspector had little interest in, and less understanding of, early years pedagogy. I well recall going to a meeting with him, accompanied by the then national lead HMI for early years and Professor Kathy Sylva, whose research work on early years at Oxford was well respected. We wanted to discuss our concerns about the early years inspection framework and found it very difficult to get the Chief Inspector's attention. He tapped the table, sighed and looked up at the ceiling, then glanced at his watch, making it very clear that he considered this meeting to be a waste of his time. Subsequently, I had reason to challenge him about an Ofsted video promoting the teaching of phonics in a reception class in Tower Hamlets. In response to my question about the evidence base for the approach, he referred me back to the video. When I looked at it again, I realized that he had focused on the young teachers, who were enthusiastically demonstrating the particular programme developed by the head of the school, whereas I had observed the children too; I saw three girls confidently engaged in the session, and the rest of the class playing with their socks, turning to forage in the drawers behind them, gazing into the middle distance and generally indicating a lack of interest. I realized then that the Chief Inspector had been impressed by the teaching, while my focus was more on the evidence for learning.

A subsequent Chief Inspector freely admitted that he did not know anything about early years. He relied on professional colleagues who were prepared to work with the sector and presided over an enlightened and very helpful definition of teaching in Ofsted's framework for the early years, which now applies to maintained schools as well as the private, voluntary and independent (PVI) sector. This definition sits comfortably with Quaker testimonies and remains in the current revised inspection framework:

> Teaching should not be taken to imply a 'top down' or formal way of working. It is a broad term that covers the many different ways in which adults help young children learn. It includes their interactions with children during planned and child-initiated play and activities: communicating and modelling language, showing, explaining, demonstrating, exploring ideas, encouraging, questioning, recalling, providing a narrative for what they are doing, facilitating and setting challenges. It takes account of the equipment adults provide and the attention given to the physical environment, as well as the structure and routines of the day that establish expectations. Integral to teaching is how practitioners assess what children know, understand and can do, as well as taking account of their interests and dispositions to learn (characteristics of effective learning), and how practitioners use this information to plan children's next steps in learning and monitor their progress.
>
> (Ofsted, 2017: 58)

I stopped working for Ofsted, as trainer as well as inspector, when it was no longer possible to invest enough time to make valid judgements, moderated within a team of experienced colleagues, and to provide constructive professional feedback. This opened up the opportunity of progressing from the voluntary role of Chair to the newly established post of Chief Executive of Early Education. By that time, I was convinced that there is nothing more important for a healthy, fair society than ensuring that all children have a good start in life. It was clear to me that the principles underpinning our traditional approach in the UK are in line with Quaker beliefs and can make a significant contribution to progress for society as a whole as well as for individuals. In addition to being in a position to foster and disseminate good early years practice across the UK, I welcomed the enhanced opportunities for advocacy, particularly with politicians.

Political issues

Political lobbying on behalf of the early years became more effective after the election of 1997, which brought in a Labour government dedicated to improving the life chances of disadvantaged families. For a while, I chaired the Early Childhood Forum, which had representation from all the organizations involved in early years care and education across the UK. Civil servants from the Education and Health departments and a senior inspector from Ofsted attended our meetings, which gave highly beneficial opportunities for growing mutual understanding, through informal contacts as well as the planned agenda items. *Quality in Diversity in Early Learning* (Early Childhood Education Forum, 1998), an enlightened curriculum framework, was co-constructed through dedicated collaborative work across the UK by practitioners working in all sectors. This deserved more attention than it received; it was bypassed in 2000 with the introduction of a statutory Early Years Foundation Stage curriculum in England, which covered provision for children from the age of 3 up to the end of the reception year, when most were 5. It was based on principles that still apply: the revised Curriculum Guidance for the Foundation Stage (DfE, 2017) addresses the education and care of all children in early years provision in England, including those with special educational needs and disabilities. Its four underpinning principles are entirely compatible with Quaker testimonies:

- Every child is a unique child, who is constantly learning and can be resilient, capable, confident and self-assured.
- Children learn to be strong and independent through positive relationships.
- Children learn and develop well in enabling environments, in which their experiences respond to their individual needs and there is a strong partnership between practitioners and parents and/or carers.
- Children develop and learn in different ways and at different rates.

Further, it is made clear that, in planning and guiding children's activities, practitioners must take into account the different ways that children learn, and reflect these in their practice. Three characteristics of effective teaching and learning are specified:

- Playing and exploring – children investigate and experience things, and 'have a go'.
- Active learning – children concentrate and keep on trying if they encounter difficulties, and enjoy achievements.
- Creating and thinking critically – children have and develop their own ideas, make links between ideas and develop strategies for doing things.

These characteristics also sit comfortably with Quaker testimonies. It is encouraging that David Carter, the National Schools Commissioner, states that good early years pedagogy should be a prerequisite of every teacher's training (George, 2017). His commendation gives significant support to the relevance of a principled approach to teaching with integrity, which goes beyond instruction, recognizes individual differences, respects each pupil and leads to learning for the teacher too.

In a drive to bring together services for children, the government established Early Years Development and Childcare Partnerships in each local authority. In 2000, I joined the Department for Children, Schools and Families (DCSF) to promote this aim in the South East Region. Quaker business methods were deeply helpful during this contentious year, when competing priorities and defensive attitudes often threatened to undermine the overarching aim of improving children's life chances. The influence of past history and the range of approaches to be found in the very different services made for widely varied rates of progress. My experience in Kensington and Chelsea soon after the Children Act in 1989 had prepared me for professional jealousies leading to some obstruction, which could only be resolved through listening, patient explanations and reassurance. Any success was achieved through a complex process resembling a multi-layered series of what Quakers call threshing meetings – extended, respectful discussions seeking to discern together the right thing to do.

The following year, I worked with the Early Excellence programme which focused very positively on inspirational settings that exemplified joint working and were models for Sure Start and then Children's Centres. At this time, government departments, including the Treasury, collaborated with each other and with the sector, in ways that enabled many difficulties to be resolved. It felt very good to be working in the DCSF at a time when every child did matter.[1]

There was extensive expansion of early years provision during the period of the Labour government. From a Quaker perspective, it was a very encouraging time, as the aim was to help the neediest families gain access to support from health and social services, as well as benefiting from high-quality educational provision. Peace and harmony were fostered through a respectful awareness of equality issues, children were helped to resolve differences with thoughtful consideration, and we worked to support shared community values through sustaining our powerful heritage of early education and care. The main difficulty at this time came from an increasing emphasis on measured outcomes, and a directive approach to assessment coupled with restrictive targets focused on literacy and mathematics.

Many of my civil service colleagues in the DCSF were able and conscientious, although most lacked experience in the field, and tended to take a simplistic view of the teaching role, assuming that if children are told something they will learn it and that this learning is linear. There was also a worrying lack of corporate memory. For example, significant issues related to staff qualifications and adult:child ratios have re-emerged some years after a detailed research project commissioned and funded by the Department itself (Munton *et al.*, 2002). This lack of continuity is exacerbated by a career structure in which few civil servants stay in any role, or indeed government department, for long enough to grasp the full implications of complex situations; this is further compounded by the increasing reliance on ambitious young special advisers, who are now commonly appointed for their political allegiance rather than specialist knowledge.

Predictably and understandably, the Treasury has prime influence on policy decisions that have to be made in the light of what is affordable. The Comprehensive Spending Review allocates resources to government departments over three years. This is reviewed biennially, but is followed by an annual internal battle within departments for funding. This, together with our oppositional political system, makes long-term strategic planning virtually impossible; I was told that my ideas for developing secure and effective early years provision over twenty years had no chance, nor did any proposal that would take longer than a single parliamentary term. This short-termism blights many aspects of policy development. In early years, the complexity and financial costs of the task in terms of staff training across different services, as well as the practical demands of building up premises and resources, make it impossible to achieve secure growth within the time available. The Sure Start initiative suffered due to the very speedy roll-out of the programme, which was necessary in political terms but did not allow enough time for development to be thoroughly embedded. Both the minister and the civil servant responsible for the project have subsequently expressed regret at the lack of emphasis on educational elements within

Sure Start Children's Centres, which relied on the PVI sector to keep up the momentum of expansion. Ten years on, austerity has led to devastating cuts; 350 Children's Centres have closed since 2010 (Jarvis, reported in *The Guardian*, 2017).

My experience of lobbying ministers was also hampered by a lack of continuity, as they, too, do not generally stay in post for long enough to develop a deep understanding of the interconnected issues involved in early years care and education. I was already aware that any communications longer than a single page of A4 would get scant attention and had realized that one of the main difficulties in gaining an effective focus on complex concerns is that the answer to any question on education, particularly in early years, tends to start with 'it depends ...'. The thoroughness of Quaker business methods contrasts strongly with what I witnessed in most encounters with politicians, who have tended, increasingly, to look at all issues through the prism of short-term political advantage.

However, in terms of advocacy for equality and opportunity, real progress was made in the ten years up to the financial crash of 2008. I am privileged to have been part of that, and remain convinced that there is nothing more important for society than addressing the needs and potential of young children and their families. I try to live in accordance with these words from *Quaker Advices and Queries*:

> Remember your responsibilities as a citizen for the conduct of local, national and international affairs. Do not shrink from the time and effort your commitment may demand.
>
> (*QF&P*, 1.02, 34)

Emerging concerns

The educational climate changed following the financial collapse in 2008 and the election of a Conservative and Liberal Democrat coalition government in 2010. The pressures on families as well as schools and nurseries have multiplied. More than 25 per cent of our children now live in poverty, with resulting instability, lack of resources and malnutrition in many families. Local authorities cannot afford to keep provision open, nor pay for enough well-qualified staff. Their moderation and training roles have almost disappeared. Government grants do not cover the real cost of places in the PVI sector, so some parents are having to subsidize entitlements to free care and education, and there are not enough daycare places to meet the offer of 30 hours' free provision for working families. In addition, the nature of early years provision is under pressure to change radically in response to a revised curriculum and assessment framework that favours performance over secure conceptual development, understanding and engagement in learning (Bate and Foster, 2017). A recent report published by the Sutton Trust examines the current state of early years policy in light of evidence about what works. Reviewing twenty years of change, it assesses the strengths and limitations of where we are today, and identifies priorities for policy attention. Key findings include concerns that:

> Early education and childcare has been a major focus of policy in this area. Of concern is that recent developments indicate a shift in funding and policy focus away from quality early education for child development toward childcare affordability for working families. Investments in affordability are welcome, but neither the tax-free childcare scheme nor the 30 hour entitlement for working families are well-designed to promote social mobility, meaning longer hours in state-funded early education for children who are already relatively advantaged, which may be expected to widen gaps in child development at school starting age. Particularly worrying, these investments are coming at the expense of the quality of provision ...
>
> One third of staff working in group-based care still lack either English or Maths GCSE or both. A current proposal to remove the requirement for maintained nursery and reception classes to have a qualified teacher is particularly worrying and could affect children in disadvantaged areas most of all.
> (Stewart and Waldfogel, 2017: 3)

The report authors' first recommendation is that the shift in focus of childcare policy away from quality towards quantity, with less focus on educational development, should be reversed, as it is ill advised. Specifically, they argue, funding should be secured to ensure that qualified teachers remain in place in school nursery and reception classes and that local authorities can return to providing support for continuing professional development. The earlier commitment to having qualified practitioners in every early years setting should be revived, as their presence is crucial for the development of disadvantaged toddlers.

Children in the UK now enter school up to a year below the statutory school starting age, which is at the beginning of the term after their fifth birthday. Current expected standards in literacy and numeracy exert significant downward pressures and make it difficult to sustain an effective play-based approach to early years education. Variations in age and life experience, as well as uneven developmental profiles, have a significant influence on children's achievement in the early years. The lack of age adjustment in the reporting of results for the Early Years Foundation Stage Profile is indefensible and is leading to many summer-born children being misdiagnosed as having special needs (Sykes *et al.*, 2009). A heavy accountability system, together with inappropriate definitions of school readiness and ill-advised approaches to the teaching of reading, are narrowing the curriculum in nurseries as well as reception classes.

Several recent initiatives pushed through by ministers go against research evidence and professional experience. The lack of respect for expertise is hard to understand, let alone accept. In 2013, as the government embarked on a review of the National Curriculum, I went with colleagues from subject associations, together with experienced primary headteachers and advisers from national associations, to meet with the relevant politician. It was agreed that I would start the meeting by explaining our reservations about the phonics check[2] that was to be applied in Year 1. The politician simply put his hands over his ears and said: 'I'm not listening.'

Clark (2017) presents strong evidence that counters simplistic claims for the effectiveness of teaching phonics without ensuring this is embedded within a rich literacy environment. Clark refers to a study where children tried to explain the function of phonics and in particular the use of 'alien' words, and their relationship to reading to Beegu, a soft toy (Carter, 2017). The children were asked: 'Is phonics about reading and will phonics help Beegu to read?' Carter pursued this with children who said 'No.' One child suggested that the purpose of books was not to read or enjoy but: 'All books are good because they help with sounds.' The children realized that if a word in the list had an alien illustration next to it then it wasn't a real word. When asked if these words helped, one child responded: 'They don't, they just confuse us!' When asked if Beegu needed these words to help her learn to read they all chorused 'No.' Some thought alien words were a 'trick'. There was a revealing comment from one child who could read:

> I learnt to read, when, so I have a book at my house which before I started school I just remembered what all the words were 'cos daddy read it to me loads and loads so I thought if Beegu's parents read to him for days and days then he could ...
>
> (Clark, 2017: 93)

Carter (2017) states: 'There is widespread teaching to the test that has nothing to do with developing children as readers ... and everything to do with raising test scores.'

As I write this, the Department for Education (DfE) has also taken an inflexible attitude to school readiness and baseline assessment, forcing through its own views without taking account of the evidence of the damaging effects, at great financial cost. This simplistic approach ignores the fact that self-regulation, engagement and confidence are the most significant contributors to children's readiness for school (Whitebread and Bingham, 2014). The government has also pressed ahead with baseline assessment at the start of the reception year, in spite of evidence that it is neither valid nor reliable, and is indeed damaging at a crucial time in children's lives (Better Without Baseline, 2017).[3] Annual entry to school is another area where policy undermines effective practice, in nurseries as well as in school.

Similar experiences have been reported in various curriculum areas, such as history, English and mathematics, where well-established truths about children's learning have been ignored in the drive for specific measurable outcomes. In his Brian Simon Memorial Lecture, Professor Robin Alexander (2011) gave a scathing account of politically driven blocking of the recommendations emerging from the rigorous independent review he led into primary education (Alexander, 2010). Andrew Pollard, one of the four experts appointed by the government to advise on curriculum reform, resigned in 2011, explaining that teachers have to take account of the needs of each child to provide a broad curriculum. He stated: 'The constraining effects on the primary curriculum as a whole are likely to be profound and the preservation of breadth, balance and quality of experience will test even the most committed of teachers' (Vasagar, 2012). When politicians do not listen to their appointed advisers, how can experienced and knowledgeable bodies speak truth to power?

Government consultations, which are enshrined in law for major social changes, should be an asset in a democracy, as they provide avenues for practitioners and interested people to contribute their views to the development of policy. However, my first experience of consultation in the mid-1990s did not inspire confidence. The event took place in a West End hotel. I knew early years care and education were at last being taken seriously, as lunch was provided and men in suits, including young political interns holding clipboards, were present. I also knew that, in line with Quaker testimonies on truth and integrity, I would have to stand up and make a particular point. With wobbly knees and shaky voice, I asked whether each response to the consultation would count as a single one. As an individual, I had no quarrel with that, but as Chief Executive of Early Education, I was representing over 6,000 members, and as Chair of the Early Childhood Forum, I was representing almost everyone in the entire country working in early years. The civil servant involved put his head in his hands and said, 'I know.' In 2015, I had reason to check whether it was still the case that each return counted as a single response and was told: 'Yes – but we read some submissions more carefully than others.' It seems that the views of individuals with little relevant experience or awareness may command the same status as the national representative bodies – or be granted even greater weighting – through this obscure process.

The DfE is commendably open about responses to consultations. Results can be found on its website for a while before they are archived. It appears that experienced and knowledgeable people are too often ignored, even if the consultation responses overwhelmingly agree with our views. For example, the introduction of baseline assessment went ahead in 2016, although it is on record that almost two-thirds of respondents disagreed with the DfE proposals.

Professional reservations about the phonics check introduced in 2012 are well founded. Phonics has a place, but makes a limited contribution to children's ability to learn to read, does not correlate with individual achievement at the end of KS1, and undermines the confidence of many children in the early stages of literacy learning (Clark, 2017). Fluent readers tend to be particularly confused by the inclusion of meaningless non-words, to be decoded mechanically; for example, 'strom' was read as 'storm' by one child who rightly expected print to make sense. As Carter commented to me in 2017, following her study in seven Bristol schools:

> The teachers' focus groups have indicated an increased pressure over the last couple of years for increased scores and this has led to some alarming practice – often in schools that already had very good KS1 reading results. This has included one school saying that, at parents' evening before the check, parents of more able readers are being told not to read books with their children in the lead up to the check but to focus on word reading and to make the children sound and blend rather than reading the whole word. And this is just one comment of many others across all of the schools …

> The children's focus groups have been even more revealing – asked why they might be reading alien words, the children speculated that it might be in case aliens came to earth, while

another thought it was because alien words might be 'slipped' into a real book to trick them. A rather wise child said it was all 'rather a waste of time'....

(Carter, 2017)

Not all children will 'see through' this test, however, and I believe it demonstrably harms their confidence and motivation to learn and to read for pleasure. Although marks in the test have risen over five years, the results of the KS1 standard assessment tasks a year later have hardly altered over the same period (Clark, 2017). The unsatisfactory nature of the process was obvious to children as well as teachers. As Sebastian Suggate (Suggate *et al.*, 2013) shows, pupils who begin formal literacy lessons at 7 achieve as well at 11 as children in the UK who are subject to premature demands for very limited and limiting literacy skills.

Quakers were among the first bodies in the UK to set up institutes for teacher training at the beginning of the twentieth century. They understood that teaching well required training and special kinds of knowledge, reflection and study as well as support in practice. As I write, that kind of education is being partially replaced by school-based training, despite Ofsted findings that university involvement in teacher education brings the best results (see Oancea, 2014). There are also concerns about variable standards and confusing information about training opportunities for NVQ Level 2 and 3 in childcare and about the lack of recognition of early years teaching status (Nutbrown, 2012).

It is salutary to remember that the 1944 Education Act explicitly left decisions about curriculum content and pedagogy to those who have the most experience, namely the teaching profession. Reducing training leads to the recycling of inadequacies, to limited 'on-the-job' performance, and also risks the loss of the critical approach that can be achieved through research and study. With this in mind, it is discouraging to know that one teacher education institution was instructed by the inspectorate to remove a particular text that challenged the current orthodoxy in teaching reading from its reading lists. The institution, contrary to norms of academic freedom, complied (personal communication, name withheld, 2017, eds).

It could be argued that successive legislation that drives towards a prescriptive curriculum, albeit allowing freedom for certain categories of schools, has also brought in approaches to accountability that limit professionalism, innovation and care for individual development and personal propensities (see also Janet Nicholls's chapter). What, then, can be said about equality in education?

Government policies over recent years have undermined one of the most effective ways to counter inequality through the provision of nurtured play, care and early learning. While politicians might vocally support the need for early input, inadequate funding means that, as I write, nursery provision is limited or being forced to close[4] and primary schools find it increasingly difficult to fund the breadth of work needed to enable all children to develop fully – not only academically, but socially, emotionally and physically. It is regrettable that many maintained nursery schools have closed and many more are at risk of closure (Riddell, 2017). In contrast to the UK's drive for early academic progress at the cost of establishing the basis for a rounded childhood, three countries in Europe that are rated highest in international comparative tests (Finland, Estonia and Switzerland) do not start formal schooling until children are 7 years old.

As an experienced professional, I have deep concerns that accountability rigidly imposed on a flawed system currently takes precedence over the real needs of individual pupils. Rising levels of mental health problems among students of all ages and undue stress on teachers are serious symptoms of the current malaise. It is very frustrating to find that, although many parents and professionals seek to speak truth to power, they are not being heard. The human cost is considerable and will cast shadows long into the future.

A Quakerly response

It became clear to me some years ago that a radical and wide-ranging change in government policy is needed in the UK, particularly in England. As a parent and grandparent as well as teacher and adviser, I could not pass by on the other side, ignoring the damage that is being done. My worries were shared by other members of Keswick Quaker Meeting. Our Area Meeting linked our concerns with Quaker testimonies, and these received widespread support among British Quakers.

We wrote a letter to *The Friend* (the British Quaker weekly journal) in April 2013, listing some specific concerns, and ending:

> We think that enlightened education is now at serious risk and ask other concerned Friends to get in touch with a view to taking these issues to Meeting for Sufferings and presenting a statement to the Secretary of State.
>
> (*The Friend*, April 2013)

Among other responses, Janet Harland, a representative on the body that oversees policy development on behalf of the Religious Society of Friends, asked: 'What do our members and attenders think, not simply about the manifold issues within education that cause them so much concern but about what, at this time, we can usefully do? We have our spiritual values and, dare I say, our moral values, on which we can stand. How can we speak to power in ways that may be effective?'

Various initiatives have followed, including the establishment of the Quaker Values in Education group, suggested questions from Friends House to be put to candidates standing for election in 2015 (Metheringham, 2014), a booklet addressing Quaker Insight in Education (QVinE, 2016) and the publication of this book.

In an effort to turn my deep concern about unfair and damaging education policies in England into positive action, my intention is to follow wise advice from fellow Quakers. Jonathan Dale, for example, considers that:

> ... to work only in the life choices within one's own – albeit partial – control, while ignoring the controlling context set by government measures, is to limit our awareness of how our testimonies are powerfully affected by public policy ... Friends have for a long time known that testimony involves working towards the expression of their testimonies in the structures of public life. ... we have to seek, both individually and corporately, locally and nationally, to express our alternative vision in ways which contribute positively to political decision making ... we aim not for a facile dissent, but to encourage a return to fundamental values despite the difficult realities of day to day politics.
>
> (Cave and Morley, 2000: 67)

Ursula Jane O'Shea advises:

> Learning to respond to the signs of our times, modern Friends have a double resource in the Quaker tradition of inward waiting and active persistence. This tradition calls for giving careful attention to the inward guide, in the inspiration of the individual and in the discernment of the community, and then matching this inward focus with the hard experience of living our testimonies that are not at home in the world.
>
> (O'Shea, 2003: 64)

A Friend at the threshing meeting held in 2014 at Woodbrooke, the Quaker Study Centre, wrote:

> Do not ask, 'What are <u>they</u> going to do about it?' 'They' needs to be you ... What are you going to do to facilitate changes in Education and support those in stress – including pupils as well as teachers?
>
> (Anonymous workshop contributor)

My intention is to harness my anger and grief and continue to inform and challenge government through my roles in several national educational organizations and through making common cause with other groups, including parents and governors. I will contribute where possible to the professional development of young teachers and early years workers. As governor of a small rural primary school, I hear at first hand the impact of current policies and can see that teachers' as well as children's opportunities and aspirations are diminished within a culture dominated by league tables and competition. However, I can encourage and support the children and parents and help staff to hold on to their principles. My hope is that future generations will be able to draw on, sustain and develop what we know about enlightened early education. Quakers can remind themselves of Parker Palmer's sage observation that 'You teach who you are' (Palmer, 1998).

For myself, I take inspiration from Helen Steven's 2005 Swarthmore Lecture *No Extraordinary Power: Prayer, stillness and activism*. She proposes:

> The important thing is the doing, the stepping out in faith. Doing our utmost, to the very limit of our being, and then being free to let go of the result; not to be bound by success, but to hold on to the confidence that the outcome will be taken up by others and the flame continue to burn. ... we ourselves being steadfast, trusting that others will be steadfast in their turn.
>
> (Steven, 2005: 97)

Notes

[1] Every Child Matters was a policy introduced by the Labour government in 2003. Its main aim was to ensure that all children, whatever their background or circumstances, should have the support they needed to stay safe, be healthy, enjoy and achieve, make a positive contribution and achieve economic well-being. It was side-lined under the 2010–15 Coalition government.

[2] This is a check on individual children to ensure schools are using a particular phonics method to teach reading – the first time a government has forced teachers to use a specific method.

[3] The Better Without Baseline campaign is an alliance of early years organizations opposing the introduction of baseline tests for 4-year-olds in England.

[4] The reply to a Freedom of Information question by Dan Jarvis MP in 2017 showed that funding for Children's Centres had almost halved since 2010 (Walker, 2017).

References

Alexander, R. (ed.) (2010) *Children, Their World, Their Education: Final report and recommendations of the Cambridge Primary Review*. London: Routledge.

Alexander, R. (2011) 'Legacies, policies and prospects: One year on from the Cambridge Primary Review'. *Forum*, 53 (1), 71–92.

Ball, C. (1994) *Start Right: The importance of early learning*. London: Royal Society of Arts.

Bate, A. and Foster, D. (2017) *Sure Start (England)* (Briefing Paper 7257). London: House of Commons Library. Online. http://researchbriefings.files.parliament.uk/documents/CBP-7257/CBP-7257.pdf (accessed 5 February 2018).

Better Without Baseline (2017) 'Government consults on rehash of failed baseline assessment proposals'. Press release, 30 March. Online. www.early-education.org.uk/press-release/government-consults-rehash-failed-baseline-assessment-proposals (accessed 25 November 2017).

Carter, J. (2017) Personal communication, 22 March, University of the West of England.

Cave, E. and Morley, R. (eds) (2000) *Faith in Action: Quaker social testimony: Writings from Friends in Britain Yearly Meeting including an essay by Jonathan Dale*. London: Quaker Home Service.

Clark, M.M. (ed.) (2017) *Reading the Evidence: Synthetic phonics and literacy learning*. Birmingham: Glendale Education.

DfE (Department for Education) (2017) *Statutory Framework for the Early Years Foundation Stage*. London: Department for Education. Online. www.foundationyears.org.uk/files/2017/03/EYFS_STATUTORY_FRAMEWORK_2017.pdf (accessed 25 November 2017).

Early Childhood Education Forum (1998) *Quality in Diversity in Early Learning: A framework for early childhood practitioners*. London: National Children's Bureau.

George, M. (2017) 'Exclusive: Early years should be "prerequisite" of all teachers' training, says Sir David Carter'. *TES*, 7 April. Online. www.tes.com/news/school-news/breaking-news/exclusive-early-years-should-be-prerequisite-all-teachers-training (accessed 25 January 2018).

Isaacs, S. (2013) *The Educational Value of the Nursery School*. New ed. London: British Association for Early Childhood Education.

Jarvis, P. (2013) *The McMillan Sisters and the 'Deptford Welfare Experiment'*. Online. www.tactyc.org.uk/wp-content/uploads/2013/11/Reflection-Jarvis.pdf (accessed 25 November 2017).

Leavitt, M. L. (1993) 'Testimonies in the Quaker tradition'. In *Quaker Peace Testimony: A workbook for individuals and groups*. London: Quaker Books, 13–18.

Metheringham, J. (2014) *Election Briefing Paper: Quaker values in education*. London: Friends House.

Munton, T., Barclay, L., Mallardo, M.R. and Barreau, S. (2002) 'Part B: Adult:child ratios for early years settings in the private/independent sector: A report of empirical research'. In *Research on Ratios, Group Size and Staff Qualifications and Training in Early Years and Childcare Settings* (Research Report RR320). London: Department for Education and Skills, 141–221. Online. http://dera.ioe.ac.uk/4642/1/RR320.pdf (accessed 25 November 2017).

Nutbrown, C. (2012) *Foundations for Quality: The independent review of early education and childcare qualifications: Final report*. London: Department for Education. Online. www.gov.uk/government/uploads/system/uploads/attachment_data/file/175463/Nutbrown-Review.pdf (accessed 25 November 2017).

Oancea, A. (2014) 'Teachers' professional knowledge and state-funded teacher education: A (hi)story of critiques and silences'. *Oxford Review of Education*, 40 (4), 497–519.

O'Donnell, E.A. (2013) 'Quakers and education'. In Angell, S.W. and Dandelion, P. (eds) *The Oxford Handbook of Quaker Studies*. Oxford: Oxford University Press, 405–19.

Ofsted (Office for Standards in Education, Children's Services and Skills) (2017) *School Inspection Handbook: Handbook for inspecting schools in England under section 5 of the Education Act 2005*. Manchester: Ofsted. Online. www.gov.uk/government/uploads/system/uploads/attachment_data/file/670083/School_inspection_handbook_section_5.pdf (accessed 25 January 2018).

O'Shea, U.J. (2003) *Living the Way: Quaker spirituality and community* (James Backhouse Lecture). London: Quaker Books.

Palmer, P.J. (1998) *The Courage to Teach: Exploring the inner landscape of a teacher's life*. San Francisco: Jossey-Bass.

Plowden, B. (1967) *Children and Their Primary Schools: A report of the Central Advisory Council for Education (England)*. London: HMSO.

QVinE (Quaker Values in Education Group) (2016) *Quaker Insight in Education*. Quaker Values in Education Group. Online. www.qvine.org.uk/wp-content/uploads/2016/02/Insight-Online.pdf (accessed 25 January 2018).

Riddell, B. (2017) 'Barbara Riddell's speech to APPG June 27th 2017'. Online. www.early-education.org.uk/sites/default/files/Barbara%20Riddell%20%20 speech%2027%20June%202017.pdf (accessed 25 November 2017).

Rumbold, A. (1990) *Starting with Quality: The report of the committee of inquiry into the quality of the educational experience offered to 3- and 4-year-olds*. London: HMSO. Online. www.educationengland.org.uk/documents/rumbold/rumbold1990.html (accessed 1 December 2017).

Santry, C. (2017) 'Exclusive: The virtually impossible task of overturning an Ofsted verdict'. *TES*, 12 June. Online. www.tes.com/news/school-news/breaking-news/exclusive-virtually-impossible-task-overturning-ofsted-verdict (accessed 25 November 2017).

SCAA (School Curriculum and Assessment Authority) (1996) *Nursery Education: Desirable Outcomes for Children's Learning on entering compulsory education*. Hayes: SCAA.

Scully, J.L. (2013) 'Quakers and ethics'. In Angell, S.W. and Dandelion, P. (eds) *The Oxford Handbook of Quaker Studies*. Oxford: Oxford University Press, 535–48.

Steven, H. (2005) *No Extraordinary Power: Prayer, stillness and activism* (Swarthmore Lecture). London: Quaker Books.

Stewart, K. and Waldfogel, J. (2017) *Closing Gaps Early: The role of early years policy in promoting social mobility in England.* London: Sutton Trust. Online. www.suttontrust.com/wp-content/uploads/2017/09/Closing-Gaps-Early_FINAL.pdf (accessed 25 January 2018).

Suggate, S.P., Schaughency, E.A. and Reese, E. (2013) 'Children learning to read later catch up to children reading earlier'. *Early Childhood Research Quarterly*, 28 (1), 33–48.

Sykes, E.D.A., Bell, J.F. and Rodeiro, C.V. (2009) *Birthdate Effects: A review of the literature from 1990–on*. Cambridge: Cambridge Assessment.

Sylva, K., Melhuish, E., Sammons, P., Siraj-Blatchford, I. and Taggart, B. (2004) *The Effective Provision of Pre-School Education (EPPE) Project: Final Report*. Online. http://discovery.ucl.ac.uk/10005309/1/sylva2004EPPEfinal.pdf (accessed 12 March 2018).

Vasagar, J. (2012) 'Michael Gove's curriculum attacked by expert who advised him'. *The Guardian*, 12 June. Online. www.theguardian.com/education/2012/jun/12/michael-gove-curriculum-attacked-adviser (accessed 7 December 2017).

Walker, P. (2017) 'More than 350 Sure Start children's centres have closed since 2010'. *The Guardian*, 2 February. Online. www.theguardian.com/society/2017/feb/02/sure-start-centres-300-closed-since-2010 (accessed 12 December 2017).

Whitebread, D. and Bingham, S. (2014) 'School readiness: Starting age, cohorts and transitions in the early years'. In Moyles, J., Payler, J. and Georgeson, J. (eds) *Early Years Foundations: Critical issues*. 2nd ed. Maidenhead: Open University Press, 179–90.

Chapter 9
Equality and the scramble for school places
Janet Nicholls

Quakers have an impressive history when it comes to the promotion of equality: campaigning to abolish slavery, supporting the rights of prisoners, upholding and promoting equality of gender and ethnicity, and being one of the first religious organizations to recognize same-sex marriage. In the seventeenth century, Quaker women and men took on equal roles within their meetings, their unusual (at that time) assumption being that women and men were equally competent and deserved equal respect. Yet today, Friends are not agreed about how equality should be expressed in a caring education system, and, in this respect, they are reflecting divisions of opinion among the wider population. This chapter presents a range of considerations and factors that might influence decisions made by anyone wishing to navigate the educational system, including Quakers making personal choices or anyone wanting to use a Quaker book to help them to think about equality. It also raises questions about what labelling a school 'Quaker' means in the UK today.

Defining equality

Equality is one of the Quaker testimonies (guiding principles by which they try to live their lives), but the word 'equality' is not being used here to deny the diversity of gifts that contributes to a functioning division of labour within society: the pursuit of equality is often dismissed as a naive failure to recognize such diversity. Rather, a Quaker recognition of equality accepts and even celebrates such diversity, and is imbued with a sense of there being a 'Light' within every person that makes them equally valuable. This applies to everyone, irrespective of ethnicity, religion, gender, sexuality, disability or educational ability:

> Equality does not mean I am not special. It means we all are.
> (Quaker Quest, 2007: 11)

In 2014, Quakers formulated an agreed statement that 'Every person is precious' (Quaker Values in Education (QVinE), 2014) in which they provided a principled critique of the state education system in Britain. While not making detailed, practical recommendations, they were nevertheless resolute in their concerns about the direction being taken at that time in the school system:

- The politicization and marketization of schooling leads to children and young people being treated as economic units. Schooling is measured by highly-selective performance data, which in turn drive excessively rapid change. Education should not be a traded commodity but a human endeavour in which people come first. Learners are beneficiaries of education, not consumers.
- The general inequality in our society has an impact on school provision and admissions practices. Equality of school provision is best managed through local oversight and fair admissions policies, and the educational disadvantages of poverty need compensation in schools.

(QVinE, 2014)

This, and the longer statement from which it is taken, could be seen as a strident assertion of the importance of the role of state education in promoting equality. Other Quaker publications, such as those produced by Quaker Quest, are also forthright in their assertion that all children should have access to the best that education can offer so that their various interests and aptitudes can be nurtured to benefit us all. However, it is still difficult to find a common understanding among Quakers about how these beliefs should be put into action, including regarding Quaker schools. Along with a dislike of anything that smacks of a rigid doctrine, Quakers tend to avoid any suggestion that they should all conform to one perspective, and education policy is no exception. Non-Quaker parents, educationists and politicians may also recognize that same diversity, but likewise have different views about the most desirable school provision and admission policies and whether or not they should be used to tackle social disadvantages.

Selection and choice

The history of educational provision in the UK generally does not reflect a belief that children are equally precious, but rather a belief that some children are more special than others. Associated problems were cited in a detailed report by the Academies Commission:

> The mission of state education is to provide access to educational excellence for all. In practice, the apparent *lack* of equal access has been a long-standing problem. The UK education system is

among the most socially segregated of OECD countries ... This is manifested in socially advantaged pupils being concentrated in the best schools ... with more teachers ... and disadvantaged children are over-represented in poorer quality schools.

(Academies Commission, 2013: 61)

In the past, most parents had little choice in deciding which schools their children would attend, decisions often being made for them by local education authorities (LEAs), based on their children's examination results. From the 1940s to the 1960s, the ideal of 'parity of esteem' was spoken of when selecting pupils at 11-Plus for secondary modern, grammar or technical schools, but parents knew that those selected for grammar schools would benefit from superior resources. Selection of this sort still exists in some areas, and discussions about increasing it are current, but today parents have more freedom of choice, albeit still limited. As Walford explains:

In England, families have the right to 'express a preference' for a school for their child. They have no automatic right to have that child accepted. In a true quasi-market of schools it is inevitable that schools would attempt to choose the students as well as the families choosing the school.

(Forsey *et al.*, 2008: 101)

Each spring, news reports give witness to the complaints of parents who find that, despite their best efforts, their children will be consigned to schools outside an easy commute, or with a poor reputation or without the specialist services that they need. In 2016, there were 62,301 appeals against allocations in England, of which 45,784 proceeded to a hearing; and 10,192 (22.3 per cent) of those heard were upheld (DfE, 2016). Appeals against allocations in England for infant years (reception and Years 1 and 2) were least likely to be successful, with 12 per cent of those heard upheld. On 1 March 2016, the ITV News described what was happening as a 'scramble' for school places.

A scramble to exert parental choice describes a scenario that can be all too familiar to parents who have been faced with a sometimes bewildering assortment of options in the school marketplace: free schools, specialist schools, comprehensives, grammar schools, trust schools, preparatory schools and crammers, as well as the ubiquitous labels of 'academy' or 'high' school. There are also many types of religious schools, some of them being free within the state system, some being accessed via scholarships and some charging fees. Quaker schools[1] are also religious schools but only one in Britain, the William Penn primary school, is within the state-funded system for all relevant children.

The concept of parental choice is often cited as a reality and a rational market principle for achieving what parents want, but is also often decried by others as unachievable in many instances. For example, parents who are dependent on the state system might prefer to send their children to an inspirational and popular local state school, yet have to accept the only place available at a less popular school that is a considerable distance from home. Various political perspectives on education have resulted in inequality becoming a key feature of the education system, and it is difficult to see where or how the Quaker belief in equality fits into the picture.

A polarity of perspectives on equality in education

The exploratory model I set out here is an attempt to link the wide variety of schooling systems in the UK to competing perspectives about social justice and individual rights and freedoms. While aware that the variety of schooling systems in this country is such that guidance cannot be provided here that is specific to readers' personal circumstances, I hope this model will, nevertheless, inform some personal deliberations.

The model simplifies issues about equality and schooling by presenting notions of equal educational opportunities as a polarity, moving from one extreme – emphasizing extra support for those who are most disadvantaged, to the other extreme – emphasizing extra support for those who are already advantaged. Individual Quakers can be found with beliefs that correspond to each of the perspectives, and it is possible to cite examples of Quaker schools that fit different points on the polarity. The model therefore challenges our understandings about the meaning of the Quaker testimony on equality and how it should be applied to education. More particularly, it may inform the deliberations of Quaker parents who want a Quaker upbringing for their children, Quaker teachers who might wish to teach in a Quaker school, and also those responsible for the provision of such schools.

Within the model there are six emphases of educational organization that can act against each other in the kinds of equality and inequality that they promote through their differing interpretations of need, fairness, equality and opportunity. At one end of the polarity, the emphasis is on more help for the disadvantaged, while at the other end the emphasis is on more help for those already advantaged (Figure 9.1).

Equality and the scramble for school places

```
┌─────────────────────────────────────┐
│   More help for the disadvantaged   │
└─────────────────────────────────────┘
                  │
┌─────────────────────────────────────────────────┐
│ Equal access and a broad highway of opportunities for all │
└─────────────────────────────────────────────────┘
                  │
┌─────────────────────────────────────┐
│ Competitive access, with scholarships and │
│ a narrow ladder to academic success │
└─────────────────────────────────────┘
                  │
┌─────────────────────────────────┐
│ A parentocracy with competition │
│ between parents in a quasi-market │
└─────────────────────────────────┘
                  │
┌─────────────────────────────────────┐
│ Private schooling outside the state system │
└─────────────────────────────────────┘
                  │
┌─────────────────────────────────────┐
│ More help for those already advantaged │
└─────────────────────────────────────┘
```

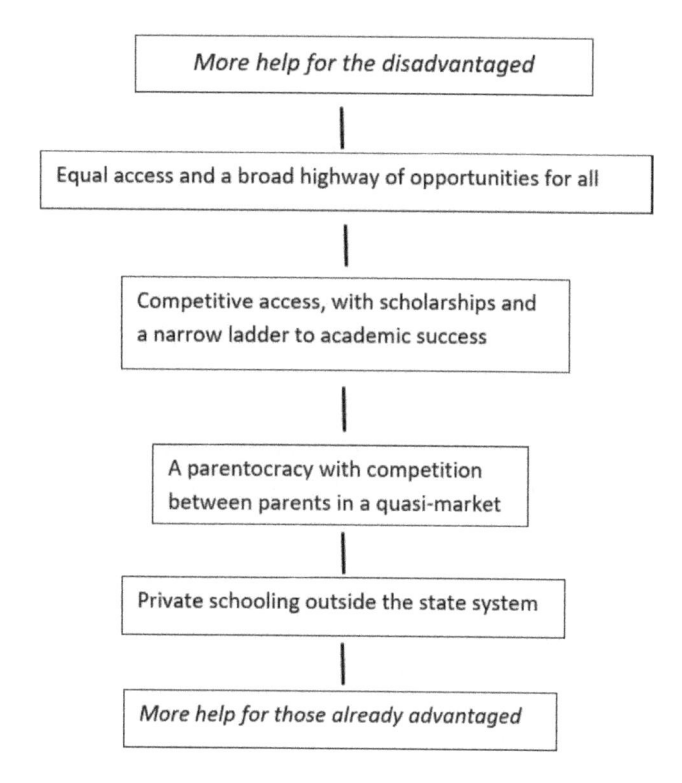

Figure 9.1: A polarity of perspectives on equal educational opportunities

Each emphasis is now examined in turn, with the role Quakers as educators, trustees and parents might play within it, and its relation to Quaker values.

An emphasis on providing more help for the disadvantaged

Extra help for children who are disadvantaged in some way may be found in individual schools when children who have special educational needs and are struggling are given specialized support, or it may constitute a whole-school ethos of compensating for various disadvantages. Central governments have also introduced schemes aiming to compensate disadvantaged children within the education system.

An emphasis on compensatory education was most noticeable in public discourse during the 1960s. For example, the 1967 Plowden Report introduced Educational Priority Areas (EPAs), where efforts were made to compensate for social deprivation within particular localities. EPAs were gradually absorbed into more generalized aid programmes for deprived areas and have been followed by similar schemes. In 1998, a Labour government introduced Education Action Zones to raise standards in disadvantaged urban and rural areas by linking clusters of schools with an action forum consisting of LEAs, local and national businesses, school governors, parents and other local groups. In 2014, a Conservative government introduced the Pupil Premium as extra funding for schools maintained by local authorities, academies, free schools and non-maintained special schools in England to raise the attainment of disadvantaged pupils of all abilities.

Breckenbrough School in North Yorkshire is a Quaker school fitting into a whole-school ethos of compensatory education. Founded in 1934 by the psychologist Arthur Fitch, it is a special school for about fifty boys with a range of learning and behavioural difficulties who are referred and paid for by their local authorities. With class sizes of no more than seven and the continuing oversight of school-leavers by an aftercare officer, it is not surprising that parents have had difficulties in getting places for their sons at Breckenbrough School. As one successful parent put it: 'It isn't a question of paying fees – no parent does that – but sticking to your guns against every argument that a budget-strapped LEA can muster' (Wainwright, 2007).

Another community influenced by Quaker ideals is Glebe House, which was established in the late 1960s as a result of the concerns of a Quaker probation officer. It is affiliated to the Religious Society of Friends (the full name of Quakers as a society) and has Quaker trustees, is an independent Friends' Therapeutic Community, a children's home registered to supply an education, and in 2016 was recognized by Ofsted as a school. Specialist interventions are provided at Glebe House for up to 17 young men who are mostly aged 16–18 years at point of entry and have a known history of harmful sexual behaviours,[2] most of them having been victims themselves and/or raised in environments in which sexual abuse was normalized. Glebe House also provides an impressive aftercare service and there is evidence of an exceptionally low rate of recidivism (Boswell *et al.*, 2014). LEAs pay the fees for Glebe House residents, although again there have been increasingly severe constraints on what LEAs can afford.

The outcomes are excellent for young men who have attended Breckenbrough School because of their learning or behavioural difficulties and for young offenders who have been residents at Glebe House. However, few places are available at these two specialist, all-male, state-funded Quaker communities.

An emphasis on equal access and a broad highway of opportunities for all

An emphasis on equal access in comprehensive schools was most popular during the 1960s and 1970s, and still exists in many areas. Such schools aim to educate children of all abilities and social classes, usually split into sets according to their attainment in some individual subjects. The large scale of such schools facilitates a wide range of subject areas and the easy movement of pupils between various sets according to their changing interests and aptitudes. They therefore purport to serve the needs of all children, irrespective of whether they arrive with disadvantages or advantages. Advocates of this emphasis on equal access argue that the social mix provides an important part of the child's education and that it is the least divisive form of schooling.

Local and national socio-economic and political contexts have nevertheless made it difficult for some comprehensive schools to provide genuinely equal access. For example, the shift away from local authority control of the schools in their areas and competition from other types of schools in or near conurbations have made it difficult or impossible to provide genuinely socially mixed comprehensive schools. The socio-economic make-up of school catchment areas also affects the socio-economic make-up of schools within those areas. Some comprehensive schools are situated in depressed areas and some parents would rather send their children to smaller schools without the wide social mix.

Comprehensive schools also have their critics. In the public perception, beliefs that the children in these schools experience nothing but 'teaching to the middle' still exist, ignoring the actual differentiation processes that aim to help both high achievers and those who benefit from careful support. The wide social mix in comprehensive schools means that they are likely to include some children who receive free school meals, children with various special needs and others who are disadvantaged in various ways; such variables can impact on the overall assessment results within a school. Remarkable personal bests by individual students are easily overlooked when the public judge schools by their students' amalgamated grades. A critical political discourse and frequent political attempts to raise aspirations and attainment for all, using performativity measures, have also created tension between the comprehensive ideal and the perceived need to compete in a market system.

The ideal of equal access for children of all abilities and social classes has proved remarkably durable in a changing social and political climate, and comprehensive schooling is found in many areas of the country. For example, when small towns have need of only one school to serve the whole population, it makes sense to provide a school that every child can attend.

I could find no example of a Quaker comprehensive secondary school, although many Quakers send their children to their local comprehensive school and some Quakers teach in comprehensive schools. Should there

Janet Nicholls

now be some Quaker-run comprehensive schools? I will say more about that later when I consider free schools.

An emphasis on competitive access, with scholarships for academic success

Selection by intelligence testing at the age of 11 was most common from the late 1940s to the 1970s, via what became known as the 11-Plus, a system of selection that still exists in some local authority areas and is currently under renewed consideration. Within this system, children compete with their peers for a limited number of places at grammar schools in which there is an academic ethos.

During the 1950s and 1960s, most of the children who failed the 11-Plus went to a secondary modern school where the emphasis was on practical skills, the planned intermediate tier of technical schools having only existed in a few areas. In some cases, children from deprived backgrounds benefited from the opportunity of a grammar school education, but the system has been heavily criticized for reinforcing existing social inequalities, and the original 1940s ideal of parity of esteem between children irrespective of what school they attended now seems naive.

The 11-Plus as a national system was challenged by mounting evidence that assessment at the age of 11 was not only unreliable as a measure of ability but also poor in predicting a child's future performance. Boys' tendency to perform less well than girls in the 11-Plus was tackled in some areas by manipulating the results to provide a gender balance within grammar schools, the assumption being that boys would catch up later. Some areas went even further in creating more grammar school places for boys than for girls, and there were many other practical difficulties.[3] A gender-neutral system would have resulted in 11-year-old boys being disadvantaged, although some parents with the means to do so would inevitably pay for their children to be privately tutored in preparation for access to a selective school.

Between 1998 and 2017, there was an arbitrary, cross-party political consensus that banned the creation of new grammar schools. Discussions about increasing their number were revived in the Conservative Party *Manifesto* of 2017, which did not use the label of 'grammar schools' but stated that the next Conservative government would '... lift the ban on the establishment of selective schools' (Conservative Party, 2017: 48) and claimed that:

> ... official research shows that slightly more children from ordinary working class families attend selective schools as a percentage of

the school intake compared to non-selective schools. While the attainment gap between rich and poor pupils stands at 25 per cent across the country, at selective schools it falls to almost zero.

(ibid.: 50)

The research cited in the *Manifesto* was not referenced in the document, and other research findings continue to support counter-claims about the impact of selective education. For example, researchers working for the independent Education Policy Institute found that:

> ... pupils who attend selective schools are far less likely to be from deprived backgrounds than pupils across all state-funded secondary schools. In selective schools 2.5 per cent of pupils are eligible for free school meals in comparison to 13.2 per cent across all state-funded secondary schools. Similarly, pupils in selective schools are slightly less likely to have a first language other than English than pupils in the wider population (13.1 per cent compared to 15.7 per cent) and far less likely to have special educational needs (4.0 per cent compared to 12.7 per cent).
>
> (Andrews *et al.*, 2016: 22)

The Education Policy Institute researchers also compared pupils' achievement of five good GCSEs, including English and mathematics:

> In 2015, 96.7 per cent of pupils in selective schools achieved that standard, compared to 57.3 per cent in non-selective local authorities, 56.2 per cent in non-selective schools in partially selective local authorities and 47.7 per cent in non-selective schools in wholly selective local authorities. So, pupils who do not attend selective schools make less progress in partially-selective and wholly selective areas than in areas without selection.
>
> (ibid.: 29)

This sort of competitive selection by means of scholarships still exists in some parts of the country, sometimes resulting in grammar schools existing side by side with schools that are labelled, inaccurately, 'comprehensive'. For example, selective schools still exist in Kent, Lincolnshire, Buckinghamshire, and Trafford in Greater Manchester. In 2015, the Kent and Medway area, which has retained and expanded its selective system, had the highest number of underachieving schools in the country – all of those being non-grammar schools. The evidence is clear, in Kent at least, that the system does not work to the overall benefit of students.

A selective system still operates in Northern Ireland, where politicians take opposing positions about the issue along party lines. Friends' School Lisburn, in Northern Ireland, is a Quaker grammar school admitting children who are selected by an examination and funded by their local authorities.

An emphasis on a parentocracy: Competition between parents

The idea of a competition between parents in an educational market has been generated by successive Labour, Coalition and Conservative governments and seems to have become normalized thinking in the early twenty-first century. In this competitive economic system, parental choice is seen as a natural and fundamental right, with access to individual state schools determined by parental influence rather than solely by the child's abilities. The assumption is that parents will know what is best for their children, that they should not have their choices stifled by the decisions of bureaucrats, and that economic laws of supply and demand will mean that educational provision will fit the consumers' requirements.

This recent emphasis on school choice has been a worldwide trend, although, as Forsey *et al.* (2008) discovered, it has spread unevenly and been interpreted differently within local contexts and according to party politics. In the UK, where the assemblies in Scotland, Wales and Northern Ireland have responsibilities for their own school systems, we can see that the impact of the quasi-market has varied according to the region's cultural and political climate.

Critics of the quasi-market system have claimed that it favours affluent and/or assertive parents and those who can move to a prestigious catchment area to take advantage of what is seen by some as 'selection by mortgage' (Gorard *et al.*, 2003). In this respect, Quaker concerns in 'Every person is precious' (QVinE, 2014), about 'children and young people being treated as economic units' and its recommendation that 'the educational disadvantages of poverty need compensation in schools', may be seen as swimming against the current educational tide.

In keeping with this quasi-market, many state schools in England have shifted from LEA control and been put into the hands of private companies or charities as academies or free schools. These labels encompass a wide range of schools, including comprehensives, grammar schools, schools specializing in particular subject areas (for example, technology, business, sport or languages) and schools aligned to particular religions. The range of schools in the marketplace could hardly be wider, but parents may still find that the sort of education they want for their children is not available within a reasonable commuting distance. For example, they may want their child's interests and abilities in the sciences to be cultivated but find that the nearest school is an academy specializing in the arts. There may also be problems in accommodating an 11-year-old child's wishes to go to the same school as friends made in his or her primary school.

Academy status for state schools was originally introduced by a Labour government for those schools in need of urgent improvement, but, since then, other schools have been given extra funding to convert to academies. Conservative governments have been particularly enthusiastic about this shift, which separates schools from the control of LEAs and puts them under the control of independent trusts (sometimes in multi-academy trusts). The label of 'academy' therefore relates to who controls and funds the school rather than to the type of school being controlled. Although they have some of the freedoms of private schools, they are expected to be socially comprehensive. This means they are required to follow the Admissions Code, which obliges academies, as well as local authorities, to ensure fair access to schooling for all pupils. The aforementioned report by the Academies Commission stated that there were some 'stunning successes' but also some problems: 'Numerous submissions to the Commission suggest some academies are finding methods to select covertly ...' (Academies Commission, 2013: 65). Furthermore: 'There is evidence that schools that control their own admissions are more likely to be socially selective than community schools' (ibid.).

Free schools are also becoming more common. According to the Department for Education:

> Free schools are funded by the government but aren't run by the local council. They have more control over how they do things. They're 'all-ability' schools, so can't use academic selection processes like a grammar school. Free schools can: set their own pay and conditions for staff, change the length of school terms and the school day. They don't have to follow the national curriculum. ... Free schools are run on a not-for-profit basis and can be set up by groups like: charities, universities, independent schools, community and faith groups, teachers, parents, businesses.
>
> (DfE, 2017b)

As with other types of school, free schools have their critics and there are concerns that they may 'socially select' pupils. Researchers at the Education Policy Institute (Green et al., 2015) found that free schools were more likely to open in deprived neighbourhoods but were less likely than other schools to take children who were eligible for free school meals. Between 2011 and 2014, for example, 15 per cent of pupils in Years 1 to 3 at free schools were entitled to free school meals, compared with 21 per cent in the schools' neighbourhoods as a whole and 18 per cent nationally.

About 21 per cent of free schools are designated to a particular faith, whereas about 34 per cent of all state schools have a religious character. Free schools could therefore provide a way for Quaker schools to get more involved in state education, and as I write there are discussions among Friends about movement in that direction.

An emphasis on private schooling outside the state system

Most parents (including Quakers) have to join the scramble with other parents in the educational marketplace, but some have been able to drop out of the state system in one of two ways.

Some parents who have not found a local school to suit their needs or values have joined others in home-schooling their children and have found an impressive array of resources to help them (DfE, 2017a). Although home-schooling does not have to follow the National Curriculum, parents must ensure that their child receives a full-time education from the age of 5. Widespread access to books, websites, television and film means that there has never been a better time for parents to educate their own children (see Keir Mitchell's chapter). LEAs can also provide some help, particularly if a child has special educational needs. Formalities for dropping out of the state system in this way involve writing to the child's headteacher, who must accept if the child is being removed from the school completely, but can refuse if the parents want to send their child to the school for some of the time. The obvious problems with the home-schooling option are that most parents have to prioritize their paid work and/or other commitments or they lack the necessary confidence to take an apparently radical step.

Other parents have been able to obtain places for their children at private schools, either because they can afford the full fees or they are able to get a bursary to contribute towards them. Although private schools are competing with some outstanding state schools, their main strength lies in the small size of their classes and the resulting extra attention from teachers, who face less pressure than their counterparts in the state system. Private schools are likely to be found in affluent areas with particularly pleasant surroundings, plenty of space and excellent facilities. It is also likely that the high status of a school will be reflected in its pupils' levels of confidence and self-esteem.

It would still be wrong for parents to assume that the education provided in a private school is inevitably superior to that in a state school. A relative lack of accountability to government systems may mean that the standard of teaching in a private school is actually lower than in a state school. There may be a narrower range of subject areas than that found in larger state schools and there has been a traditional tendency for private schools to emphasize academic subjects at the expense of more vocational subjects and life skills. Some parents may find that schools in the state system are better equipped to address their children's special educational needs. Private schools are also criticized for not providing a healthy social environment in which children from many backgrounds can mix and learn together.

An emphasis on providing more help for those already advantaged

In the UK, there is a well-established, self-perpetuating cycle of high-achieving adults being able to buy privileged education for their equally high-achieving children. Their confidence and the useful contacts made at school have led the privately educated to be over-represented in the British political system, as well as in the upper levels of the judiciary, finance and other influential and well-paid positions (evidenced in books by Dorling, 2017, and Atkinson, 2015, both of which point to current educational provision as perpetuating privilege).

The problem when considering equality and the market for private education is that most parents are severely constrained by their personal finances. A cursory look at incomes indicates that no amount of careful budgeting would help more families to live in a desirable catchment area or pay fees for a school outside the state system. The median average full-time wage in 2016 was about £28,000 per annum,[4] while fees for just *one* child to attend a private school on a daily basis could be half that amount or more. If part-time workers and those living on benefits were added to the half of full-timers who were below that median wage, it could be seen that most of the population had an annual income well below £28,000.

Most schools that are formally associated with the Society of Friends in Britain are private schools and accessed by parents who can pay fees or can have fees supplemented by a scholarship or bursary, based on their child's existing outstanding achievements in specific subjects. Scholarships typically contribute from 5 per cent to 10 per cent of the school's day fees and entitle schools to claim to the Charity Commission that they have a charitable remit, which entitles them to tax exemptions. However, most British Quaker schools tend to be very expensive,[5] and some of them are regarded as 'public schools' – that is, the elite of all private schools by virtue of membership of the Headmasters' and Headmistresses' Conference. Their high fees are defended as a response to the sort of financial pressures experienced by most private schools, but personal choice or impediments in access to such schools have resulted in very few of their pupils and staff being Quakers, while increasing numbers of pupils have come from other faiths and other countries. At the time of writing, in the seven nominally Quaker secondary schools, only 11 teachers belong to the Society of Friends and only 48 pupils are from Quaker families, 33 of whom are supported by bursaries for various reasons. What, then, makes these schools Quaker?

Quaker schools were established before the provision of state schools in the nineteenth century, and were then regarded as progressive in providing education equally for Quaker boys and girls. With the advance of universal education, most Quaker schools closed, but some have remained and become institutions largely for those who are already advantaged. They still maintain a commitment to Quaker values (Newton, 2016), although some interpretations of equality have become problematic. The Quaker testimony of equality is still expressed as valuing the good in everyone and leading a life that benefits society as a whole. Quaker schools also provide an environment in which the other Quaker testimonies of peace, truth and simplicity are taught and valued, and quiet moments are provided each day for worship, stillness or reflection.

There has been no agreement about how to tackle some Quakers' concerns about how expensive private schools fit, or don't fit, within the Quaker testimony on equality. In any case, nearly all Quaker schools are totally independent of the Religious Society of Friends, which is not in a position to dictate to them corporately about their governance or values. All of them have a responsible body of (usually Quaker) governors but they tend to be linked to different Quaker Area Meetings and independent of each other, and it would be difficult for the national Quaker Yearly Meeting to initiate changes to the schools without their agreement. Schools with an illustrious history of educational provision, and with a strong, supportive sense of community, are hardly likely to agree to their own demise, although recent changes in the state system may have generated opportunities for the integration of some private Quaker schools within the state system or for the creation of new Quaker free schools.

Discussion: Personal beliefs and actions

This review of options and school systems, and application of an exploratory model, may leave us wondering if equality means anything at all with regard to personal and political decisions about school systems and the scramble for school places. The desire to make the right decisions for our own children can unintentionally skew opportunities for others. In a world in which resources are scarce, should the educationally disadvantaged or advantaged take priority? Should success for some take priority over access for all? Should parents who cannot afford to pay have any choice in school access? The various perspectives about equality in schooling do not seem to provide an easy answer to accommodate the values of all Quakers. Maybe the most obvious conclusion is that Quakers' statement that 'every person is precious' is incompatible with a system in which the most privileged children become more privileged and the most disadvantaged become more disadvantaged. This leaves parents, governors, teachers and others involved in education to decide whether to accept the inequalities of provision that currently exist in such a fragmented system or swim against the tide of inequality.

Any such shift away from acceptance would include enhancing the self-awareness of all (Quakers and non-Quakers) who are involved in the education system. For example, the Academies Commission (2013) cited evidence from David Braybook, a consultant for special educational needs who 'observed covert practices of steering SEN pupils toward other schools, along the lines of "This school is not for you. Your child would be happier elsewhere"' (2013: 74). Similarly, the Academies Commission cited a study by the ISOS Partnership, which concluded that 'effective engagement with Fair Access arrangements depended more on the commitment of individual headteachers and governors than on the type of school (academy or otherwise)' (2013: 71).

Lack of engagement with the issues raised here means that the absence of equality from public discourse leads education further and further away from serving the needs of all of our children. It also means that the anomalous position of privately funded Quaker schools within the school marketplace becomes increasingly challenging to Quaker values. Moreover, doing nothing does not match many statements found in various Quaker readings. For example, the following quotes can be found in *Twelve Quakers and Equality*:

> We try to have no regard to social status or any of those other criteria which come so easily to our minds, and can lead us to discriminate between people.
>
> (Quaker Quest, 2007: 12)

> I should check if I am seeking my advantage at another's cost, or who is really paying for my standard of living.
>
> (ibid.: 18)
>
> Gandhi advised that before taking actions we should consider their effect on the poorest people in society.
>
> (ibid.: 19)

Swimming with the tide may be the most comfortable response, but Quakers have not always taken the comfortable option. In the seventeenth century, George Fox and early Friends challenged hitherto unquestioned assumptions behind social inequalities and spoke 'truth to power' – when doing so meant they could not only have been labelled crazy upstarts but also have lost their liberty or even their lives. In the twenty-first-century scramble for school places, parents must work out issues within a public discourse that presents a good quality of education as a scarce resource and a school place for their child as something for which they have to compete against other parents. Quakers have to work with their own consciences and let their lives speak (QF&P, 1.02, 27).

Individuals and groups can strive to influence policies as parents, teachers, school governors, members of various action groups or in other capacities. An example could be seen in March 2015 when more than 80 Quaker meetings across Britain took part in a Week of Action to demand greater political action to tackle inequality. Their activities included vigils and other events, highlighting their concerns to the media, and putting pressure on local authorities, councillors and parliamentary candidates. Doing something, therefore, involves confronting the issue of equality and education or at least maintaining a place for it in public discourse. For Quakers it also involves critical reflection on their personal beliefs. Susan Rooke-Matthews (1993) expressed concern that Quakers had an image of being a 'white, middle-class, well-educated group of heterosexual people, preferably in stable marriages with children that behave in socially acceptable ways' (Rooke-Matthews, 1993, 953: QF&P, 23.46) and that people who did not fit that image might feel marginalized. Among the lengthy concerns that she associated with this perception, she observed that:

> ... many problems faced by a large proportion of people are seen as separate: people who are poor, facing oppression, living in poor housing, experiencing prejudice are 'others'. This enables us to be very caring but distant (and sometimes patronising) and

also makes it difficult to be conscious of prejudice behind some of the normally accepted assumptions of our society/Society.

(ibid.)

She continues:

> Until we as the Religious Society begin to question our assumptions, until we look at the prejudices, often very deeply hidden, within our own Society, how are we going to be able to confront the inequalities within the wider society? We are very good at feeling bad about injustice, we put a lot of energy into sticking-plaster activity ... but we are not having any effect in challenging the causes of inequality and oppression. I do sometimes wonder if this is because we are not able to do this within and amongst ourselves.
>
> (ibid.)

We can reflect carefully on our personal beliefs and actions, even when choices are constrained by their social, economic and political contexts.

Perhaps one way of making sense of the myriad of competing assumptions about equality and schooling described in this chapter involves reflecting on what education could be teaching future generations. It may provide some children with an impressive list of qualifications, and even help them to achieve remarkable careers, but if it has not instilled compassion for the least fortunate in society then it has not provided one of life's most precious lessons: the importance of not forgetting those who are trodden underfoot in the scramble.

Notes

[1] When Friends' (Quaker) schools started to be established in the seventeenth century, they could be seen as champions of equality, providing education for children who would otherwise be denied it. Quakers at that time operated like an unorthodox society, within the more socially acceptable wider society, in which mixing socially, or being educated alongside non-Quakers, was not encouraged for fear of contamination. Today's Quaker or Friends' schools operate independently of the Yearly Meeting of the Religious Society of Friends, but most of their governors or trustees are Quakers and many have Friends who sit on General Councils. Some Quaker schools report to a general meeting, which is open to all Friends in Membership and to others who are invited. Some Quaker schools also report to local area meetings of Quakers, although the schools are autonomous in their own day-to-day running. The Yearly Meeting recently ended its uniquely close link with Ackworth School, in West Yorkshire, when it ceased to be the body that appointed the school's governing body.

[2] See: Glebe House Children's Home, *Statement of Purpose* (January 2016: 3). Online. www.ftctrust.org.uk/imgstore/ftct_sop.pdf (accessed 12 March 2018).

[3] In 1988, the Court of Appeal found Birmingham City Council guilty of sex discrimination, because in Birmingham there were a total of 520 grammar school places available for boys and only 360 such places available for girls. Regional disparities in the number of grammar school places elsewhere also made it more difficult to 'pass' the 11-Plus in some areas than others. When a fixed number of grammar school places is combined with varying standards of cohort performance, it is possible for a child to 'fail' the 11-Plus one year with a score that would have provided a 'pass' the next year.

[4] Comparisons between the incomes of men and women working full time and without overtime consistently report that women earn an average of about £100 less per week than men. The median average income of £28,000 is calculated from the incomes of both men and women (ONS, 2016).

[5] Fees for Quaker schools in 2017 varied from £13,383 per annum for day pupils aged 11 and over and £26,256 per annum for boarders aged 11 and over (both at Ackworth School in West Yorkshire) to £21,654 per annum for day pupils aged 11 and over and £34,044 for boarders aged 11 and over (at Leighton Park School in Reading). Costs for children of primary school age at these Quaker schools tend to be lower and costs for sixth formers tend to be higher. Extra charges are usually made in the form of acceptance and registration fees and for such extras as the costs of instrumental music lessons. These Quaker schools provide a limited number of means-tested bursaries of between 50 per cent and 100 per cent of fees, which may be varied up or down during the child's time in the school, in line with changes in their parents' incomes.

References

Academies Commission (2013) *Unleashing Greatness: Getting the best from an academised system*. London: RSA/Pearson. Online. http://www.educationengland.org.uk/documents/pdfs/2013-academies-commission.pdf (accessed 14 March 2018).

Andrews, J., Hutchinson, J. and Johnes, R. (2016) *Grammar Schools and Social Mobility*. London: Education Policy Institute.

Atkinson, A.B. (2015) *Inequality: What can be done?* Cambridge, MA: Harvard University Press.

Boswell, G., Wedge, P., Moseley, A., Dominey, J. and Poland, F. (2014) *Treating Sexually Harmful Teenage Males: A longitudinal evaluation of a therapeutic community*. Norwich: University of East Anglia.

Conservative Party (2017) *Manifesto*. Online. www.conservatives.com/manifesto (accessed 14 March 2018).

DfE (Department for Education) (2016) *Admissions Appeals for Maintained and Academy Primary and Secondary Schools in England: 2015 to 2016* (SFR 40/2016). London: Department for Education. Online. www.gov.uk/government/uploads/system/uploads/attachment_data/file/551936/SFR40_2016_Appeals_Text.pdf (accessed 5 February 2018).

DfE (Department for Education) (2017a) 'Home education'. Online. www.gov.uk/home-education (accessed 26 November 2017).

DfE (Department for Education) (2017b) 'Types of school: Free schools'. Online. www.gov.uk/types-of-school/free-schools (accessed 7 December 2017).

Dorling, D. (2017) *The Equality Effect: Improving life for everyone*. Oxford: New Internationalist.

Forsey, M., Davies, S. and Walford, G. (eds) (2008) *The Globalisation of School Choice?* Oxford: Symposium Books.

Gorard, S., Taylor, C. and Fitz, J. (2003) *Schools, Markets and Choice Policies.* London: RoutledgeFalmer.

Green, F., Allen, R. and Jenkins, A. (2015) 'Are free schools socially selective? A quantitative analysis'. *British Educational Research Journal*, 41 (6), 907–24.

Newton, N. (2016) 'Schools for Well-being: The educational significance of Quaker school culture – based on a mixed methods study in secondary level Quaker schools in England'. PhD thesis. Online. http://ethos.bl.uk/OrderDetails.do?uin=uk.bl.ethos.730837 (accessed 1 March 2018).

ONS (Office for National Statistics) (2016) *Annual Survey of Hours and Earnings: 2016 provisional results* (Statistical Bulletin). London: Office for National Statistics. Online. www.ons.gov.uk/employmentandlabourmarket/peopleinwork/earningsandworkinghours/bulletins/annualsurveyofhoursandearnings/2016provisionalresults/pdf (accessed 5 February 2018).

Plowden, B. (1967) *Children and Their Primary Schools: A report of the Central Advisory Council for Education (England).* London: HMSO.

Quaker Quest (2007) *Twelve Quakers and Equality* (Pamphlet 7). London: Quaker Quest.

QVinE (Quaker Values in Education Group) (2014) 'Welcome to the Quaker Values in Education Group'. Online. www.qvine.org.uk (accessed 26 November 2017).

Rooke-Matthews, S. (1993) Letter, *The Friend*, 151.

Wainwright, M. (2007) 'In search of lost boys'. *The Guardian*, 13 February. Online. www.theguardian.com/education/2007/feb/13/schools.specialeducationneeds (accessed 25 January 2018).

Chapter 10

Reflecting on values emerging from practice and the value of reflecting on practice

John Mason

Looking back over my career in education, it is possible to detect certain developments in the way I work, whether with learners, teachers or colleagues. At the time, these were – at least for me – mostly below the surface. However, over time, as I have tried to articulate various practices so as to be able to draw attention to them as possibilities for others, I have become increasingly aware of how those practices focus on (and are based on) what I value in terms of fostering and sustaining the development of, in my case, mathematical thinking. However, I suspect that they apply in some form or other to all subjects or disciplines, whether in school or university or in less formal educational contexts.

Offering practices to others, whether experientially or in some more explicit form, always runs the risk that they will be adopted superficially, simply by going through the motions. In my experience, it seems that effective adoption of practices requires bringing what one values in the way of learner behaviour into alignment with what underpins those practices.

My aim in this chapter is to bring to the surface various values that are behind some of the practices of which I am aware, and to draw on these to consider both the value of reflecting on my own actions and the value of getting learners to reflect on their actions. It turns out that these detected values are in alignment with Quaker values. Indeed much of what attracted me to Quakers is that alignment! Writing this chapter has brought about further awareness of that alignment.

I begin with some practices that have become established components of the way I see myself interacting with learners and colleagues. Each begins with a short description of some pedagogic action or actions, followed by some historical remarks about how I recall becoming aware of them as practices. That is followed by a reflection on what it seems to me is being valued. At the end, I align these with Quaker values, as expressed by others. Perhaps the most obvious and self-referent example is the value I place on respecting learners as learners, by providing time and stimulus for reflection on experience.

Practices

I offer here descriptions of some pedagogical actions of which I am aware, together with some historical recollections and an attempt to identify what it is that I value in those practices.

Conjecturing and convincing

When I meet a group for the first time, I stress that everything said by them or by me is to be treated as a conjecture. It must either be tested in experience if it is about pedagogy, or by finding a convincing justification or counter-example if it is knowledge-based. Everything is said (or done) with the intention of modifying conjectures as necessary. I even praise the first few times someone modifies their conjecture, signalling modification as an instance of disciplinary thinking.

I urge those who are confident about their thinking to listen carefully to others, offering suggestions or counter-examples, or asking questions that might help redirect attention appropriately according to their thinking. I urge those who are unsure not to hold back, but rather to try to express what they are thinking so that they can separate themselves from the conjecture, consider it dispassionately and modify it as seems necessary.

As a graduate student I encountered a film called *Let Us Teach Guessing* (1965) featuring George Pólya teaching some prospective high school teachers. It released in me a way of working that only later did I realize had been what I experienced in high school with my mathematics teacher, Geoff Steele. First and foremost is the importance of establishing a conjecturing atmosphere. I do not know when or how this became such a core part of my ways of working with people, but I always stress two things: firstly, participants in workshops must not believe anything I say and, secondly, that proper 'thinking' only really starts when people make and then modify their conjecture.

In a conjecturing atmosphere, no one is ever 'wrong', but it may be that their conjecture needs modifying. It is the conjecture, not the person, that is being judged. Learners can be praised for making a conjecture, without passing judgement on the appropriateness of that conjecture. Others may offer possible counter-examples, or ask questions, or even propose or invite modifications to the conjecture. The interaction becomes collaborative rather than competitive, because the justifiability of a conjecture is not an

John Mason

indication of an individual's prowess. The purpose of making a conjecture is to examine it critically and then to modify it appropriately.

Mathematics is often associated with right/wrong answers, when in fact it is more usefully and practically seen as a comprehensive way of perceiving and thinking about the world, featuring opportunities for experiencing a flow of creative energy. Insights and 'bright ideas' are but one manifestation of access to creative energy and are best treated as conjectures. Conjecturing and convincing are two of the natural powers that all learners possess. So mathematics can be experienced as a domain in which to develop and refine those powers (see also Anne Watson's chapter).

I soon discovered the positive benefits of developing an ethos in the classroom in which learners treat everything that is said, whether by me or by others, as conjectures. The purpose of making a conjecture is to try to express what one is thinking to get it 'outside of oneself' and then modifying as seems necessary. I noticed that when I tried to keep a thought inside me until I was sure it was correct, it was like clothes in a tumble drier: thoughts went round and round, sometimes changing, sometimes stuck in a ball. By externalizing a thought, it becomes available to be looked at dispassionately, to be considered in repose, without commitment. As Pólya (1965) says, 'make a conjecture but do not believe your conjecture'.

The flip side of conjecturing lies in convincing yourself, then a friend, then a sceptic, who by their questions can assist in refining your articulation. A good deal about justifying conjectures can be learnt by developing appropriate scepticism towards other people's reasoning. It has long been my practice to resist confirming or refuting learners' conjectures, because this reinforces their dependency on me in particular, and on textbooks and other teachers in general, for judging the correctness of their thinking. One of the really important transitions in upper primary and lower secondary students is from a belief that truth (correctness) resides in adults, to an understanding that truth resides within disciplines and through reasoning. It lies in consistency and coherence within the discipline through adopting the established methods of justifying and validating claims according to that discipline.

WHAT I VALUE

What I value is learners developing their thinking, making and refuting conjectures, modifying them and attempting to justify them. All participants are equal in this respect, even though not all conjectures are of equal validity. I find that the only way to develop a particular manner of thinking is to engage with that thinking myself; and the only way to sensitize myself to what it is to be a learner is to be exploring and learning myself.

Doing for learners only what they cannot yet do for themselves

I try my best, not always successfully by any means, to do for learners only what they cannot yet do for themselves. To do otherwise is to usurp the use of their own powers, which can block the impetus for learners to make real personal connection with the current topic and activity. This means holding back and allowing learners to struggle to express themselves. It also means making the effort to hear what they are *trying* to express rather than assuming that what is *actually* expressed is their best thinking.

Another version is to refuse to confirm or deny learners' answers to questions. I tell them that *they* are collectively responsible for answers, while *my* attention is on the processes.

I don't now know when I became aware of doing this, or at least trying to. My awareness of it as a useful principle gradually emerged over a long period of time. It certainly came to the fore when various forms of constructivism became a focus in education. To prompt and support learners in constructing meaning for themselves, whether collectively or individually or both, involves getting out of their way, letting them do what they need to do to learn effectively. It involves respecting them as learners. I cannot do the learning for them, tempting as it is sometimes to try, urged on by the merciless pressure of time!

A conjecturing ethos includes trying not to do things for learners that they can already do for themselves. Sometimes it is painful to watch them struggle and sometimes it is appropriate to demonstrate a different way of thinking, a different focus of attention, but on the whole I try not to intervene. I must, for example, respect a learner's choice not to engage, as long as that is an informed choice. Every act of a teacher is an intervention in the flow of learner experience and intervention can all too easily turn into interference. This is not to say that the learner has to struggle to reconstruct the whole of a topic for themselves, but great care is needed to direct attention appropriately and to provide space and time for personal reconstruction.

WHAT I VALUE

Acknowledging the natural powers of another human being is a small but significant part of 'acknowledging that of God' in them; it is their birthright. When I am tempted to try to do the thinking for learners, tempted to make use of my powers rather than prompting them to use their own, I am at best

John Mason

creating dependency and at worst usurping their powers and even indicating that those powers are not wanted in my classroom. This is disrespectful.

All of this depends on prompting and supporting learners to take initiative.

Taking initiative

I expect and intend that learners will take initiative rather than wait passively for some action to be cued. When they ask for help because they are stuck, I am as likely to ask them 'what question am I going to ask you?' as I am to ask a directive question or offer a prompt for further action. This, for me, is the essence of 'scaffolding and fading' – that is, the process of giving pedagogic support but gradually removing it as learners become competent (Seely Brown *et al.*, 1989; Love and Mason, 1992).

When I began tutoring, I soon realized that people often had no idea of what to do when they were stuck, so drawing on my own experience and on the articulations of George Pólya (1962), I emphasized ways in which learners can take initiative. First, they can construct or seek out particular examples or special cases (*specializing*), which helps to get a sense of underlying structural relationships. Second, they can attempt to express these as general properties (*generalizing*) being instantiated in the particular example. This developed through extending and varying routine problems or exercises, in which learners constructed examples and near-examples of concepts for themselves, to posing their own problems arising from situations they had encountered, whether in the material world or in the world of mathematics itself.

I use the terms *assenting* and *asserting* to distinguish between, on the one hand, behaviour in which learners wait until they know exactly what they are supposed to do before acting, and, on the other hand, taking initiative to make conjectures and to anticipate what might be coming next (Mason, 2009). Learners content to assent to what happens in class are much less likely to succeed on subsequent tests than those who make conjectures, who assert and then test and check their assertions. It is vital that learners and teachers alike are aware of the status of what they say and do, whether as guesses, intuitions, conjectures based on evidence, or conjectures that can be justified or substantiated.

WHAT I VALUE

I value learners taking initiative, drawing on energy from their own desires and will, rather than waiting passively for me to tell them exactly what to do. This applies equally to working on novel problems, to practising skills through doing exercises and to appreciating and comprehending new concepts.

Taking initiative as something to encourage developed, for me, through the experience of trying to get learners to make choices for themselves about how they worked and on what.

Making choices

I try to get learners to make choices, especially choices that can become significant. Thus, I expect them to develop a personal narrative concerning a situation, phenomenon or event that needs to be explained or exemplified. In mathematics, I might ask someone to choose a letter to be used as the preferred variable name for the lesson instead of the usual 'x' (not very profound, but effective nevertheless); I may ask someone for a particular example to use as a worked example for the topic; I expect them to choose, from a set of exercises or questions, which ones they feel they need to do to appreciate and comprehend the general class of problems of that type. I have found that I engage learners by having them make some commitment to the activity through these choices, sometimes referred to as 'taking ownership'.

The cliché 'practice makes perfect' holds sufficient truth to keep it alive, generation after generation, but it is not always clear what is being practised. Allowing learners to choose which, and how many, tasks to work on enables them to take initiative in deciding when, and how much, to practise. Of course, they need to develop criteria for what constitutes 'sufficient practice' and they need to know how to recognize situations in which their fluency will be useful.

WHAT I VALUE

I value full participation. I value learners anticipating what is coming rather than struggling to catch up by, for example, copying notes from a screen. I also value learners trying to construct their own examples of concepts or problem types, so as to enrich the range of examples to which they have access for their specializing and generalizing – for their sense-making.

I value learners enriching their example space by identifying or constructing examples that have different features. I find it useful to follow Caleb Gattegno (1987), an educator of languages and mathematics, in thinking in terms of: *awareness,* as what an expert has that enables them to behave expertly; *awareness of awareness,* as what a teacher needs so they can intervene usefully; *awareness of awareness of awareness,* as what teacher educators require, so as to be able to work effectively with teachers and would-be teachers (Mason, 1998).

John Mason

Specializing and generalizing

I look for opportunities to state generalities, with the intention and expectation that learners will construct particular cases for themselves, to make sense of the general and re-generalize for themselves. I may offer specific instances of something with the intention that they then express a generality for themselves. Again, I expect and intend that they will check and modify their conjecture(s) as necessary.

I don't know when I began to enact these for myself, but it was, again, in the film by George Pólya that I recognized and became explicitly aware of them. Pólya's words 'specialize' and 'generalize' provided labels around which a variety of experiences could be clustered, with associated pedagogical actions or practices.

Generalizing is a natural human act. Even the foetus in the womb displays evidence of generalizing, when it responds similarly to similar outside forces. The neonate recognizes mother, no matter how she is dressed, what she is doing or what perfume she is using, which requires generalizing. A 2-year-old, having been given a doll that makes a variety of sounds when different parts of the body are squeezed, starts squeezing similar parts of the body of her new-born sister! Recognizing repetitions of situations or events involves generalizing, and is necessary for – indeed, it is the basis of – language. It is also essential for coping with the material world. To be respectful of learners behoves me to do everything I can to stimulate them to make use of their own powers within my discipline. 'Seeing the general through the particular' (that is, seeing the particular as an instance of something more general) and 'seeing the particular in the general' (that is, recognizing something particular as an instance of some more general principle) are both essential for our participation in human society.

One of the possible reasons that many people do not make use of their undoubted powers in the domain of mathematics may be that they have been induced to leave some of their powers at the classroom door. As long as textbooks continue to do most of the specializing and generalizing, there is little reason for learners to use their own powers. A teacher who, pressured by a drive for efficiency and visible effectiveness, is tempted to usurp learners' powers is actually likely to disempower learners and even to generate negative emotions associated with the subject matter. For other subjects, these effects may not be so strong, but it is still the case that if learners are not expected to, or allowed to, be themselves in a full sense in lessons (thinking, creating, generalizing, imagining) they are unlikely to enjoy learning.

What I value

The intricate interplay between specializing and generalizing, for me, is where I think sense-making – and hence appreciation and comprehension of concepts – actually takes place, in addition to letting ideas mature in the back of the mind while sleeping, and over time. I have often said that teaching takes place *in* time and learning takes place *over* time. Acts of teaching are about directing learner attention to what is salient; acts of learning are about strengthening neural connections and letting go of extraneous connections. Through specializing and generalizing for themselves, learners strengthen and develop their natural powers to do this, in preparation for having to use these capacities in the future, whether in mathematics or in some other context.

Imagining and expressing

I try to begin a new topic or task by inviting learners to imagine something. It may be a way of working that is perhaps a bit unusual, or it may be a specific mathematical situation or material-world situation that is to be thought about mathematically. When we have been imagining a mathematical situation (often a diagram), I then invite people to say to each other what they are 'seeing'.

When I took up my post as a lecturer at the Open University, I encountered a group of teachers and teacher educators who were working on mental imagery. I quickly saw how important my mental imagery was and I discovered how powerful it is to stimulate people to try to imagine things, whether in anticipation of imminent or of future action.

I build up the image verbally until people are desperate to depict what they are imagining. This, I conjecture, may help to release their power of depiction by increasing their desire. I then get them to express what they are experiencing in words, symbols, diagrams, gestures, rhythms – indeed in any art form (see also Janet Sturge's chapter in this book). To this end, I ask people to try to convey to each other what they are imagining, without using their hands. The idea is to get them to grapple with being more precise about their language, to 'say what they are seeing' so that others might be able to 'see what they are saying'.

What I value

One insight that has emerged for me relatively recently when thinking about forms of expression is the distinction between *babbling* (Malara and Navarra, 2003; Berger, 2006) and *gargling*. Babbling refers to the child in the cot making sequences of sounds that sound like a sentence but with no evident content. More generally, babbling refers to the attempt to express oneself in whatever medium or media, where the expression is jumbled, incomplete, inarticulate and not yet conforming to the expression of experts. This applies equally well to all structured forms of expression, whether in music, art or dance, as well as to words, such as, for example, a child making initial sounds with a musical instrument. By contrast, gargling refers to attempts to impress a teacher or other person by using technical terms in a superficial manner, without commitment or deep meaning.

Talking in pairs

When I notice that I have said something complicated, or perhaps a bit abstract, or when I have posed a problem for individual consideration, I often pause and invite learners to try to say to each other what they have comprehended.

I use *talking in pairs* as a regular practice in workshops, seminars and lectures. This practice merges with two frames that we used at the Open University in some of our courses for teachers: Do–Talk–Record and Manipulating–Construing–Articulating (Open University, 1982; see also Mason and Johnston-Wilder, 2006). The first of these emphasized that, to support learners in writing or making other records of their thinking, it is really helpful both for them to have something to do, whether with material objects, physical action or written symbols, and also to talk about what they are doing. The other frame draws attention to the purpose of 'doing', namely to make sense of what they are doing and to experience and express underlying relationships. In other words, learners need something specific to be doing and some goal or question to be addressing.

What I value

Again, what I value in this practice is the opportunity for learners to try to express themselves, because it is only through struggling to articulate that clarity emerges. As the well-known adage has it, 'you learn most by teaching'. That is, you learn most by expressing it to someone else.

Freezing (pausing)

When I ask learners a question to prompt them to think about something, I often 'freeze' by becoming motionless. This reduces the distractions induced by movement in peripheral vision and indicates that the question is about something important. At first I draw their attention to the freeze and ask them what they are doing and what they *could* be doing during that time. The purpose of this pause, as well as to consider what to do next, is to provide an opportunity for learners to reconstruct or review what has been happening and, in so doing, perhaps encounter some uncertainties that they can then ask about. So freezing, or pausing, becomes an invitation to seek clarification.

At some point I realized that I found it difficult to keep up with a torrent of talking from a teacher or tutor, and then I realized that learners might have difficulty keeping up with my torrents of articulation. Becoming articulate requires effort on the part of the learner and does not simply arise from being in the presence of an articulate teacher. I began to encourage learners to ask me to pause, to 'press the pause button' whenever they wish. Of course this takes time to develop, because people are reluctant to interfere. They think they are the only ones who are struggling to keep up.

One alternative approach is for me to use the 'pause button' myself when learners are expressing their thinking, reminding them that others may not be keeping up, so modelling requests for a pause. However, I also discovered that people often do not know what to do when I pause: some feel anxious, while others simply 'wait for something to happen', so I draw their attention to the possibility that they can take every opportunity to say to themselves what they think was just being said and I may even suggest trying to articulate it to others near them. That way, really sensible, productive questions can emerge.

I find that when I ask a question or invite learners to ponder something, their actions are often affected by where *my* attention is. So I developed the habit of deliberately freezing, so that no movement of mine would distract them.

WHAT I VALUE

I value time to reconstruct things for myself, to allow possible connections and associations to come to the fore. If I think learners would benefit from a similar action, I have to provide space, time and opportunity for it.

Speaking to experience

I trust participants in my sessions to work for themselves, to attend to what is important for them and to make of their experience what they can. In this way I respect them as learners. I try to work with people's experience, but to do this I need not only to have recent and relevant experience of my own, but also to be aware of that experience myself. Through being aware of my own experience I seem to be able to speak to the experience of others.

When I began working with teachers, I was immediately challenged as to whether I had 'walked in their shoes', whether I had myself been a teacher, when in fact I had never taught in schools. I soon overcame this lack by working hard at 'speaking to teachers' condition'. For this it is not necessary to have been a teacher, but to listen and learn and not to preach at teachers, especially on matters of specific detail about which I am ignorant. I work hard at describing only what I practise myself. I concentrate on mathematical thinking and associated pedagogical actions and not on managing behaviour, or covering a curriculum, or preparing for inspections or any other myriad concerns of day-to-day school life.

WHAT I VALUE

I value the undoubted prior experience of learners using, and having used, their own natural powers. Underpinning this is the conviction that everyone could think mathematically if they could use those powers appropriately. I value personal experience of teaching and learning as a major source of knowledge. But learning from experience does not often happen by itself: some further action is usually required.

Reflecting on experience

I end every lecture, workshop and class with a few moments during which I invite participants to consider what struck them during the session: the main points for them; dominant emotions evoked; actions they might want to try out for themselves in the future; initiatives they might take; what to look out for in the future; what to pay particular attention to in the future; what aspects of their teaching require particular care.

Each of these probes refers to an aspect of the human psyche (cognition, affect, enaction, will, witness, attention and conscience). It is my belief that, unless the whole of the human psyche is engaged, learning is going to be, at best, partial. For a long time, I focused explicitly on the traditional aspects of the psyche (cognition, affect and enaction) and only implicitly on the other four, without realizing that they are equally important and significant.

At one point I coined the expression for myself 'One thing that we do not seem to learn from experience, is that we do not often learn from experience alone'. Something more is required, and that 'more' is reflection. Not simply thinking back, but intentionally bringing to mind specific incidents, extracting useful actions or cautions for the future, and then imagining myself in the future acting differently in a similar situation.

WHAT I VALUE

I value providing myself opportunities and sufficient energy to reflect on recent experience to imagine possible future actions and to remember to offer learners similar opportunities. Explaining to yourself, reconstructing in your own words, developing inner incantations to accompany practices so as to internalize them – these are all forms of effective reflection that make a vital contribution to the maturation process known as 'learning'.

Underlying values

These reflections on the values underpinning my practices have reminded me that I begin with the assumption that everyone can think mathematically if they choose to do so. Over time, I developed a way of articulating this, at first in the language of *processes* involved in thinking mathematically (Mason *et al.*, 1982) and more recently recast as getting learners to make use of, and to develop, their natural powers. This is no new idea, being found in the writings of various philosophers such as Alfred North Whitehead (1932), Caleb Gattegno (1970) and others.

Creating a conjecturing atmosphere and supporting learners in making, testing, modifying and justifying their conjectures have much in common with being a seeker after spiritual truth. A conjecturing atmosphere depends on everyone listening and observing attentively, not simply to what is said and done, but to what might be behind those manifestations generating them. This aligns with Quaker values, for ministry is not truth, but a manifestation of attempts to be in touch with 'the spirit'. As such, every act of ministry is a conjecture.

As Quakers, we are advised to 'Think it possible that [we] may be mistaken' (*QF&P*, 1.02, 17), but we are also advised to consider carefully before ministering whether what we might say really needs to be said. Yet there are strong alignments:

> A Friends' Meeting for Worship finds no room for debate or for answering (still less for contradicting) one another; if this is desirable, it will be left for another occasion.
> (Brayshaw, 1921, 103: *QF&P*, 2.69)

> ... [being part of a meeting and taken beyond it] can only be done if there is a willingness to be led by each of the ones ministering into a deeper level of what they were not only saying but what they were meaning to say, and perhaps even beyond into what something beneath us all was meaning to have said through what we were saying.
> (Steere, 1872, 11: *QF&P*, 2.70)

> The intent of all speaking is to bring into the life, and to walk in, and to possess the same, and to live in and enjoy it, and to feel God's presence.
> (Fox, 1657, 103: *QF&P*, 2.73)

John Mason

I find that George Fox's assertion applies to the classroom, lecture hall and tutorial just as it does to a meeting for worship:

> When language is used unthinkingly, without being related to the experience of either the speaker or the listener, it is meaningless. Words are only symbols and when there is no shared experience the symbolism breaks down. When we speak of our own experience, our feelings are always involved. The same is true when we listen to others: we may read into their words meanings which are not intended but which reflect our own emotions ... The more important and profound the subject matter, the greater the need for sensitivity in choosing our words.
> (Conference: *Exploring the fundamental elements of Quakerism*, 1986: QF&P, 2.63)

But the notion of a conjecturing ethos in a classroom might therefore be seen to contradict the avoidance of debate; my practice is to urge participants to try to articulate what is not yet quite clear for them and to restate what others have said, in their own words. Yet Quaker Advice 13 offers 'Do not let a sense of your own unworthiness hold you back,' while Quaker Advice 15 asks: 'Are you prepared to let your insights and personal wishes take their place alongside those of others or be set aside as the meeting seeks the right way forward?'. In other words, 'don't believe your conjecture', but test it in the light of what others say. Quaker Advice 11 also applies: 'When you recognise your shortcomings, do not let that discourage you.'

It is a positive event when your conjecture needs modifying, because there is the possibility for both individual and collective growth. Maintaining a conjecturing atmosphere in the way in which one responds to the conjectures of others can be seen as a version of Quaker Advice 3: 'Hold yourself and others in the Light, knowing that all are cherished by God.'

Underpinning the use of prompts to imagine and express is a recognition that people have much richer and more extensive inner experiences than can ever be articulated in public. The power to imagine is the basis for planning and the channel through which it is possible to make contact with a source of creative energy that has parallels in the effect of regular participation in Quaker meetings for worship – 'that inner space of various kinds has called my attention and has been a large and enlivening place' (Holdsworth, 1985, 10: QF&P, 26.28).

An important connection for me with Quaker values lies in developing sensitivity to what people are trying to express, rather than taking their words (or other expressions) at face value as being exactly what is intended.

Different people express similar experiences in very different vocabulary, and what matters is the experience, not the utterance. By encouraging people to speak from their experience rather than from imagined generalities (a Quaker value), others are enabled to hear behind the words, to see behind the display something of what is generating that expression, something of what is being imagined. Conflict often arises not from hearing or seeing what is generating the expression, but rather by being triggered by differences in how it is expressed compared with how one might express oneself or to what one is accustomed to or expecting.

Many teachers have found that getting learners *talking in pairs* or small groups has the effect of releasing contributions from learners who otherwise might be reluctant to expose their ideas publicly and in a large group. I see this as one way of easing people into ministry in a Quaker context, perhaps by participating in discussion groups held in a worship-sharing manner.

Teaching as a caringly respectful profession

I spent some twenty years writing a book about the ways of working that we developed at the Open University, namely the *discipline of noticing* (Mason, 2002). It was my reconstruction of a single lecture by Bennett (1976) translated into the teaching of mathematics, but I soon realized that it applied to any caring profession, of which teaching is but one. At its core is the adage that 'I cannot change others; what I can do is work at changing myself'.

The book outlines a method of turning reflection on one's practice into a discipline, which can be used as a research method, as professional development or as personal awakening. At its core, it describes techniques for awakening oneself to notice – and to exploit that noticing so as to alter one's behaviour in the future. All of this I consider consistent with, and in alignment with, the Quaker notion of transformation (Dandelion, 2014).

The difficulty is that the teacher needs to maintain a balance between caring for the learner and caring for the subject. Putting *all* one's attention on the learner, trying to ease their passage into a complex topic, is just as unhelpful as putting all one's attention on the subject matter so as to convey it in its clearest and purest form. Neither extreme does justice to the learner or the subject. Neither calls upon inherent powers. As the saying goes, 'every stick has two ends'. Working with only one leaves the other end wagging about dangerously.

Care for the learner can mean sometimes not giving answers, or even feedback, to reduce dependency on the teacher. Caring for the subject or topic can mean not trying to reveal all the beauty and complexity of which the teacher is aware when learners are not yet ready. Anne Watson writes more about this in Chapter 6.

For me, caring for learners begins with respecting each individual, assuming that they have the intention to seek truth. It means seeing each learner as possessing enormous powers – powers that can be deployed in many different contexts and that may need to be honed and developed. This way of seeing acknowledges 'the powers of ordinary men and women; in their immense potentialities; in their capacity to rise higher than themselves; in their essential creativeness' (Tanner, 1989, 3: *QF&P*, 21.36).

Caring for learners includes promoting (even provoking) withdrawal from action, followed by reflection on that action, to learn from experience. For example, pausing and remaining outwardly and inwardly still provides a brief respite for learners and even contributes to an implicit stillness for them. Quaker practices are centred around experiencing stillness as a means to accessing deeper insights.

Caring includes offering structure, even discipline, in ways of thinking. And here there are strong parallels with Quaker thinking:

> We may have a firm hold on old truth ourselves, but unless we are eager to find new ways of expressing it we may be unable to speak the word of life to others just when they most need it.
> (Fawell, 1987, 9: *QF&P*, 26.18)

> A living truth, if it is to stay alive, must speak to the conditions of the times. Once it is tied up in concise terms, bound by the words used and thought to be the last word, it is already on the decline. Life means growth – and death. We should not cling to words that have lost their life.
> (West, 1988, 40: *QF&P*, 26.20)

Care for learners means prompting them to construct their own narrative, their own inner incantations for procedures, their own explanations for why procedures work, and their own articulation of connections between otherwise apparently disparate concepts and examples.

For me, caring for the discipline means not trying to reduce complexity to the point of trivializing. It means not downplaying the power of the disciplined ways of thinking. It means being conscientious about displaying and using disciplined ways of thinking, so that others learn to participate.

Balancing the two forms of care can sometimes be difficult, but is nevertheless essential, because letting go of either diminishes learners' experience of the discipline as a whole. One way to maintain such a balance is to provide moments of silence, of quiet, during which what has been said and done can be allowed to settle. William Penn (1699) famously offered a Quaker parallel: 'True silence is the rest of the mind, and is to the spirit what sleep is to the body: nourishment and refreshment' (Penn, 1699: QF&P, 20.11).

Reflecting

The main force for reflecting on my own experience arose during my time at the Open University. I was asked to develop written course materials, summer school programmes, and radio and television content linked to the written materials. Unlike my previous experience, where I was responsible for giving lectures to undergraduates using an imposed textbook, I now had to make choices: what concepts to introduce, in what order and even through what medium. This made me question what is involved in learning (and doing) mathematics: what was I actually doing? What actions had been effective in what circumstances? It was this questioning that led me to reflect on my own experience. Combined with an experience of a sabbatical year with a well-travelled scholar (J.G. Bennett), during which I experienced and became aware of the value and importance of experiential learning, I developed what I later came to understand as a phenomenological approach to teaching and learning: immersing people in activity through which they might experience the concepts, procedures and ways of thinking that constitute *mathematical* thinking.

As time has gone on, I have appreciated more and more the importance of promoting reflection as an integral, perhaps key, part of learning: getting people to consider what actions they have taken that have been effective, and in what way; getting people to construct their own narrative as part of their sense-making; getting people to imagine themselves in the future acting in a similar way when it seems appropriate.

The power to imagine and to express what is being imagined is what makes planning for the future possible. An important application of this power is reflection: looking back in critical tranquillity, isolating actions that appear to have been effective and imagining oneself as fully and completely as possible re-enacting a similar action in the future. The power to do this is what can save us from endlessly repeating unhelpful habits. The deeper the habit is ingrained, the harder it is to catch it before it is enacted in order to respond differently.

The impulse to speak or, more generally, to express oneself can be seen as the release of pent-up energy. To experience a desire or need to express that which comes from deeper inside, from insight rather than from an automatic reaction to something seen or heard – from some source of creative energy – it helps greatly to have time to sit quietly with it, even to put it to the back of the mind so that it can mature naturally. Of course, this is what can happen in meeting for worship: putting thoughts, feelings and desires to one side, to allow something deeper or higher or more transcendent to enter.

I see every act as a teacher as an intervention in what would otherwise be the movements of learner attention. Each teacher-act offers learners an opportunity to focus their attention on something and to attend in particular ways. What I am attending to, both in caring for learners and in caring for the subject matter, displays to learners a value system, and it is important to me that learners are helped to become aware of those values. It is all too easy to:

> ... get distracted by the intellectual claim to our interest in a thousand and one good things ... Quaker simplicity needs to be expressed ... in the structure of a relatively simplified and co-ordinated life-programme ...
>
> (Kelly, 1941, 110: *QF&P*, 20.36)

I regard teaching as a profession in which it is possible to experience moments of freedom, when a choice to act is participated in freshly, even if only for a moment. These moments are also opportunities for creativity, for acting non-habitually, by being sensitive to learners' states. They usually correspond to moments in which learners have opportunities to experience freedom through making choices, through taking initiative, through experiencing the flow of creative energy and expressing insights in a conjecturing atmosphere.

It behoves me, not only as teacher but in general, to become aware of what others imagine I value and to note and work on any contrasts between that and what I claim to value.

Summary of my personal values

Among the values I hold most dear in my educational work are:

- Nurturing and sustaining the use and development of each person's natural powers. These, if employed and developed in any particular discipline, enable them to engage with that discipline. This value is part of 'that of God' in everyone.
- Fostering a respectful conjecturing atmosphere. This is likely to enrich participation and engagement in which those who are confident

choose to listen and comment, while those who are uncertain choose to try to articulate that uncertainty. What matters most is the making of conjectures with the intention of modifying them as and when necessary, and seeking to justify or provide evidence for those conjectures.
- Encouraging participants to construct their own narratives, their own examples and their own questions, and to make their own discipline-significant choices.
- Immersing learners and colleagues in practices that respect values and enable them to come together in a spirit of cooperation and mutual support, blending expertise and insight to develop together.
- Working to balance caring for learners with caring for the discipline, so that neither overpowers nor displaces the other.
- Doing for learners only what they cannot yet do for themselves.
- Drawing on, and relating to, the full human psyche, including enaction, affect, cognition, attention, will, witness and conscience.
- Providing opportunities for, and being seen to value, specific acts of reflection, of reconstruction and re-articulation, of appreciation and comprehension of topics and methods of approaching problems: in short, of thinking mathematically.
- Engaging with others with respect.

Afterword

I know of no better expression of how to work effectively in education than this:

> We must look to our meetings, to our love for each other, and our corporate discipline. We must look to ourselves, to speak of our lives and to let our lives speak. Above all we must look to the truth. We have an Inward Teacher who teaches, guides and commands us. When we know what we have to do, how to do it will come.
>
> (*QF&P*, 1992: 29.02)

I act with, and in front of, learners in ways that are as consistent as I can manage with my view of mathematics, of how mathematical thinking develops. I do not experience my pedagogic choices as being informed by Quaker testimonies, but, on reflection, I find that the behaviour I value is consistent with Quaker values. Thus, it is not that I teach in a particular way because I am a Quaker, but more that I am a Quaker because what I value is consistent with espoused Quaker values.

References

Bennett, J.G. (1976) *Noticing* (Sherborne Theme Talks Series 2). Sherborne: Coombe Springs Press.

Berger, M. (2006) 'Making mathematical meaning: From preconcepts to pseudoconcepts to concepts'. *Pythagoras*, 63, 14–21.

Brayshaw, A.N. (1921) *The Quakers, Their Story and Message*. London: George Allen and Unwin.

Dandelion, B.P. (2014) *Open for Transformation: Being Quaker* (Swarthmore Lecture). London: Quaker Books.

Fawell, R. (1987) *Courage to Grow*. London: Quaker Books.

Fox, G. (1657) *Something concerning silent meetings*. Reprinted in Fox, G. (1831). *The Works of George Fox, Vol. IV*. Philadelphia: Marcus T.C. Gould; New York: Isaac T. Hopper.

Gattegno, C. (1970) *What We Owe Children: The subordination of teaching to learning*. London: Routledge and Kegan Paul.

Gattegno, C. (1987) *The Science of Education: Part 1: Theoretical considerations*. New York: Educational Solutions.

Holdsworth, C. (1985) *Steps in a Large Room* (SwarthmoreLecture). London: Quaker Books.

Kelly, T. (1941) *A Testament of Devotion*. NY: HarperCollins.

Love, E. and Mason, J. (1992) *Teaching Mathematics: Action and awareness* (EM236). Milton Keynes: Open University.

Malara, N.A. and Navarra, G. (2003) *ArAl Project: Arithmetic pathways towards favouring pre-algebraic thinking*. Bologna: Pitagora.

Mason, J. (1998) 'Enabling teachers to be real teachers: Necessary levels of awareness and structure of attention'. *Journal of Mathematics Teacher Education*, 1 (3), 243–67.

Mason, J. (2002) *Researching Your Own Practice: The discipline of noticing*. London: RoutledgeFalmer.

Mason, J. (2009) 'From assenting to asserting: Promoting active learning'. In Skovsmose, O., Valero, P. and Christensen, O.R. (eds) *University Science and Mathematics Education in Transition*. New York: Springer, 17–40.

Mason, J., Burton L. and Stacey K. (1982) *Thinking Mathematically*. London: Addison-Wesley.

Mason, J. and Johnston-Wilder, S. (2006) *Designing and Using Mathematical Tasks*. 2nd ed. St. Albans: Tarquin Publications.

Open University (1982) *Developing Mathematical Thinking* (EM235). Milton Keynes: Open University.

Penn, W. (1699) 'Advice to his children', 2(27). In *A Collection of the Works*, 1726, Vol. 1. London: J. Sowle.

Pólya, G. (1962) *Mathematical Discovery: On understanding, learning and teaching problem solving*. Combined ed. New York: John Wiley and Sons.

Pólya, G. (1965) *Let Us Teach Guessing* (Mathematical Association of America Lecture Film). Washington, DC: Mathematical Association of America.

Seely Brown, J., Collins, A. and Duguid, P. (1989) 'Situated cognition and the culture of learning'. *Educational Researcher*, 18 (1), 32–42.

Steere, D. (1872) *On Speaking Out of the Silence*. Pendle Hill Pamphlet 182. Philadelphia, USA: Pendle Hill.

Tanner, R. (1989) *What I Believe: Lectures and other writings*. Holburne: Crafts Study Centre.

West, J. (1988) 'Reason and mystery'. *Friends Quarterly*, 25, 40–41.

Whitehead, A.N. (1932) *The Aims of Education and Other Essays*. London: Williams and Norgate.

Chapter 11
When school won't do
Keir Mitchell

Sometimes seeing a thing to be wrong carries with it an obligation to endeavour to mend it, however big the task. In my small way, I realize that this is what I have tried to do since my children came of school age. And I struggle to do it because in doing so I must make an 'unpopular stand' (*QF&P*, 1.02, 38).

I believed school to be good.

Up to the age of 35, I was thoroughly immersed in school and education, first as an academic child and teenager, then at university and, later, in the world of work. I became a project manager for an education charity and worked with local education authorities and government departments in the UK and overseas. I helped schools get built and staffed, because schools were a good thing; this was, at that time, a self-evident truth to me, so wholeheartedly had I bought into the school system.

Then, bored with sitting at a desk, I became a teacher myself, working in three primary schools with children aged 4 to 11, and I trained as a Forest School leader as well. I was tired and stressed, though rewarded by the children.

And then it came to my turn to send my children to school. It was, indeed, my own school, as at the time I had chosen to live in the community in which I worked. But I realized that I couldn't. I couldn't send my children to that school and, as the truth of the matter became plain to me over time, I realized I couldn't send them to any school, because, being convinced by Quaker testimonies, I wished my children to grow up to be Quakers. I wanted them to grow up in an environment where the prerequisites for peace were present and modelled by adults. I wanted them to seek truth for themselves and to be empowered to tell what they found to their peers, to adults and to power. I wanted them to be treated, their needs to be met and their voices to be heard as equals, not subordinates. But I had come to understand – and now here contend – that the school context and current system are at odds with that. I should add here that it is easy and psychologically comfortable for teachers and others who are deeply involved in the education system to attempt to make a caricature of anyone who does not wish to participate in their system as afraid of the ideas the children may come across, or the company they might keep. That is in no way the case here. Ideas we welcome, we consider and we argue over; and the company we keep ranges from penniless travellers to rich industrialists, from atheists to the most devout. No, it is not the company or the ideas that are the problem. The problem is the unconsidered actions that the system takes, the unwitting maltreatment that it perpetrates and perpetuates. That is the problem. To use a metaphor: the education system drove up to my family and offered us a lift. We refused, not because of the loud music they were enjoying, nor because of the other passengers, nor even because of the route they wished to take. We refused because the driver was oblivious to the fact that the car was unroadworthy (a fact I could see only too clearly as a driver myself).

That realization, that the actions of the education system are at odds with my children growing up as Quakers, had, and continues to have, a daily effect both on our family life (as our children are educated at home) and on my career (which I'll come to). But first I should explain the truth that I saw and how, over time, it was revealed more fully to me. And as the Quaker peace testimony is what first drew me to the Society of Friends and was the first place where I realized that my working life and beliefs were at odds, I'll start with that.

Questioning belief in school

By my fifth year of classroom teaching, my mind was already disquieted; my daughter was approaching school age but my partner was expressing reservations about sending her to school even though I taught in the school to which we would send her and I knew from experience that it was the most child-focused and friendly school I had ever encountered. For my part, I knew that I deeply desired to see more of my children through their being at school with me, but couldn't unpick this from a nagging doubt that school would be any better for them than their life at home.

Then a new head was selected, a head who promised much administratively but had no teaching experience with very young children. As a staff, we held our breath expecting to have to argue every point of the school's sound pedagogy. But when it came, the storm actually opened my eyes in an unexpected way and exposed to me problems that ran deeper than the school pedagogy.

In an opening gambit on behaviour, the new head likened his school sanctions for misbehaviour to an arsenal, with a trip to his office standing proud as a nuclear deterrent; and, abhorrent though the comment was to me, it immediately, and inescapably, rang true. Having proudly spoken for pacifism since my teens and the first Iraq War and chosen what I thought was a peaceful profession, it was as if I had looked down to notice that the tool in my hand that I daily bandied around to get my own way in the classroom was a gun, and I had carried it all along.

I was pained, distressed and disbelieving. I brooded on my misfortune in meeting for worship. Slowly, and piece by piece, I began holding my practice as a teacher and a parent up to The Light to see if it was peaceful. It was a painful process and it took time.

I looked more closely and more empathetically at the 4-, 5- and 6-year-olds who were subject to the sanctions of the behaviour policy and saw now, not irrationality and wilful disobedience that I had seen before, but instead fear, anger, repressed hatred and depression in their faces and tears. These were the very same emotions that I had always felt myself when I had been forced or cornered into compliance.

I asked myself whether the threat of lost privileges, lost playtime or an unknown fate at the hands of the head was, for a young child who doesn't yet understand about life and death (and to whom an hour may seem an eternity), comparably terrifying as a threat to an adult from a gun. I found that, given how young and inexperienced the children were, how much they valued their free time and how scared they could be of the unknown, it was shockingly comparable. Then I looked at the children who were never subject to behaviour sanctions and saw that the knowledge of the existence of the sanctions also affected them deeply; they were frozen into obedience and silence lest they should have to face them.

Beginning school life by obtaining obedience to authority through fear seems to me at odds with an individual seeking and speaking truth and working towards developing an understanding of peace. It also strikes me as inherently unequal in treating young children without respect. But this realization did not come all at once.

First, I questioned my role in the situation, but I could not find a way to see behaviour management within the school as a step towards peace. I take the prerequisites for peace to be care, justice and the respect and tolerance embodied in human rights, but the methods of managing children's behaviour seemed to fall far short of these qualities; in fact they offered many children limited care and respect, considerable fear and a lack of tolerance. Moreover, they gave access to justice only with respect to interaction with peers, never in relation to interactions with adults.

The lot of boys

The lot of active boys caused me particular concern. Every year, a significant proportion of the boys of all ages in my classes had learnt best and been happiest when they could move, run around, investigate objects physically, touch things, throw them and learn by playing (including play-fighting). I knew this from the many Forest School sessions that I had run during which children were allowed, in a rich outdoor environment such as woodland, to direct their own social, physical and scientific learning and to consciously take risks as long as everyone remained happy and safe.

But in a classroom set up for reading, writing and maths, these active boys' preferred ways of learning were highly inconvenient. With the best will in the world I could (and did) set up the most spectacular role-play areas or sensory tables in a classroom, but still these boys would not be able to learn in the way they learnt best, because they were constrained by the rules of the classroom. They could not, for example, see how strong the pine cones were by standing on them (a reasonable scientific test for a 5-year-old, but inconvenient because it is messy and destructive); and nor could they actually storm the cardboard role-play castle, because other children needed it after them.

Or rather they *could* do these things, indeed (and this is crucial in terms of the tolerance, respect and care that were *not* given to them) some would be *unable to stop themselves* testing the strength of the pine cones or storming the castle in the flow and excitement of ideas, learning and discovery, but when they did it they would become subject to the behaviour sanctions.

The same boys often also found it hardest to sit still or to hold a pencil, and later in their school career they could be seen missing their playtimes and standing or sitting outside the staff room waiting to be chastised, perhaps just having their time wasted, or now, chillingly, to have their medication for modifying behaviour 'signed off'.

There are many effective adult men whom I could imagine being active boys when they were 5 years old. In their natural state, these boys are neither physically ill, nor distressed, nor a serious danger to themselves or others. I also know, and have known, a great many teachers and they, almost without exception, are essentially kind and well meaning; so I asked myself why active 7-year-olds could be so misunderstood and shown so little respect for their person that they should have a medication programme forced on them rather than accommodation be made for their needs. Such needs are consistent across generations of boys: the need to move, the need to follow their own interests, the need to play, have fun and be funny.

A fruitless search for support and guidance

I was deeply disturbed, and questions flooded my mind in meeting for worship and other quiet moments. And while looking at the questions helped, resolutions and guidance seemed more remote than ever.

At that time, the advice about children in *QF&P* seemed quiet to me, or perhaps in retrospect it was too wordy and equivocal. It also contained allusions to arguments that, in my mind, were long dead (such as being against corporal punishment). I could not see the wood for the trees. Parental dilemmas? Yes, I could see those in the text. Schooling and advice to teachers? Yes. But, having been deeply immersed in the lives and thoughts of young children for a long time, I felt the children themselves were strangely absent. Children were being talked about, but with no real presence, like an uninspiring review of a play, or a staged Facebook post; the texts were centred on the adults, but the support that I needed to improve my ways of working with children eluded me. It took a long time for me to see beyond that point, but still, because I was convinced by the testimonies, and my partner and I wanted our children to grow up as Quakers, we attended meeting for worship whenever we could.

Simplicity enters the argument

At the same time, I was looking closely into other aspects of schooling in the light of the testimonies.

I had long been concerned with living simply, and my partner and I had endeavoured to ensure that much of our food was grown locally. We walked or cycled if we could, and tried not to amass ostentatious possessions (where we sadly still struggle in the realm of books and musical instruments), but it took a conversation with a Muslim friend of mine to point out the relationship of all this to school. He, as an Imam working for peace in state prisons and a father of a 4-year-old, was weighing up whether he could send his children to state schools and, by this time, I was working as a part-time Year 1 teacher and helping my partner to educate our eldest children at home. 'It's the curriculum,' my friend explained, 'it says at one point that the school should teach children to be good consumers; that doesn't translate well into Arabic.' 'Why not?' I asked. 'Well, the Devil, Satan, consumes. It's really hard not to translate "consumer" as "devil". I don't want that for my children.'

And so I looked, and I realized the hallmarks of consumer society were everywhere in school. I saw children showing off their possessions in 'show and tell' sessions, and the parental competition of their purchased birthday parties. I saw the emphasis on ever greater targets and endless productivity in the classroom (to what end and for what real purpose? I wondered) and the extrinsic rewards of stickers and throw-away treats that were given for effort or obedience, in preference to allowing a child satisfaction in the act and beauty of creation itself. The subtext to this, the example set by the school culture, seemed to me to be 'want more, make more, grab your reward, wave it with pride and move on'. Indeed, a need to make school reflect television now had children waving their achievement certificates at each other like wrestlers after a bout. But of more concern was that the children seemed to become so deeply involved in this system and pattern of external rewards that they lacked the internal motivation that I saw in my own and other home-educated children and in 4-year-olds when they started school. Somehow, within a year or so, that internal motivation seemed to leak away or have been so suppressed that it didn't show.

No. Even discarding allusions to demons, I still didn't want that for my children, and was relieved that we hadn't enrolled our children in school and had chosen to educate them ourselves. But that was still not the end of what was revealed to me.

Some disturbing light on what was wrong

In a quiet moment late one evening, I saw with clarity what I was doing as a teacher and knew that I would have to make sweeping changes to my relationship with schooling.

I saw that my job as a Year 1 teacher was twofold: first, to take self-motivated young children with ideas and a will of their own and institutionalize them so that for an enormous proportion of their time they would submit to the will of the teacher; and second, to make the job of subsequent teachers easier by ensuring that as many children as possible could communicate through written language (including written maths).

In my personal experience, which now includes many children in school and many who have not attended school, I can find no reason why children should learn to read, write and count by the age of 6. No developmental window closes on these capabilities.

Children all over the world start to learn to read, write and count later; for example they start at 7 in Germany, while home-educated and Montessori-educated children may be 9 or older. Essentially, waiting until they are ready, self-motivated and the symbols make sense to them means they can then learn very quickly. My own son learnt to read in about a week at age 9.

No child of 6 genuinely needs to read, write or count *except* at school. Six-year-olds do not have to fill in tax returns, or even navigate by road signs or work out their own change. The aim to get everyone reading, writing and counting by the age of 6 is a peculiarity of this country's schooling system, but it is highly convenient for schools because it means, from Year 2, teachers can give written instructions, set quiet written tasks, do not have to be experts in deciphering developmental writing, and the messiness of direct experience in learning can be replaced with books and screens.

This realization led to a further series of questions. If I was, first, institutionalizing the children not for their own benefit but instead so that they would be conveniently obedient to subsequent teachers and, second, teaching them to read and write at that young age not because they needed those skills at that age but because that, too, was convenient for subsequent teachers, then what else in the school system was set up for the convenience of adults and not for the benefit of the children?

Over time, as my children and their friends grew and learnt outside school, while I remained connected to it, I identified more aspects of the school system that primarily served adults at the expense of the children:

- There was the clean, tidy, crowded classroom. It was warm and comfortable for an adult, but I knew from my, now extensive, Forest School experience that most children between the ages of 3 and 13 would be happier outside with plenty of space in all but the wildest weathers.
- There was the need for constant productivity; schoolchildren were kept constantly busy with directed tasks. Outside school, I saw children learning without such tasks, so those tasks were not an essential part of learning as I had previously thought. Instead it now seemed that the adult-directed tasks prevented the children from learning in their preferred, but less convenient, ways. Children given directed tasks looked tidy and purposeful (just as the school management liked) but by comparing them with children outside school I could see that they missed out on empowering, self-initiated, learning.
- There was the breaking down of learning into standardized small steps and targets that helped make children's learning more intelligible to adults and indeed made it appear that the adult was in control of the child's learning. But was this of any benefit to the child? From experience, I now knew that children do not naturally see their

learning as *the* 'next step' or 'target' but instead see a broad vista of areas in which they can develop and choose appropriately. The sheen of control created by the breaking down of learning appeared to make the child's actual learning worthless unless it was focused on the teacher's target. And when the learning did focus on the target, the teacher won as much reward as the child. This seemed wrong and dishonest. Outside school, *all* the learning my children and their peers did was valuable, not just that focused on an adult-dictated target, and the credit for their learning was all their own.
- Another aspect of the breakdown of learning into targets was that it made it possible for a teacher to keep a bureaucratic trail of progress, make comparisons and report on children. These things were undoubtedly interesting for adults (and devastating or elating for parents), but were they of any actual benefit to the child? Did they not risk creating arrogance and complacency in those who were ahead of the game, and anxiety and depression in those who were behind?

But the system being set up to serve the wrong people went beyond the relationship between adults and children. The inversion went on up to government:

- Standard assessment tasks (SATs) appeared to me primarily a convenient way for government to prove the success of their policies, of very little benefit to teachers and done at the cost of children.
- Teachers themselves (unlike doctors) were employed on a professional contract, which allowed the management of the school and the government to make almost any demand of them and expect it to be implemented regardless of the time teachers might have to spend doing it. I'd contend that it is not good for children to have a teacher who is exhausted by ever-changing bureaucracy, nor is it good to be that teacher.
- And, it seems to me, the state school system itself exists more to enable parents to go to work and enable the state to control the learning of children, than it does to provide those children with education that is 'civil and useful', as the early Quaker George Fox suggested (*QF&P*, 23.71).

Increasingly, as I meditated on what I had found, it seemed that the school system had been designed by adults for the convenience of adults, with appropriate education of the children taking second place. So, I wondered how that squared with the fundamental equality of all members of the human race (*QF&P*, 23.36).

In school, children are expected to be obedient to adults and are punished if they refuse or rebel. Children are expected to listen respectfully to adults and act on adult criticism. Children are expected to thus submit uncomplainingly to the will of adults for many hours each day, inhabit spaces designed for adults' comfort according to rules made by adults, and learn ways to communicate with adults so that they may perform the work designated by adults to the adults' specification. Adults are expected to keep children in order and provide them with the tasks that the adults believe will help them develop and then monitor them exclusively in those tasks.

Many years ago, when working with education ministries of developing countries, I was shown the little trick of changing the names of groups to something more familiar and then rereading a text to see if it might be unfair or perhaps cause offence. So, if you will, try reading the preceding paragraph again and replace 'children' with 'women' and 'adults' with 'men'. The inequality, to me, seems far more extreme than the difference in understanding and wisdom between adults and children could possibly justify, and so I would contend that it lacks respect for, and tolerance of, children, which again brings us back to the prerequisites for peace.

Indeed, the relationship between this type of unequal obedience and peace appeared to me extremely problematic. I could not see how children coerced into daily obedience to a teacher who both formed the questions and was in the position to judge the answers could possibly develop the habits that would make them feel at home with ministry in a Quaker meeting, or develop the confidence and skills to speak truth to power without feeling that they were wrong to do so.

The institutionalization and obedience that I was required to engender as a Year 1 teacher, the adult-centred design of the school system and the mismatch between obedience and speaking truth jangled together in my mind disconcertingly for a long time. Perhaps I had missed something.

In the end, I considered what I knew of the history of the state education system – its birth in a time of empire, nationalism and industrialization and the consequent need for obedient, productive soldiers and workers – and concluded that no match between the school system and Quaker testimony had ever been intended. And, in sadness, that in the century and a half since the 1870 Education Act, no significant match had been achieved.

Light shines through everyone, including children

I didn't know what to do next, but, having held up so much of my practice to the light of the testimonies, and my beliefs about my practice having changed so markedly, I was in the tightest of spots with relation to honesty and integrity. If asked, I could not now give children honest reasons to justify their obedience or their work.

Over and again, and in every generation, Quaker ministry speaks of the examples we set and particularly the examples we set for children (*QF&P*, 23.72; 23.82; 23.83). I wanted to be an example but, if I remained within the school system, then I would be called upon to condone actions and to work and behave in ways that were now at odds with my beliefs. Whatever personal adaptations I might bring to my practice, I felt that, if I remained a teacher, my foremost example would be that of hypocrisy.

It took many quiet moments in meetings and outside to come to terms with the reality of the situation. I felt I had been blind and, through my blindness, I had done wrong. I felt that, as a teacher, I had not provided a good pattern or example to children because I had not understood that the requirements of a teacher in the school system were at odds with the example I wished to be. I was no pattern (Fox, 1656, in *QF&P*, 19.32), I was only contradiction.

Finally, I opened *QF&P* quite randomly and read 'The Light: The Inward Light is the light of Christ. It is a universal Light, which can be known by anyone, of either sex, of any age, of whatever religion' (*QF&P*, 19.25) and it dawned on me that when, earlier, I had looked for advice and guidance about children, I had restricted my search. I had been adult-centred in my search for advice. Advice and guidance throughout *QF&P* applied to my relationship with everyone including children, because the light shines through everyone including children. Then I found support for being loving and peaceful with children. I found support for listening, understanding and encouraging children in their own thoughts and talents, whatever they were, because all the testimonies, advice and guidance applied equally to my relationship with children as to my relationship with anything or anyone else.

And so, like a conscientious objector, I decided to refuse to surrender moral responsibility for my actions as a teacher, because I now had no doubt that some of them were wrong and damaging to children. But, unlike conscientious objection to military service, I could have easily walked away from teaching. I could have left schools behind; there would have been no legal consequences for me. Except that the Quaker testimonies urged me 'to mend the world, to live better in it, to keep the helm and guide the vessel to port, not to steal out at the stern' (Penn, 1682, in *QF&P*, 23.02). And here the absence of legal consequences became a blight; if I refused to be a teacher there would be no court case in which to take a stand, there would be no magistrate required to listen to my reason and make judgement on it and there would be no newspaper waiting to report my fate.

So, if the system would not make an example of me, then I wondered what I should do. And the answer, when it came, was simple but required me to walk two paths at the same time. I wanted my children to be Quakers. Therefore, I should be the best example I could be, and, as I felt that was impossible within the system, then I must work outside the system with them. But I also wanted to help change the system and so I must also be an example *within* it.

Respectful attention in school and out

Therefore, I have created two small and imperfect spaces in which I can strive to set the best example I can. One involves working with home-educated children outside school and the other is within school. But the path I am treading is not an easy one.

You see, what I realized that I enjoyed as an adult and as a teacher was that the children attended respectfully to what I said and what I asked them to do and appeared to develop through attending to what I said and did. That made me feel important, respected and loved. Let's call this 'respectful attention'. But that respectful attention, when achieved as a teacher in a school, was based on obedience and the threats implicit in the behaviour management system. I didn't want to use those any more, because I consider they are at odds with the Quaker testimonies.

It is a humbling thing to admit, but I now believe I should earn respectful attention through equality, peacefulness and friendship rather than demand it through obedience. Hence, both my space within school and the space that I have developed for home educators are built on the following ideas:

- I only encumber the children with one rule: to love one another. Except that phrase is normally far too humorous or scary or both for most children, so I approximate it as 'keep everyone happy and safe', both of which can be checked by one child simply by looking at another. And what a complex rule that is. To keep everyone happy the children must empathize with, listen to and negotiate fairly with each other at the very least; and to keep everyone safe they need to predict the consequences of their own and other people's actions. These are challenges for most adults, but they are achieved by all of the children most of the time. Of course, I am bound by the same rule too (that is only honest and equal).

- I freely share my power as an adult with the children. I do not lay down what they are to learn and the way they are to learn it, but instead I empower them to choose and direct their own activities (this way they are happy, they are not in awe of power). I then:
  - watch the children carefully to ensure that what they have chosen to do is purposeful and that they are, in fact, learning something through their activity
  - listen carefully to the children for clues and indications that they may be ready to learn, understand or practise an important concept or convention within their own activities, and come forward with the relevant assistance, explanation or tools at the appropriate moment. In doing this, I find scope to encourage them to do things that I think they should do within their own ideas for learning (because I care for them and their development).
- Because I share my power in this way, it is easy to treat the children, from the very youngest (who at some Forest Schools are too young to talk), with the utmost respect and tolerance of their personality and developmental stage in the expectation that respect will, in time, be reciprocated. This includes:
  - trusting them to make decisions
  - physically getting to their level to converse (I spend a lot of time on my knees)
  - making friendly eye contact (rather than the domineering sort frequently used by adults in the classroom)
  - smiling and making jokes
  - and crucially listening wholeheartedly to the important things that they want to tell me, prioritizing the children's conversation over the babble of adults.
- In the same respectful, reciprocating ways, sharing power freely enables me to do the following:
  - I admit my mistakes and, consequently, when the children make mistakes (perhaps by taking a joke too far or upsetting another), I can justly and readily complain.
  - I am honest about my internal states to the children. If I am enjoying myself or tired or irritable, I say so, and, therefore, it does not seem

odd if I point out their states. When they are upset or angry I can say how they seem to me and listen to their experience of it.
- I respect their humour as humour (not a waste of my time or an affront to my status) in the expectation that they will then endure and engage with mine.

- If I must use my power as an adult over a child, for example to prevent an upset child from hurting others or to create some justice, I explain my actions privately to the child as soon as possible to maintain equality and respect.

Within school, I now teach one day a week providing Forest School for all the children on a class-by-class basis with teachers in attendance as my assistants. In this I have opportunities to model different ways of being with the children that are not based on adult dominance and obedience. The sessions begin and end in a classroom but take place predominantly in a woodland where most of the children's time is spent in self-directed and self-selected, intrinsically motivating, activities such as lighting fires, using knives, climbing or imaginative social role-play, with the remainder of the time being taken up with carefully selected cooperative games, nature activities and stories. There is no curriculum to be adhered to and the sessions are so loved by the children I have no need for behaviour sanctions because they will control their own behaviour, keeping everyone happy and safe in order to be able to get on with the things they want to do. In fact, with the one rule securely in place and a few pieces of safety advice for novice knife, fire and other tool users, there has never been a serious accident in seven years.

In this way, the children are given real responsibility, freed from obedience of the classroom and empowered to make their own decisions and instruct me on how to help them. Their class teacher is required to step away from dominating the class and can see the children and their behaviour in a different light. The class teachers have the opportunity to develop their skills and confidence so they can use this way of working for themselves.

Outside school, working with my own and other home-educated children, my project is, again, based in woodland and the outdoors (this is where the children are happiest). And, because there is no school attached, we add back in all the good things we have indoors: some warm, dry shelter, opportunities for writing, maths, science, sport and art, a kitchen, computers, music, books, strategic games, things to make and things to take apart.

The children's session is begun with a meeting that they run and in which they each decide what to do that day, make suggestions for the future and deal with any problems. I then enable them to get on with the things that most interest them that day. From this, we have children developing into enthusiastic engineers, artists, chefs, strategists, writers, climbers, entrepreneurs, actors and theatre directors.

The learners in school and out, according to their own will, take risks and experiment (both scientifically and with social situations). They explore and investigate the things that interest them, gaining deep experience and mastering skills through their own effort. They imagine and create artefacts and their own worlds.

What emerges is a different relationship with learning and the power embodied in adults, in which the learners are themselves empowered rather than obedient. Empowerment, in my view, is a much better starting point both for ministry and speaking truth – both important in Quaker living. Help for any of this learning is always on hand, but crucially the relationship between those doing the learning and those facilitating the learning is a model of equality; and because learners are deeply involved fulfilling their own ideas and creating their own successes, it reduces the drive to compare, compete and consume that mars our attempts to live simply and honestly.

So, does all this produce the respectful attention that I still love? Well, sometimes the children grant me it, particularly when I hit the right note with a story that I have written for them or can give them the assistance they need to succeed with a particular project. But it's a good thing for it to be like that, because the respectful attention I now receive is granted not through obedience but in response to something I have myself done, or created, and I find that change, in itself, is more honest. Along with it, I am now reluctant to claim vicarious plaudits for the children's development; those rightly belong entirely to them. Moreover, the whole relationship between me and the children has changed. It is no longer based on their attention to my ideas. Instead it seems to be more like the relationships between respectful, caring, tolerant friends.

And, for me, the best thing is that I can see nothing bad about that.

References

All references in this chapter are from:

Religious Society of Friends (2013) *Quaker Faith and Practice: The book of Christian discipline of the Yearly Meeting of the Religious Society of Friends (Quakers) in Britain.* 5th ed. London: Religious Society of Friends. Online. qfp.quaker.org.uk (accessed 13 December 2017).

Chapter 12
Natality and Quaker education
Giles Barrow

This chapter offers a theoretical basis for a contemporary vision of Quaker education. Central to this work is the idea of natality, which is a symbol of birth and renewal. My intention in the following discussion is to explore the potential of natality as a foundation for a Quaker view of education. In doing so, I will draw on the work of Hannah Arendt and of Quaker thinkers including Grace Jantzen, Parker Palmer and John Macmurray, among others. My own view is that the spiritual relevance of natality to the educational experience has not been fully recognized and that there is value in framing it within the context of Quaker faith and practice. The range of this chapter is to primarily outline the key features and character of a natality-based view of Quaker education and spirituality. A secondary consideration in the chapter is to offer some thoughts on how to apply the idea of natality to the work of the contemporary Quaker educator.

Bringing a Quaker view of teaching and learning to bear on modern schooling is a new exercise, and my hope in doing so is to bring about fresh insights and possibilities for educators and students. In preparing this chapter, I have set out to live adventurously in the realm of the theory and philosophy of education, and the work of Grace Jantzen will prove to be essential for informing my central argument. I suggest that, while Jantzen, a convinced Quaker, provides an extended, rich and dynamic account of natality, as an academic theologian-philosopher she does not extend her ideas into the field of education. Meanwhile, Hannah Arendt, one of the first modern philosophers to provide a comprehensive treatment of natality, contained her discussion within the general territory of sociology and politics, and did not address the connection with the spiritual and theological. So, part of my purpose in this chapter is to make links between the work of these two distinctive narratives on natality. In most respects, what follows is a 'giving birth' to a new way of framing Quaker education.

To summarize the following discussion, I am proposing that a Quaker vision of education involves the gradual unfolding of personhood, in direct communion within a sense of place and in relationship with others.

Furthermore, the notion of natality provides a robust and kaleidoscopic basis on which to ground ecological, sociological and spiritual development for both teachers and students, in addition to forging educational institutional culture. I present here a discussion of ideas, educational theory and philosophy that might offer a new way for Quakers to view education.

Natality: An introduction

For the purposes of my exploration, the term 'natality' is used in its metaphorical, existential and symbolic sense. Throughout this discussion, I am suggesting that natality is used synonymously with birth, becoming, renewal and beginning. Furthermore, I use it to describe the process by which students increasingly become expressions of their deepest selves, whereby what Quakers describe as 'that of God in everyone' is uniquely rendered. In philosophical terms, this process is pregnant with potential for framing the educational relationship, situating the educator as a midwife, or cultivator, in a process of renewal. Natality stands in contrast to mortality, the predominant existential end-point that has preoccupied philosophers and theologians for centuries. The first modern philosopher to refer to natality was Heidegger, who used it to emphasize the major thrust of his argument that centred on movement towards death. It was Hannah Arendt, a pupil of Heidegger, who reversed the focus and developed a philosophy of natality. For Arendt, natality became one of several important themes in her writing spanning several decades during the mid-twentieth century. Born in Germany in 1906, Arendt, a Jew, escaped National Socialism by travelling to the USA and developed a career as a political theorist. It is in her most influential work, *The Human Condition* (1958), that she discusses natality:

> The miracle that saves the world, the realm of human affairs, from its 'normal' ruin is ultimately the fact of natality ... It is in other words, the birth of new men [sic] and the new beginning, the action they are capable of by virtue of being born. Only the full experience of this capacity can bestow upon human affairs faith and hope ... It is this faith in and hope for the world that found perhaps its most glorious and most succinct expression in the few words with which the gospels announced their 'glad tidings': 'A child has been born unto us.'
>
> (Arendt, 1958: 247)

The references here to a Christian frame of reference are entirely symbolic; Arendt was secular in terms of her own beliefs, but nevertheless she sees the importance of the cultural significance of natality. In addition to hope and faith, Arendt writes elsewhere of how the fact of our birth is what gives rise to identity, a desire to act in the world and to create meaning to life. Although generally Arendt's work is concerned with political theory, in a short collection of essays she considers the connection between natality and education, particularly that of the younger generation:

> Basically we are always educating for a world that is or is becoming out of joint, for this is the basic human situation, in which the world is created by mortal hands to serve mortals for a limited time as home. Because the world is made by mortals it wears out; and because it continuously changes its inhabitants it runs the risk of becoming as mortal as they. To preserve the world against the mortality of its creators and inhabitants it must be constantly set right anew. The problem is simply to educate in such a way that a setting-right remains actually possible, even though it can of course, never be assured. Our hope hangs on the new which every generation brings ...
>
> (Arendt, 1961: 192)

That penultimate sentence is possibly the most significant in terms of the educator–student relationship. Here, Arendt captures the risk, or uncertainty, that is a quintessential quality in the educational experience. As in any birthing process, there is the possibility of failure that accompanies the hope for a new life, but Arendt's educational objective is for the new generation to be taught so that they might be sufficiently critical of what has gone before with a view to being resourced for the future. This carries the capacity to question the status quo, to upturn established conventions and continue to thrive anew. Her more substantive observation is that education functions as a cross-generational transaction through which the 'becoming' generation are provided with their inheritance of what has previously accrued, with the invitation to make it of their own for their time.

Natality: Learning to be human and the work of John Macmurray

At around the same time as Arendt was developing her ideas on natality, the Scottish philosopher (and Quaker later in life) John Macmurray presented his view on the purpose of education. While he did not refer explicitly to natality, his perspective echoes several themes implicit in the concept. In 1958, he delivered a lecture entitled 'Learning to be human' (Macmurray, 2012). Reading it today, the paper is still an astonishingly clear declaration of educational purpose. Macmurray centres his discussion

Natality and Quaker education

on two observations: that learning to be human presents a paradox for educationists and that the pace of societal change requires educators to prepare students for a world with which they, the educator, will be unfamiliar. Significantly for the purpose of this chapter, Macmurray talks in terms and phrases that speak directly to the natal experience. In reference to the 'educational paradox', he explains that, while we may be born human, individuals need then to learn to *be* so:

> We are born human and nothing can rob us of our human birthright. Nevertheless, we have to learn to be human, and we can only learn by being taught ... He [sic] can only survive by being cared for ... He has to learn everything ...
>
> (Macmurray, 2012: 666)

Macmurray goes on to outline three areas critical in pursuing this educational purpose, the task of learning to be human, which connect to a feature of natality – relatedness:

> The first principle of human nature is mutuality ... For this reason the first priority in education – if by education we mean learning to be human – is learning to live in personal relation to other people.
>
> (ibid.: 670)

He continues with a remark that resonates with the embodied nature of learning:

> What I have in mind includes the development of our capacity for sense experience, and through this, the education of the emotions ... But to learn to live in our senses is to enjoy both our seeing and our hearing and what we see and hear.
>
> (ibid.: 671)

This appraisal of the sensory becomes extended into a call for contemplation. From this point Macmurray reaches into what might be considered territory closer to the divine:

> There is one other consequence of learning to live in our senses. Besides the education of emotional capacities, and indeed through this, it provides a discipline of the imagination ... To learn to be human is to learn to be creative. The imaginativeness of children is their birthright. And the discipline of the imagination cannot be intellectual; it must be rooted in contemplation, in the life

of the senses and the reflective activities that spring from it – contemplation, valuation and imaginative expression.

(ibid.: 672)

Although Macmurray does not make explicit mention of Quaker faith and practice, his remarks on contemplation, of being in the world and attentive to beauty, are indicators wholly in line with a Quaker frame of reference. Perhaps more specifically, Macmurray mirrors the socio-political aspects of Arendt's theory when he talks of the limitations of the role of schools in their relation to wider society. He challenges those teachers who would attempt to disconnect their students from their families and community so that the negativity of these influences might be eliminated. This, he argues, is mistaken. The 'agency of education is the society in which we live and nothing less; and that when we think of schools it should be to consider what part they should play in the scheme of education' (ibid.: 669). In other words, education cannot be fully delivered by schools alone – it is more than a public, civic project and is in a co-dependent relationship with the private, the personal, the communal and domestic spheres of life.

Jantzen's Quaker perspective

Moving on from the mid-twentieth century, a more contemporary Quaker position on natality and the associated experience of learning to be human can be found in the work of Grace Jantzen. While Arendt's account of natality might inspire educators in preparing to meet the new generation, it remains essentially a sociological perspective. Despite influences and language borrowed from religious traditions, Arendt remains concerned primarily with the secular world and pays little attention to religious, theological or spiritual matters in her writing on natality. It is the work of Jantzen, born in 1948, that offers an elaboration beyond the sociological, initially in her pivotal work, *Becoming Divine* (1999), and in her final series of writings in which she sets out a feminist theological framework, with natality at the heart of a new spiritual imaginary. Jantzen was raised in the Canadian Mennonite community before moving to the UK, where she lived in the Lake District working as an academic theologian, eventually at Manchester University, before her death in 2006. As a convinced Quaker, Jantzen provides a dynamic, radical and feminist perspective on the sacred. Despite working as an academic for much of her life, she does not deal specifically with education theory or practice, and so her discussion of natality is restricted to theological territory. However, although my concern in this discussion is on pedagogy, Jantzen's commentary on the spiritual possibilities of natality are valuable in the context of establishing a Quaker education vision.

Jantzen's main contention is that theology and, by extension, Christian liturgy, doctrine and scripture have been dominated by a patriarchal ideology in which mortality has been the existential point of reference. The implication of this, in Jantzen's view, has been a history and culture utterly fixated on death, the symptoms of which take forms of both necrophilia and necrophobia in Western habits of mind and spirit. Jantzen critiques a familiar Western narrative in which war must be waged to subjugate that which is not true, human and natural resources are subject to exploitation so as to satisfy insatiable acquisitive appetites, and new territories are colonized in pursuit of man's desire for mastery. Such a narrative is accompanied by the destruction of natural resources, the objectification of 'the other', including specific oppression of the feminine and, important to this discussion, the complete eclipsing of natality as an alternative original point from which to understand the human condition.

Before moving into the detail of Jantzen's perspective on natality, it is important to briefly take account of her understanding of Quakerism because this will support a deeper appreciation of its link with natality and an intimation of her wider argument. Bearing in mind that the main focus of Jantzen's writing is to establish the architecture of a feminist spirituality, much of her argument contends that mainstream theology is dominated by a patriarchy that engenders a preoccupation with mastery and, ultimately, violence. In contrast, she identifies examples of exceptions to this in the Christian tradition. In doing so, she argues that some non-conformist movements demonstrated a different frame of reference; this includes the emergence of Quakerism.

Using a recurrent turn of phrase, Jantzen refers to Quakerism as being 'at an angle' to the society of seventeenth-century England. By this she identifies Quakerism as developing a spiritual perspective that set it apart from the conformist mainstream protestant tradition. One of the differentiations in Jantzen's view was a Quaker concept of the divine that resided within the individual, as opposed to a purely, or solely, externalized concept of God:

> Whereas the rest of society – for all their religious differences – held to a concept of God sharply other than the world ... Quakers believed that the divine was *within* human persons, a life and light and seed and fountain – they mixed their metaphors happily – in everyone.
>
> (Jantzen, 2010: 87)

A second principle was an emphasis that focused on life in the 'meantime', on earth: '[The early Quakers] saw the task of their lives as bringing about social and religious change in this world, rather than merely preparing themselves for the next' (ibid.: 80). Jantzen recognizes that some aspects of mainstream religious conventions continued into Quaker methods. For instance, she tracks the extensive crusading polemics in early Quaker tracts, in which dread and fear, in the form of Hell, will come to those who turn away from inner Light and life. In this regard, Jantzen picks up how, even within this non-conformist movement, the signs of death and violence persisted.

However, where Jantzen finds most potential for a new theology is in the specific works of early Quaker women. While acknowledging Quakerism as being at an angle, she contends that Quaker women 'were just a little farther out on the same limb as the men in the development of a symbolic of life as against the symbolic of violence and death' (ibid.: 149). In supporting this observation, Jantzen cites writings from several female writers in early Quaker history, including Margaret Fell, Dorothy White, Sarah Blackbarrow, Katherine Evans and Sarah Chevers. Jantzen notices that in the writings of these women there are significant differences in their language from that of some of the male writers of the time:

> If they aimed to 'answer that of God in everyone' it could not be by violence ... Moreover, while a Quaker stance would make for delight in and appreciation of the physical world, and thus for an enthusiasm for scientific investigation and discovery, this enthusiasm would not be on a removal of God from the world, as in the increasing secularism of the time. Rather, they sought to discern and cooperate with the divine Life. Hence their approach left room for ecological concern rather than exploitation and domination of the physical world.
>
> (ibid.: 91)

It is in the context of this understanding of Quakerism that Jantzen positions natality as an alternative spiritual centre-point. If natality had been the predominant 'symbolic' at the time, she suggests, modern culture would be utterly different and, by extension, so would implications for educational theory, policy and practice. The importance of the voice of women in the framing of natality becomes more apparent as I turn now to its principal characteristics.

Natality: Key features

In this section, I want to share the core dimensions of natality. These are drawn mainly from Jantzen's work but also incorporate observations from my own experience in education. To some extent, each feature combines some of the emphasis in the earlier work of Arendt and Macmurray.

Relational

It is the fact of our birth that makes us relational beings. No one as yet has ever been born alone – birth has always arisen through relationship and takes place accompanied, even if it is only the mother who is present. Mortality emphasizes the individual, it atomizes one from another – it is possible to die alone. Human capacity – indeed hunger – for connection is a central feature of natality. The individual arrives out of, and in, relationship to another and this evidently matters, given that so many people spend their life seeking out and recreating relational experience. The term 'relational' has a general appeal but I want to look closer at its specific implications within a natal frame of reference.

The important feature of relationship here is to be prepared to be impacted by the arrival of an 'Other' who has never existed before. It means to start from a position of not knowing who it is that will arrive. By implication it means suspending, even for a brief time, the possibility of stability, familiarity and knowingness, even though we might hold out a hope to return to certainty. For educators, this type of relational process can be especially challenging. Can the teacher really hold this risk in the face of a culture that insists on certainty, where the teacher must be 'in charge' of the student, the curriculum and the teaching and learning dynamic? Can there be room for this fertile space between teacher and student? Biesta (2014) refers to this moment, or place, as the 'beautiful risk of education' and explains that it involves educators engaging in education as a 'weak' concept. He explains that:

> ... education only works through weak connections of communication and interpretation, of interruption and response, and ... this weakness matters if our educational endeavours are informed by a concern for those we educate to be subjects of their own actions – which is as much about being the author and originator of one's actions as it is about being responsible for what one's actions bring about.
>
> (Biesta, 2014: 4)

This, in my view, describes succinctly one of the qualities of being a Quaker educator. It echoes the quiet waiting of meeting for worship, the collective anticipation of what is yet to be known – the natal moment.

Embodiment

Incorporated in natality is a recognition and appreciation of embodiment. Neither is a mind born, nor can a soul emerge, without being integrated within a body. Unlike discourses on mortality whereby there are tendencies to separate mind, body and soul, being natal means wholeness. As I type these words, the activity of my mind is simultaneously enmeshed with the movement of my fingers, the ache in my shoulder, and the wistful part of me that glances up and out of the window towards the bright winter sunshine. The importance of embodiment within a natal framework is better understood when put alongside the idea of human flourishing, which in most respects is at the heart of the natal purpose. Arguably this acknowledgement of body–mind–spirit integration reflects the Quaker commitment to trusting an inner Light; truth is lived, not simply believed. 'Belief' and matters of truth can exist solely in the cognitive realm and, in doing so, appropriate religious faith and practice away from the holistic experience of being human. Again, for Quaker educators, I suggest that this commitment to embodiment presents significant challenges. In schooling systems that tend to prize cognitive ability and assess success by academic performance to the exclusion of other qualities, how does the teacher resist teaching students solely from the 'neck up'?

Flourishing

I have already referred to the concept of flourishing as a prime objective of a natality-inspired approach, and this, in turn, I believe, should become foundational for a Quaker vision of education. While this is another term – like relational – which has a general usage, I want to explain it more specifically in the context of natality. Here the meaning is linked to the task of becoming as fully individuated as we can be. I see this as being essentially about the irreplaceability of the individual. In more common usage the notion of flourishing can be expressed simply as realizing the potential of each individual, but in educational terms, this does not bear scrutiny. Simply pursuing the personal potential carries a shadow that harbours potential narcissistic tendencies, a tendency to acquisitiveness and exploitative behaviour; to be all I can be (at others' expense). Of course, when individual teachers and schools and colleges seek to realize the potential of their students they do not intend to initiate or encourage the development of these shadow tendencies – that is not what I am arguing here. My important point is to help students calibrate the innate and natal desire to thrive and flourish alongside the natal appetite for relatedness. In other words, how does the student grow more of themselves, *in relationship with others* who are similarly engaged? To paraphrase a question of Arendt: how might individuals reconcile themselves in the world to make themselves at home in the world?

Flourishing is problematic as an educational objective, albeit a tantalizing one. A prerequisite is the previous commitment to embodiment, but even then the desire to thrive can be thwarted by the more immediate challenge of survival:

> The notion of flourishing does not begin to make sense unless bodiliness is taken into account: dualism is ruled out from the start. The concept of flourishing is one which involves thriving, luxuriant growth, diversity, obvious and exuberant good health: all of these are rooted in bodily well-being, including both physical health and adequate material provision. Sick people, starving people, people whose existence is miserable because they lack the necessities of physical and psychological well-being cannot be said to be flourishing.
>
> (Jantzen, 1999: 167)

These latter comments bring to the foreground issues to be addressed if a Quaker view of education is to be founded on natality. Social injustice and inequality are familiar themes among the work of Quakers generally and those engaged in education specifically. If natality is taken as the basis of such a vision, then part of the role of educator is to create conditions in which learners can flourish. For Quakers, peace education is not only necessary to pursue because of a general aspiration on behalf of the wider world, but it is also vital within a teaching and learning space so that an educational vision of natality can be achieved.

Intimacy

In being alongside the natal process, the educator enters a peculiarly specialist relational realm. On the one hand, most education takes place in a public arena – the classroom, training area, school or college. These are places unlike a medical or therapeutic space, which intentionally affords a degree of privacy in which the practitioner carries out their intervention. For the teacher, there are often others observing the work – colleagues, students, inspectors – and witnessing the interaction between the one taught and the other who teaches. Despite this open aspect, there is nevertheless the potential for a peculiar type of intimacy in the educational encounter. In my experience, it creates an exquisite tension in the work of the teacher. This topic of intimacy is perhaps an unusual and sensitive one to discuss in modern-day education. So often when asked to recall teachers from the past, people can recount the capacity of individual school teachers to reach into their lives and create lasting impact. (For further consideration on the impact of schooling and personal development, see Barrow, 2009.) Such an imprint might not always be welcome or positive, leading to shame, guilt or anger that lingers long after school days are over. Conversely, the sensitivity of the teacher, an insight shared by someone who has chosen to support us, can be remembered as the motivation behind an entire career.

To relate these discussions back to Quaker faith and practice, if there is 'that of God' in everyone, then such moments of intimacy represent the possibility of Light emerging in the classroom or training room. 'Becoming divine', or experiencing the sacred, is not restricted to the Meeting House, but is also at the heart of the educational encounter.

Co-creativity

What is sometimes lost in the academic writings of Arendt and Jantzen is that the actual phenomenon of natality is rather messy. It is messy in the sense that the process of arrival, cultivation or midwifery and emergence into new life rarely fits into a neat structure or process. The agency of the new may bring with it volatility, activism, appetites of enquiry and curiosity, in addition to impetuousness. Combined with the intention, experience and knowledge of the educator, the involvement in natal interplay demands fluidity from all partners, complete with give and take. What results is the sum of respective energies and is unique, belonging to the distinct moment and place in which learning arises. Notions of a single truth, a prescribed canon of knowledge or exclusive way of doing things must be rapidly abandoned in the face of a natal process.

Betwixt and between

Associated with co-creativity is the accompanying uncertainty of natality. What, or who, might emerge? How will this experience change me in the process? Can I be open to the impact and possibility of being transformed through this experience? While these questions are pertinent to the wider experience of Quaker faith and practice, they have particular relevance for educators and students. This experience of not knowing, or being in between places, can be explained through the notion of *liminality*. The origin of the word relates to 'threshold' and refers to the phase during which the individual is neither in one clearly defined state or role, nor another clearly defined position. Adolescence, for example, is a liminal phase in the life cycle. In relation to education, liminality can be used to understand the episode in which the student is in between not knowing and knowing, or incompetency and competency.

Holding uncertainty is similar to the task of managing risk in education, discussed earlier. The discombobulation so typical of liminal processes can be felt by both teacher and student alike. Self-doubt, reduced confidence, fear and bewilderment are common features at this time. There is a real prospect of failure, of not eventually reaching the other side of whatever threshold is being crossed. Supporting students during this phase is a particularly important task for the teacher, in which they hold out hope on behalf of the student when the learner has lost sight of it themselves.

Education as interruption, and the interiority of the teacher

Natality, by definition, involves an arrival, and in relation to educational encounters this relates to the student's initial becoming. However, natality can also be understood in terms of the 'arrival' of the teacher into the awareness of the student. In effect, the teacher *interrupts* the continuity of the student's experience of the world. It is this action of 'breaking into' that features so strongly in Biesta's rendition of the role of the teacher:

> My point is that *to learn from someone is a radically different experience from the experience of being taught by someone …* When we [say] that 'this person has really taught me something' – we would more often than not refer to experiences where someone showed us something or made us realize something *that really entered our being from the outside.* Such teachings often provide insights about ourselves and our ways of doing and being – insights that we were not aware of or rather did not want to be aware of.
> (Biesta, 2014: 53 – emphasis in the original)

This is a challenge for educators raised exclusively on a student-centred methodology, in that it positions the teacher as having a role beyond that of enabling or facilitating the 'release' of what is already within the student. Furthermore, it is not simply the new intelligence, or knowledge, that the teacher brings to the student's world. Most importantly, the teacher is representative of a will that is not that of the student. Education is a process whereby the Other – and by this I refer to the more than human otherness – is encountered and demands to be reconciled with. I see in this a parallel with what can happen in meeting for worship when the spoken ministry of another Friend – or indeed the entirely silent meeting – disrupts the continuity of individual stillness (or agitation) and creates dissonance, out of which a new engagement with the world emerges.

One of the qualities of the educational interruption is that it has significant potential for intimacy. At its most potent, it is as if the teacher has reached into the interior life of the student and touches the individual process of becoming human. What a position to be in, what power comes with such a role! Readers, I am sure, will be keenly aware of the teachers in their lives who have achieved such an intimate reach, whose influence has continued many years after the event. The interruptions I refer to are those that lead to a transcending of the student's sense of self, when we are taught into a world we would not have otherwise found or have named a dimension of ourselves that was hitherto out of our own sight. In either the positive or negative sense, the power of the teacher's interruption is clear, and this leads to what I think is the most significant challenge for the Quaker educator: if the teacher does indeed engage in an interruption into the world of the student, then perhaps they had best be sure of *who* it is that does the interruption. Who is the self that teaches?

The work of Parker Palmer is arguably the most thorough and sustained approach to exploring the interiority of the teacher. He opens his seminal text, *The Courage to Teach* (1998), by explaining that, more often than not, the questions that preoccupy most teachers are about 'what' to teach and, secondarily, 'how' to teach. Occasionally there might be a prompt to consider 'why' teach?:

> But seldom, if ever, do we ask the 'who' question – who is the self that teaches? How does the quality of my selfhood form – or deform – the way I relate to my students, my subjects, my colleagues, my world? How can educational institutions sustain and deepen the selfhood from which good teaching comes?
>
> (Palmer, 1998: 4)

What follows in Palmer's exploration is an account of what it is like *inside* the teacher, identifying the challenges and dilemmas, alongside the joy of gifting ourselves through enacting – embodying – education. At the heart of his approach is a reflective journey that borrows heavily, although not exclusively, from his own faith and practice as a Quaker. Consequently, there is an emphasis on personal journeying, reclaiming, or establishing, professional vocation and the task of 'integrating soul with role'. This latter phrase is a distinctive marker in Palmer's writing, the notion that an individual's sense of self, or soul, is revealed through how they live out their professional role; there is no split between work and life because 'I am what I do'. To this end, Palmer has written extensively on living life 'divided no more' in which the call is to integrate the whole self in pursuing an authentic, true path in life (see, for example, Palmer, 2004). The connection with holism sits well within a natal-based educational perspective and, emerging out of a Quaker-based frame of reference, Palmer provides an authentic basis for a Quaker vision of holistic education. The goal of spiritual integration of the student that lies at the heart of educational purpose is less likely to be realized if not reflected in that of the teacher.

A Quaker view of educational philosophy and theory

There is a recurrent interplay of themes throughout the works of Arendt, Macmurray, Jantzen and now Palmer, which, in my view, form a powerful spiritual, socially just and ecologically sensitive educational model. I believe that this might form a distinctive Quaker vision of educational philosophy and the basis of a Quaker theory of education. Furthermore, I hold that such a view reflects a *creational turn* in educational discourse. In other words, this is a view of education founded on the principle that a kind of birth takes place during the teaching and learning process. While it is an incremental, organic process, never completed in a single episode, this unfolding of self is not something that is found solely from 'out there' in the world, or in the curriculum. Barbara Windle (1988) expresses it thus:

> To confirm the deepest thing in our students is the educator's special privilege ... It demands that we see ... the possibility of something untangled, clear, directed. It asks us to sustain that faith ... and indeed to find... the ground for hope. It requires us to love freely, readily; unconditionally but truly ... Above all, we must water the ground of the student's being with faith in that deepest self – to do so constantly, tirelessly, patiently – and to love enough to know what one should demand from the student in response and how and when to ask it.
> (Windle, 1988: *QF&P*, 23.75)

The work of Arendt, Macmurray and Jantzen has been central in preparing the ground for establishing natality as the basis out of which Quaker educators might grow an education vision that is sufficient for our time and place. Whether the teacher is a spectator, an instigator, an accompanist or a combination of these, relative to the educational process, is the point at which I bring my exploration to a close. In doing so, I am endeavouring to enact the primary exchange in a natal-based education process. The task might now be that the reader decides for themselves – in relation to the context of where they practise and with whom they teach – how to make best use of what they know, for now. My intention in this chapter has been to do no more than share one way of knowing about natality, an idea that celebrates life, recognizes the significance of the present moment and holds out hope for what might happen next.

References

Arendt, H. (1958) *The Human Condition*. Chicago: University of Chicago Press.

Arendt, H. (1961) *Between Past and Future*. London: Faber and Faber.

Barrow, G. (2009) 'Teaching, learning, schooling, and script'. *Transactional Analysis Journal*, 39 (4), 298–304.

Biesta, G.J.J. (2014) *The Beautiful Risk of Education*. Boulder, CO: Paradigm Publishers.

Jantzen, G.M. (1999) *Becoming Divine: Towards a feminist philosophy of religion*. Bloomington: Indiana University Press.

Jantzen, G.M. (2010) *A Place of Springs* (Death and the Displacement of Beauty 3). London: Routledge.

Macmurray, J. (2012) 'Learning to be human'. *Oxford Review of Education*, 38 (6), 661–74.

Palmer, P.J. (1998) *The Courage to Teach: Exploring the inner landscape of a teacher's life*. San Francisco: Jossey-Bass.

Palmer, P.J. (2004) *A Hidden Wholeness: The journey toward an undivided life*. San Francisco: Jossey-Bass.

Windle, B. (1988) in E. Perkins (ed.) *Affirmation, Communication and Cooperation*. London: Quaker Home Service.

Chapter 13
Friends' education: A reflective commentary
Kathy Bickmore

It is an honour to participate in this volume by offering this reflective commentary on some ideas resonating in the preceding chapters. To introduce myself: I am a convinced Friend, teaching and conducting research in Canada and abroad around questions of how publicly funded education may contribute to building young people's capacities and confidence to contribute to democratic peacebuilding transformation.

I will briefly discuss four core themes that have arisen, intersected and returned to me continually in reading these chapters. The first, and perhaps the most unexpected to me in my first reading, is the value of uncertainty, nurtured in unprogrammed open space for learning and improving on 'truths for now' in the context of inevitable change. Second is the challenge and necessity of nurturing learners' relationships and practices for sustainable (just) peace, in schools and classrooms and as peacebuilding citizens in society. Third is the question of justice, including equity of access to high-quality, inclusive learning opportunities that respect the capacities of all to (learn to) discern for themselves. Last, woven throughout the others, is the theme of critical reflexivity for generating insight, motivation and capacity for contributing to personal and social change.

Uncertainty: Unprogrammed and unprogrammable educational space

A central theme running through this book that speaks strongly to me is the importance, for Friends and for education, of uncertainty and unprogrammed or even unplannable learning opportunities. Such opportunities create spaces for hearing the small voices within, for openness to others and alternative perspectives, and for consequent reflective processes of discernment. This openness to the unknown is even more crucial in educational dealings with young people, and more delicate: educators are, by definition, responsible for acting as guides, yet our eventual goal is for the learners to guide themselves, to contribute their Light to remaking the world:

> How do you share your deepest beliefs with [children and young people], while leaving them free to develop as the spirit of God may lead them? ... Are you ready to learn from them and to accept your responsibilities towards them?
>
> (QF&P, 1.02, 19)

Several chapters affirm the fundamental value, rooted in Quaker faith and practice, of thinking it possible that we may be mistaken. The late Canadian Quaker scholar Ursula Franklin, in a 1993 talk to an Acoustic Ecology conference, reminds us that, in worship, '[Friends make] the collective decision ... to be silent in order to let the unforeseen, unforeseeable, and unprogrammed happen'. She further argues, consistent with the concerns voiced by authors in this volume about schooling, that 'this environment is very much at risk ... Our present technological trends drive us toward a decrease in the space ... for the unplanned and unplannable to happen' (Franklin, 2006: 160). Such unprogrammed and unplannable spaces are crucial, Ursula argues, for creativity, discernment and even individual and collective sanity.

In contrast to contemporary mainstream schooling's obsession with assessment of predefined learning objectives, education that is not overly pre-programmed can reap the benefits of uncertainty, which in turn opens the way for listening and for honouring diversity. Anne Watson, in Chapter 6 of this book, points out that conflict, which generates and may emerge from uncertainty, can spark creativity. For instance, if people's views about a maths idea conflict, she observes that 'we can talk about it and maybe both learn more through the experience, even imagining [a new understanding] ... Thus, the task for teachers ... rather than correcting or avoiding misconceptions ... [is] to engender a willingness to use concepts ... that society accepts as "truths for now" within a subject' (pages 110–11). Such a cognitive care pedagogy resonates with Anne's Quaker sense of uncertainty, which is the familiar ground for listening to others, questioning experience and thinking it possible that one is mistaken. Recognizing truths as partial (both incomplete and formed through particular human perspectives) and 'for now' admits that the not-knowing continues, leaving space for further discernment and for inclusion of future learners. Janet Sturge's chapter on arts in the curriculum also exemplifies a teaching approach that puts children's perceptions at the heart of learning (Chapter 7).

Similarly, John Mason, in Chapter 10, encourages his students to think for themselves rather than seeking certainty. He emphasizes that 'everything said by them or by [the teacher] is to be treated as a conjecture.

… I urge those who are confident about their thinking to listen carefully to others … I urge those who are unsure not to hold back, but rather to try to express what they are thinking …' (page 183). Quaker values guide John to include contrasting (novice as well as confident) voices alongside one another, and to help his students develop '… sensitivity to what people are trying to express, rather than taking their words (or other expressions) at face value as being exactly what is intended' (page 194). Thus, uncertainty and imperfection are accepted as inevitable in the learning process, even as gifts for the journey towards collective discernment through reflective dialogue. Canadian Quaker *Faith and Practice* (1.66) affirms that, in contrast with predictable knowing, 'even *trying* to discern works for us as it brings our spirit closer to God'. Ideally, education would help all people learn to (try to) discern: to be kind to themselves and others in the process of seeking to understand what seems obscure, to make distinctions and perceive options and potential consequences, and consequently to arrive at sound, caring, right judgements. Education that presents knowledge as partial and provisional, embracing ongoing uncertainty, rejects the notion that knowledge is fixed, that the teacher is merely a programmer and that students are mere collectors and repositories of predetermined pearls of wisdom (as in Freire, 1970).

Building sustainable peace

Another core theme in this book is the Friends' peace testimony. Building peace and reconciliation among individuals, groups or nations involves internal reflexivity as well as collective effort: 'Bring into God's light those emotions, attitudes and prejudices in yourself which lie at the root of destructive conflict, acknowledging your need for forgiveness and grace' (*QF&P*, 1.02, 32). As Ursula Franklin (2006: 76–7) explained: 'Peace is indivisible. We have to come to terms with the fact that, like the sun, the rain, and God's grace, peace will be there … both for those we love and for those we can't stand.' Nobody will have sustainable peace – in schools or beyond in the wide world – until all have peace, with justice, so that neither they (we) nor ostensible adversaries have anything to fear. Peacebuilding education in, and through, schools is therefore a complex and long-term endeavour. As Tim Small argues (Chapter 5), educational environments that can support these lofty goals are values-led, meta-cognitively reflective and responsive to individuals' concerns and feelings, 'offering the most fertile ground for growing learning power' (page 86). Building students' capabilities, inclinations and experiences of positive, sustainable peace requires transformation of school and classroom relationships, including

– but reaching well beyond – instituting non-violent conflict education and resolution practices.

In contrast, typical government schooling unfortunately tends to avoid this work of listening, reflecting, thinking together and reconciling – instead institutionalizing demands for perpetual obedience, backed by punishment. Formal curriculum guidelines, as implemented, tend to avoid recognizing conflicts (or their resolution, transformation or reconciliation) as learning opportunities. Wendy Scott tells the sad story of a shift in early years practice from an internationally respected ethic of nurture to institutionalization of obedience to formal guidelines (Chapter 8). Tim Small notes that his work towards 'enabling people to become the authors of their own lives' had placed him 'on a collision course with the apparatus of an educational system' (page 78). Similarly, Keir Mitchell reflects (Chapter 11) on the troubling mismatch between schools' demands for obedience and institutionalization, on the one hand, and Quaker commitments to speaking truth, equality and peace, on the other.

Thus, the Friends participating in this volume direct our peace education efforts towards different spaces. Some (myself included) have chosen to try to transform publicly funded schools and classrooms from within, to support the diverse and often non-privileged communities who populate them and the large-scale democratic inclusion they (try to) represent. Other Friends (also represented in this volume) opt to redirect their best energies away from bureaucratic, control-oriented school systems, towards creating and supporting more flexible and positively peaceful educational spaces.

Anna Gregory and the Peacemaker team (Chapter 4) outline the multiple dimensions of creating peaceful school cultures from these ordinarily constraining and compliance-oriented starting points. They talk of building a peaceful and mutually supportive school culture, maintaining it through constructive conflict resolution and conflict resolution education and repairing the peace where necessary through restorative justice practices, which take into account multiple perspectives, stories and histories. Belinda Hopkins (Chapter 3) articulates how transformation of school conflict management into formative and restorative 'community-led encounters' that emphasize story-sharing, emotional expression, collaborative problem-solving and inclusive practice with constructive conflict communication may foster individual and community development, and also challenge existing power hierarchies.

Citizenship capacities for positive peace are intrinsically autonomous (democratic) as well as relational: if peaceful behaviour were merely inculcated by 'knowers' to 'novices', it would not be sustainable, without surveillance, in ever-changing complex contexts. Thus, Belinda explains the importance of teachers having opportunities to learn how to help students develop their own 'inner moral compass' (self-motivated self-regulation), along with the skills and processes to build and repair relationships or resolve conflicts. Similarly, Don Rowe (Chapter 2) calls for educators to directly nurture children's ability to think and talk morally, rather than merely trying to achieve or impose a moral ethos in a school.

Transforming power requires exercise of power, in particular with (and on behalf of) those most marginalized and harmed by unjust systems. The blame and power-over norms that Belinda, Anna and the Peacemakers team find rife in school cultures disproportionately oppress visible minority and economically marginalized students (USA evidence includes Skiba *et al.*, 2002). My own research teams in the Americas, too, have found that school peacemaking initiatives often have not resisted the inequitable power relations embedded in patterns of social conflict (Bickmore, 1993, 2002, 2011, 2013; Nieto and Bickmore, 2016), and thus have not formed a sustainable fabric of just social relations.

Feminist pacifist activist Barbara Deming, who attended a Friends school in the USA, reminds us that action for peace requires challenging the violent status quo of injustice. She often referred to non-violent action as two hands working together, combining impulses traditionally assumed feminine and masculine – one hand calming (expressing gentle sympathy), the other speaking truth to power and pushing for movement (expressing assertiveness):

> The most effective action [for change] both resorts to power and engages conscience. ... We can put more pressure on the antagonist for whom we show human concern ... (precisely in our acting both with *love*, if you will – in the sense that we respect her human rights – and *truthfulness*, in the sense that we act out fully our objections to her violating our rights) ... it happens that in combination these two pressures are uniquely effective.
> (Deming, 1984: 175–7)

This confluence of re-educative clarity, caring and human agency encompasses teaching for, and through, positive peace.

Towards justice: Equity, openness and discernment, within and between learning spaces

Closely aligned to building peace, then, is to build primary justice. Beyond secondary justice – that is, redress after incidents of harm – primary justice refers to proactive, reciprocal and comprehensive pursuit of dignity and well-being for all: the creation of the just society (Evans and Vaandering, 2016: 43). This means facing conflict constructively, to transform the roots of destructive conflict: 'Bear witness to the humanity of all people, including those who break society's conventions or its laws ... *Seek to understand the causes* of injustice, social unrest and fear' (*QF&P*, 1.02, 33, emphasis added). A crucial dimension of this primary justice is the provision of equitable access to high-quality education for all. Canadian Friend Ursula Franklin, mentioned earlier, reflected that:

> ... the power of the old order rested in large measure on the restriction of knowledge and vital information to certain classes and castes. The struggle to gain access to education has always been part of the struggle to overcome the old order.
>
> (Franklin, 2006: 260)

As we have seen, there is little consensus among Friends about how best to practise Quaker testimony on equality, in the context of a demonstrably unequal system that includes elite private (including Quaker independent) schools as well as resource-stressed government-funded schools. In particular, Janet Nicholls (Chapter 9) articulates a challenge: 'Quakers' statement that 'every person is precious' is incompatible with a system in which the most privileged children become more privileged and the most disadvantaged become more disadvantaged' (page 177). How can Quaker educators nurture creativity, experimentation and humanizing environments without exacerbating social inequality – including exclusion from those very environments?

Educational equity, as part of primary justice, includes not only public provision of schooling, but also the achievement of high-quality, inspiring and humanizing education for all, within whatever circumstances and institutional spaces we find ourselves. Anne Watson (Chapter 6) explains how cognitive care pedagogies can enhance social justice by embracing multiple perspectives and methods to make space for all to learn fundamental principles (truths) in their own ways. These are 'forms of teaching that do not create anxiety, but enhance confidence and self-actualization – teaching that cares about the cognitive efforts of different individuals as well as their emotional and social development' (page 109). Here, again, the prompting of love opens the way for justice. Similarly, Tim Small (Chapter 5) calls for Authentic Enquiry pedagogy, embracing Friends' affirmation of diversity, inspiration and processes of discernment. He argues that Authentic Enquiry 'challenges the status quo because it is anchored in personal interest rather than didactic intent' (page 95). Enquiry and cognitive caring, as in Freire's (1970) pedagogy of problem-posing dialogue and praxis, disrupt the usual power differential between teacher and student, enabling each to learn from, and with, the other.

Quakers believe strongly in each person's ability to discern right or good ways forward, distinguishing these from harmful or misleading choices. In all of us, and especially in schools that routinely deprive learners (and often teachers) of this respect and opportunity, these discernment abilities may, at times, be hidden or buried – requiring excavation, un-learning and re-learning. John Mason (Chapter 10) elaborates the idea that learners may un-learn dependency to increase justice, through pedagogies recognizing and developing each learner's inherent capacity to learn, reinvent and create knowledge: 'a small but significant part of "acknowledging that of God" in them' (page 185). As in Anne Watson's cognitive caring approach and Tim Small's Authentic Enquiry approach, Friends' values are embodied in the way diverse (confident and novice) learners' ideas and insights are invited alongside one another's, in a spirit of equal respect for all. John expects learners to take initiative and to ask for help, while he also supports equitable access by implementing pedagogies of 'scaffolding and fading' – providing learners with temporary structures of support (such as questioning patterns and pauses for collectively reflecting on key ideas) that they can eventually learn to conduct autonomously (allowing the teacher's guidance and their own dependency to fade away). It is daunting, yet tremendously exciting, to imagine and enable the kinds of high-quality education for cognitive autonomy and mutual care (key elements of agency for democracy and justice) that have primarily been available to (some) elites, now taking shape in educational spaces available to diverse people in the general public.

Reflection, reflexivity and community responsibility for social change

The brilliant and loving authors in this volume have provided me an opportunity to conduct, inside myself with their help, some of the critical yet caring reflection that they identify as a crucial element of Quakerly education. Through sharing their experiences and reflections, they have guided my own reflections on my philosophies and practices in education. As several authors in this volume point out, such reflexivity is, itself, a crucial tool and insight that Friends value and promote in education. As Giles Barrow (Chapter 12) explains, citing Quaker educator Parker Palmer (1998), quality education that can help to foster social change integrates 'soul' with 'role', combining leadership with caring, courage and hope born of faith in what the learners can create for their present and future.

On this premise, and based on the thinking of Gert Biesta (2014), who, in turn, is influenced by Derrida's (2000) philosophy of unconditional hospitality, Giles articulates the foundational goal of relationality in education. Interesting: this takes us back around to the principle of expecting and valuing uncertainty, as well as inclusion. Because humans generally want and need relational connections with others, education is challenged to prepare students to welcome the encounter with somebody new: 'It means to start from a position of not knowing who it is that will arrive. By implication it means suspending, even for a brief time, the possibility for stability, familiarity and knowingness …' (page 223).

Giles quotes an essential insight from philosopher Hannah Arendt, which is worth repeating here. She contends that education must always anticipate and try to prepare for social change:

> Basically we are always educating for a world that is or is becoming out of joint … To preserve the world against the mortality of its creators and inhabitants [that is, in view of the problem that what works in the world 'wears out' over time] it must be constantly set right anew. The problem is simply to educate in such a way that a setting-right remains actually possible …
> (Arendt, 1961: 192)

This book, indeed, begins to articulate what it might mean to educate to make it possible to set things right, to progress from our violent and topsy-turvy world towards something more humane. Ursula Franklin emphasizes the essential role played by criticality and diversity in this process of educating to set things right:

> If within the society there are failures in compassion, knowledge, or tolerance, it is not the job of schools to produce students who can comfortably fit in. On the contrary, the schools ought to draw attention to these failures and stress that they require correction.
> (Franklin, 2006: 354)

I am grateful for this opportunity to think together with the Friends in this volume, reflecting on some of the many problems that 'require correction' in education, while inspired with hope by discerning some possibilities for the 'setting-right'. For me, this book has opened several new reflective windows between my Quaker self and my educator self, which I'm sure will continue to shed and share light for the future.

References

Arendt, H. (1961) *Between Past and Future*. London: Faber and Faber.

Bickmore, K. (1993) 'Learning inclusion/inclusion in learning: Citizenship education for a pluralistic society'. *Theory and Research in Social Education*, 21 (4), 341–84.

Bickmore, K. (2002) 'Peer mediation training and program implementation in elementary schools: Research results'. *Conflict Resolution Quarterly*, 20 (2), 137–60.

Bickmore, K. (2011) 'Policies and programming for safer schools: Are "anti-bullying" approaches impeding education for peacebuilding?'. *Educational Policy*, 25 (4), 648–87.

Bickmore, K. (2013) 'Peacebuilding through circle dialogue processes in primary classrooms: Locations for restorative and educative work'. In Sellman, E., Cremin, H. and McCluskey, G. (eds) *Restorative Approaches to Conflict in Schools: Interdisciplinary perspectives on whole school approaches to managing relationships*. London: Routledge, 175–91.

Biesta, G.J.J. (2014) *The Beautiful Risk of Education*. Boulder, CO: Paradigm Publishers.

Canadian Friends (2010) *Faith and Practice*. Ottowa: Canadian Yearly Meeting of the Religious Society of Friends.

Deming, B. (1984) 'On revolution and equilibrium'. In Meyerding, J. (ed.) *We Are All Part of One Another: A Barbara Deming reader*. Philadelphia: New Society Publishers, 168–88.

Derrida, J. (2000) *Of Hospitality*. Trans. Bowlby, R. Stanford: Stanford University Press.

Evans, K. and Vaandering, D. (2016) *The Little Book of Restorative Justice in Education: Fostering responsibility, healing, and hope in schools*. New York: Good Books.

Franklin, U.M. (2006) *The Ursula Franklin Reader: Pacifism as a map*. Toronto: Between the Lines.

Freire, P. (1970) *Pedagogy of the Oppressed*. Trans. Ramos, M.B. New York: Seabury Press.

Nieto, D. and Bickmore, K. (2016) 'Citizenship and "convivencia" education in contexts of violence: Transnational challenges to peacebuilding education in Mexican schools'. *Revista Española de Educación Comparada*, 28, 109–34.

Palmer, P.J. (1998) *The Courage to Teach: Exploring the inner landscape of a teacher's life*. San Francisco: Jossey-Bass.

Skiba, R.J., Michael, R.S., Nardo, A.C. and Peterson, R.L. (2002) 'The color of discipline: Sources of racial and gender disproportionality in school punishment'. *Urban Review*, 34 (4), 317–42.

Index

academic   20, 25, 27, 31, 88, 90, 119, 134, 135, 156, 157, 170
academies   164ff., 172ff.
adolescence   14, 17, 86, 107, 119, 127ff., 133, 227
adults   37ff., 45, 48, 58, 60ff., 65, 67ff., 73, 107, 110, 119, 147, 184, 202ff., 206, 208ff., 212ff.
ambiguity   14, 22, 79, 107, 115, 135
Arendt, Hannah   7, 9, 216ff., 238
arts   101, 104, 119ff., 173, 232
assessment   28, 79, 95, 126, 133ff., 144, 150, 154ff., 169, 170, 209, 232
authenticity   6ff., 22, 25, 50, 66, 88, 91ff., 125, 229, 236
authority   37, 45, 48ff., 67, 72, 80, 95, 129, 130, 204
autonomy   2, 6ff., 14, 42, 91, 129, 234, 237

Barnes, Kenneth   105, 106, 123
behaviour management   7, 16, 19, 24ff., 39, 41ff., 49ff., 53ff., 63, 66, 69, 71, 72ff., 104, 109, 122, 168, 182, 186, 192, 195, 203ff., 212ff., 224, 234
Bible   3, 18, 120
Bickmore, Kathy   9, 14, 61, 231ff.
Biesta, Gert   223, 227, 238
birth   9, 103, 126, 152, 216ff.
boys' education   87, 125, 168, 170, 205ff.
brain   24, 84, 119ff., 127ff.
Bruner, Jerome   96
bullying   42, 45, 71

care   6, 13ff., 20, 23, 30, 69, 100ff., 125, 150ff., 156, 185, 192, 195ff., 204ff., 219, 232, 236
carers   36, 46, 52, 148
change   5, 20, 37ff., 39, 47ff., 52, 58ff., 71, 73ff., 80, 83, 87ff., 90, 94ff., 108, 112, 129, 144, 152, 195, 207, 211ff., 218, 226, 231, 235, 237ff.
character education   22ff., 124, 126ff., 136
children   childhood   5, 9, 125, 157; children of God   2, 9, 125, 126, 141, 185, 198, 217, 222, 226, 237; economic unit   102, 119, 125, 164, 172; Quaker children   2, 45, 79, 177, 203, 206
children's centres   144ff.
circle time   14, 28, 39, 43ff., 52ff., 61ff.
citizenship   11ff., 44, 89, 102, 151, 231, 234
Claxton, Guy   79ff.
cognition   13, 26, 53, 84, 100ff., 122, 192, 199, 224, 232ff.
cognitive care   100ff., 232ff.
collaboration   40, 49ff., 73, 85ff., 112, 128, 145, 183, 234

community   7, 13–15, 22ff., 28, 30, 36, 39ff., 46ff., 53, 58ff., 67ff., 85, 95, 103, 122, 140, 143, 150, 158, 168, 173, 176, 202, 220, 234, 237
compassion   23, 27, 43, 75, 179, 238
competition   126, 159, 169, 170ff., 183, 207
conflict   12, 14, 16, 18ff., 22, 30, 36ff., 42ff., 51ff., 63ff., 79, 110, 126
conflict resolution   5, 20ff., 30, 37, 39, 43ff., 46, 57ff., 69, 70ff., 139, 143, 145, 195, 232ff.
crafts   101, 123, 128, 132
creativity   6, 22, 42, 48, 57, 59, 79, 84, 90, 93, 95, 110, 117ff., 149, 184, 188, 194, 196, 198, 219, 226ff., 232, 236
Cremin, Hilary   21, 43, 68, 71
criminal justice   36, 40, 44, 48, 70ff.
culture   39, 45ff., 57ff., 86, 89, 91, 103, 105ff., 122, 131, 144, 146, 207, 217, 221, 223, 234
curiosity   14, 69, 78, 84ff., 94, 122, 226; see also enquiry, inquiry
current system   1, 8, 103, 202
curriculum   3, 7, 11ff., 17ff., 47, 61, 65, 67, 89, 91, 95, 102, 104, 115, 120, 122, 125, 130, 141, 144, 148, 152ff., 173, 206, 214, 223, 229, 234

dance   121, 123, 125, 130ff., 190
Deakin Crick, Ruth   79ff., 86, 96
Deming, Barbara   235
democracy   12, 16, 19, 25, 29, 60ff., 142, 154, 231, 234, 237
Department for Education   19, 148ff., 154, 202
Dewey, John   53, 122
discernment   6, 63, 95, 108, 124ff., 130, 134ff., 149, 158, 222, 231ff., 235, 237ff.
drawing   116, 120ff., 129, 132

early childhood   14, 66, 120, 139ff.
education ministries   12, 140, 150, 198, 206, 210
emancipation   78ff.
emotion   5, 17, 38, 43, 48, 50, 57, 63ff., 73, 85, 105, 109, 112, 119, 122ff., 128, 131ff., 141, 157, 188, 192, 194, 219, 233ff.
empowerment   43, 49, 67ff., 116, 202, 208, 214ff.
enquiry   78, 89, 91ff., 101, 104, 116, 120, 121, 226, 237; see also curiosity, inquiry
environment   school   4ff., 47ff., 58ff., 86, 211; classroom   24ff., 91, 104, 110; surrounding   124, 129, 132, 134, 143, 147ff., 153, 168, 175, 202, 205, 236; global   20, 29, 232; see also culture
equality   2, 4, 7ff., 20, 26ff., 30, 49, 54, 59, 61ff., 100ff., 119, 124ff., 135, 140ff., 145, 150, 156ff., 163ff., 184, 202, 210, 212ff., 225, 234ff.
ethics   7, 24ff., 30, 139
ethos   3, 19, 24ff., 52, 59, 167ff., 184ff., 235; see also culture

Index

examinations 103, 112, 136, 165, 172; *see also* tests
exclusion 39, 42, 44, 54, 65, 69ff., 236
experience 1, 6, 9, 16, 46, 48, 57, 64ff., 73, 80, 84ff., 88, 90ff., 93, 95, 102ff., 125ff., 133, 139, 141ff., 148ff., 153, 154ff., 158, 169, 178, 182ff., 191ff., 227, 232, 237

failure 5, 20, 85, 93, 146, 170, 227, 238
feminist spirituality 220ff., 235
Fox, George 1, 29, 111, 139, 178, 193, 209, 211
Friends 1ff., 11, 20, 26ff., 37, 42, 45ff., 100ff., 120ff., 143, 157ff., 163, 168ff., 174ff., 178, 193, 203, 228, 231ff.; *see also* Quaker
friendship 14, 212

gender 132, 145, 163, 170
government national 8, 12, 17, 19, 31, 41, 60, 80, 102, 119, 129, 141ff., 149ff., 157ff., 167ff., 202, 209, 234, 236
governance of schools *see* management
Graham, Lydia 128, 132
Guild of Friends in Education 100, 123

Habermas, Jürgen 80
Hawkes, Neil 16, 24ff.
Heidegger, Martin 217
home school 174, 203ff.
Hopkins, Belinda 16, 36ff., 58, 72, 126, 234
human rights 13, 16, 18, 20ff., 30, 204, 235

inclusion 13, 57, 63, 65ff., 69ff., 106, 112, 120, 124, 159, 169, 211, 213, 231ff., 234, 236
inner light 2ff., 30, 222, 224
inquiry 17, 63, 69, 83, 87ff.; *see also* enquiry, curiosity
integrity 6, 20, 29, 46, 57, 66, 116, 120, 125ff., 140, 143, 149, 154, 211

Jaggar, Trevor 104, 144
Jantzen, Grace 216ff.
judgement 13ff., 28ff., 49ff., 64ff., 94, 120, 126, 128, 146ff., 183ff., 210, 212, 233
justice 2, 5ff., 7ff., 11ff., 36ff., 59, 67ff., 73ff., 103, 166, 179, 204, 214, 225, 231, 233ff.

knowledge 6, 11, 14, 19, 68, 80, 92, 95, 100, 102ff., 105ff., 108ff., 124ff., 128, 136, 156, 183, 192, 226ff., 233, 236
Kohlberg, Lawrence 13, 24

Lampen, John 4ff.
law 12, 15ff., 29, 39, 101, 154, 236
leadership 36, 53ff., 66ff., 84, 91, 145, 202, 238

learning 1, 7, 11, 26ff., 43, 46, 53, 58, 61, 64, 70, 78ff., 101ff., 105ff., 112ff., 125, 127, 131ff., 136, 141ff., 147ff., 150ff., 168, 185, 189ff., 197, 205, 208ff., 213ff., 216, 219ff., 225ff., 231ff., 235ff.
learning power 78ff.
listening 2, 6, 21ff., 37ff., 40ff., 51ff., 62ff., 65ff., 85, 91, 106, 110ff., 124ff., 130, 134, 145, 149, 183, 191, 194, 199, 210ff., 232ff.
literacy 3, 18, 43, 119, 133, 144, 150ff.
local authorities 146, 149, 151, 168ff., 171ff., 178
Loukes, Harold 5
love 5ff., 16, 23ff., 29, 100ff., 124, 127, 133, 199, 212, 229, 223, 235

Macmurray, John 111, 216ff., 223, 229ff.
management of schools 47, 119, 208ff.
mathematics 100ff., 182ff.
military ethos 19
mind, mindful 18, 27ff., 47ff., 51, 83ff., 87, 89, 93, 102, 105ff., 107ff., 110, 112, 119, 122ff., 127ff., 135, 189, 197ff., 203, 206, 210, 221, 224
ministry 122, 193, 195, 210ff., 215, 228
mistake 37, 106, 109ff., 116, 142, 193, 213, 232
moral education 3, 6ff., 11ff., 38, 50, 72ff., 158, 211, 235
motivation 38, 79, 134, 156, 207, 214, 226, 231
music 108, 111, 119ff., 190, 206, 214
mutuality 18, 45, 50, 66, 70, 85, 110ff., 134, 199, 219, 237

natality 216ff.
national curriculum 12, 19ff., 86, 102, 123, 135, 144, 153, 173
Newton, Nigel 4, 176
Noddings, Nel 13, 111ff.
numeracy 3, 101, 119, 144, 152

O'Donnell, Liz 3, 131
Ofsted 144ff., 156, 168

Palmer, Parker 6, 78, 159, 216, 228ff., 237
parents 3, 13, 17ff., 24, 36, 46, 49, 58, 66, 134, 140ff., 148, 153ff., 157, 159, 164ff., 170ff., 209; *see also* carers
peace education 11ff., 37, 42ff., 57ff., 225, 234
peace testimony *see* testimony
pedagogy 7, 25, 91, 134, 140, 146, 149, 156, 183, 203, 220, 232, 236
peer mediation 5, 21, 24, 41, 43ff., 58, 67ff.
Penn, William 3, 120, 122, 166, 197, 212
philosophy 2, 9, 14, 18ff., 28, 87, 111, 193, 216ff., 229, 238
phonics 146, 153ff.

241

Index

Piaget, Jean   13, 105ff.
Plowden, Bridget   140, 167
police   11ff., 40ff.
policy   1, 6, 9, 16, 26, 38, 44, 47, 52ff., 65, 69, 94ff., 101, 136, 150ff., 157ff., 164, 178, 204, 209, 222
politics   11ff., 100, 128, 129, 139ff., 163ff., 216ff.
Pollard, Francis   4, 7, 122
power   37, 41, 45, 49, 60, 68, 89, 108, 122, 130, 154, 157ff., 178, 184ff., 193ff., 202, 210, 213ff., 228, 234ff.; *see also* empowerment, learning
prison   2, 21, 44, 142, 206
punishment   2, 5, 24, 38, 47ff., 55, 58, 72, 206, 210, 234

Quaker   values   1, 4, 11, 20, 78, 102, 124, 139, 158, 163ff., 167, 176ff., 182, 193ff., 233;   worship   2, 7, 26, 121, 123, 143, 176, 193ff., 204, 206, 224, 228, 232;   business method   149, 151;   school *see* schools;   children *see* children
QVinE: Quaker Values in Education   1, 158, 172

Reader, John   4, 101
reflection   7, 9, 23, 25ff., 36, 52, 65, 80, 91, 95, 130, 143, 156, 176, 179, 182ff., 220, 228, 231ff.; *see also* reflexivity
reflexivity   17, 95, 231, 233, 237ff.; *see also* reflection
relationships   5ff., 16, 23, 26, 36ff., 57ff., 78, 85ff., 95, 110ff., 131, 139, 148, 209, 211, 215ff., 223ff., 231, 233ff.
Religious Education   3, 11, 18, 20, 165, 174
Religious Society of Friends (see Quaker)   1, 29, 120ff., 123, 157, 168, 176
respect   6, 13, 16, 19, 24, 25ff., 30, 38, 43ff., 49ff., 62ff., 68, 112, 116, 126, 134, 137, 149ff., 163, 183, 185ff., 195ff., 198ff., 204ff., 210, 212ff., 231, 235, 237
responsibility   5, 12ff., 24, 25ff., 30, 46, 59, 64ff., 71ff., 79, 83, 88, 106, 115, 141, 151, 185, 211, 214, 223, 231, 232, 237ff.
restorative   approach   36ff.;   justice   57ff.
rights *see* human rights
Rogers, Carl   78, 96

school   classroom   11, 16, 46ff., 53, 61, 65, 69ff., 73, 86, 91, 93, 104, 109, 112ff., 143, 184, 186, 194, 203, 205, 208, 213ff., 225, 234;   comprehensive   136, 165, 168ff.;   faith   18;   free   165, 168, 170, 172ff., 176;   grammar   3, 165, 170ff.;   nursery   139ff.;   primary   3, 4, 9, 12ff., 16, 28, 44, 60, 84, 105, 113, 139ff., 166, 184, 202ff.;   Quaker   2, 3ff., 7, 101, 120, 164ff., 174ff.;   secondary   3, 12ff., 52ff., 86, 89, 122, 135ff., 165, 170ff., 176, 184
selection   5, 136, 164ff., 170ff.
silence   26ff., 63, 108, 121, 131, 197, 204, 228, 232
simplicity   198, 206;   *see* testimony
social justice   36, 44, 49, 54, 67, 103, 166, 236
subject teaching   20, 86, 100ff., 120, 123, 126, 134, 135ff., 153, 169, 175, 188, 195

testimony   2, 4, 57, 78, 127, 139ff., 158, 166, 176, 198, 203, 206, 210, 233, 236
tests (see examinations)   1, 5, 79, 84, 87, 109, 119, 135, 154ff., 186, 205
therapeutic   4ff., 123, 132, 168, 225
transformation   7, 18, 47, 74, 79ff., 195, 231ff.
trust   6ff., 14, 19, 38, 50, 61ff., 66ff., 112, 159, 191, 213, 224
truth   2, 6ff., 16, 19ff., 29ff., 51, 78, 100ff., 119, 122ff., 125ff., 134ff., 139ff., 154, 176, 178, 184, 193, 196, 199, 202ff., 210, 224ff., 231ff.;   *see* testimony

uncertainty   6, 9, 63, 79, 95, 110, 199, 218, 226ff., 231ff.

values-based education   11ff., 36ff.
visual (including imagery)   89, 105, 119, 121, 124ff., 129ff., 132ff., 189
Vygotsky, Lev   96, 105, 107ff.

West Midlands Quaker Peace Education Project WMQPEP   21, 57
Whitehead, Alfred North   122, 193
Windle, Barbara   127, 229
Wingate, Jim   42, 46, 113
worship *see* Quaker worship